THE ROUGH GUIDE to
THE TITANIC

Credits

The Rough Guide to the Titanic

Editing: Joe Staines & Richie Unterberger
Picture research: Joe Staines & Greg Ward
Typesetting: Ankur Guha
Diagrams: Katie Lloyd-Jones
Proofreading: Jason Freeman
Production: Erika Pepe

Rough Guides Reference

Editors: Kate Berens, Tom Cabot,
Tracy Hopkins, Matthew Milton,
Joe Staines
Director: Andrew Lockett

Publishing Information

Published February 2012 by
Rough Guides Ltd, 80 Strand, London WC2R 0RL

Penguin Group (USA), 375 Hudson Street, NY 10014, USA
Penguin Group (India), 11, Community Centre, Panchsheel Park, New Delhi 110017, India
Penguin Group (Australia), 250 Camberwell Road, Camberwell, Victoria 3124, Australia
Penguin Group (New Zealand), 67 Apollo Drive, Rosedale, Auckland 0632, New Zealand
Email: mail@roughguides.com

Rough Guides is represented in Canada by Tourmaline Editions Inc.,
662 King Street West, Suite 304, Toronto, Ontario, M5V 1M7

Printed in Singapore by Toppan Security Printing Pte. Ltd.

The publishers and authors have done their best to ensure the accuracy and currency
of all information in *The Rough Guide to the Titanic*; however, they can accept no
responsibility for any loss or inconvenience sustained by any reader as a result of
its information or advice.

280 pages; includes index

A catalogue record for this book is available from the British Library

ISBN: 978-1-40538-699-9

1 3 5 7 9 8 6 4 2

THE ROUGH GUIDE to
THE TITANIC

Greg Ward

www.roughguides.com

Contents

Introduction

Shortly before midnight on Sunday 14 April 1912, the White Star liner *Titanic*, on her maiden voyage from Southampton to New York, struck an iceberg in the North Atlantic. Two hours and forty minutes later, she sank. Just over seven hundred survivors found their way into lifeboats, and were picked up the next morning by the Cunard liner *Carpathia*. Meanwhile, fifteen hundred men, women and children died. Many froze to death in the open ocean, adrift in their lifebelts and crying out for help that never came.

That appalling catastrophe captivated the attention of the world. There's no mystery as to why – the largest ship on Earth, sailing between the two wealthiest nations, was destroyed in a disaster that claimed the lives of prominent citizens and humble emigrants alike. It was the ultimate news story, in an era when the newfound ability of news to race around the world seemed all but magical.

What's not so obvious is why the *Titanic* still exerts such a hold on popular imagination a hundred years later. The crucial factor may be that the disaster happened beyond the usual confines of time and space. It took place in neither the old world nor the new, but in a liminal space between the two. Having vanished below the horizon west of Ireland, the *Titanic* never reappeared. Instead, unseen in the witching hour of a moonless night, for the eternity between the collision and the final plunge, her passengers and crew found themselves poised between life and death.

Even as the *Carpathia* returned to New York, the *Titanic* was entering the realm of myth. During those three days, the only information to be released was a slowly accumulating list of survivors. Newspapers, which had at first

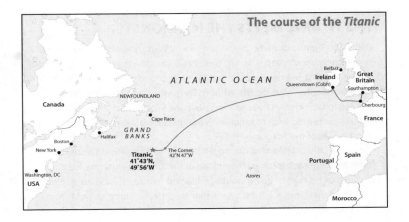

The course of the *Titanic*

reported the *Titanic* being towed towards Canada, now filled the void by extrapolating from small snippets. The fact no husband had survived his wife was interpreted as proof that the general conduct aboard the *Titanic* was a "splendid tribute to the Anglo-Saxon sense of duty". After a bewildered White Star Line spokesman told reporters that he'd thought the ship was "unsinkable", it came to be believed that the world at large had shared his opinion. Over the coming weeks, as the survivors described their experiences, some of the initial stories turned out to be true. Some did not, but remained in the public consciousness anyway.

The tragedy tapped into many of the crucial concerns of the era. What did it mean to be a man? What did it mean to be British? It also posed more timeless questions. We all live in the awareness of death, but how should we – and how would we – behave when confronted with its imminent certainty?

The passengers and crew of the *Titanic* represented a cross-section of contemporary society. Their social stratification was echoed in its physical structure, from the millionaires in their upper-deck staterooms to the stokers shovelling coal far below. In a stark, elemental arena of ice and darkness, far from all that was familiar, rich and poor alike were subjected to a hideous ordeal from which less than a third emerged alive.

In the crucible of the disaster, the rules and conventions by which the Edwardian world operated were put to the test. Who survived, and who did not, was taken to reflect intrinsic truths about gender, class and race. Where the actual statistics failed to bear out cherished beliefs, they were largely ignored. Rhetoric about bravery and self-sacrifice served to obscure simple facts, such as that if the ship had had an appropriate number of

THE *TITANIC* MEETS THE ICE-MONSTER

That the *Titanic* disaster possessed an almost unearthly quality was immediately recognized. On 17 April 1912, the day that the *Daily Sketch* carried the first full news of the sinking, it also published an article about the "**ice-monster**" that destroyed her: "To most of us icebergs have always seemed to be merely extravagant details in the fairy tales of science. We were as little concerned with them as with the glass mountains of Grimm or the flying horses of the Arabian Nights."

Second Officer Lightoller, during what was clearly rehearsed testimony to the British inquiry, described the sinking in similarly mythic terms. Hoping to ensure that no human being would be blamed for the collision, he depicted a night of malevolent enchantment that might have come straight from a fairy tale:

"Of course we know now the extraordinary combination of circumstances that existed at that time which **you would not meet again in a hundred years**; that they should all have existed just on that particular night shows of course that everything was against us … In the first place there was no moon … Then there was no wind, not the slightest breath of air. And most particular of all in my estimation is the fact, a most extraordinary circumstance, that there was not any swell. Had there been the slightest degree of swell I have no doubt that berg would have been seen in plenty of time to clear it … The moon we knew of, the wind we knew of, but the absence of swell we did not know of."

lifeboats and a fully trained crew, everyone would have been saved. In Britain, Captain Smith, who went down with his ship, and the musicians who played as the *Titanic* slipped beneath the waves, were hailed as heroes. In America, Benjamin Guggenheim, dressed in his finest clothes, and John Jacob Astor IV, bidding his young wife farewell, were seen to have died like gentlemen. The press in both countries rejoiced that their citizens had passed the test of gallantry.

Despite those religious commentators who insisted the sinking of the *Titanic* was a divine judgement – whether on humanity's misplaced faith in new technology, or simply the decadence of the first-class passengers – it came more widely to be seen as a triumph as well as a tragedy, a vindication of Anglo-Saxon character and fortitude. Less than two weeks after the disaster, *Lloyd's Weekly News* published a forty-page booklet called "The Deathless Story of the *Titanic*", although if there's one thing the story was not, it was deathless.

The *Titanic* reappears

It's easy to assume that the *Titanic* has simply remained in popular consciousness ever since she sank. However, the evidence suggests that she faded
from prominence with the coming of the Great War in 1914, and especially
after the sinking of the Cunard liner *Lusitania* by a German U-Boat, just off
Ireland, in May 1915.

It's surely significant that after 1913, no new books about the tragedy
appeared until the 1950s, by which time another world war had come and
gone. The revival of interest was spurred by the publication in 1955 of American author Walter Lord's classic *A Night to Remember*, which was made into
a successful British film three years later.

By now, the Edwardian era was remembered more for the rigidity of its
class and gender divisions than for its moral rectitude. While the heroism of
many aboard the *Titanic* was still recognized, uncomfortable undercurrents
were rising to the surface. There had always been a lurking suspicion that
the *Titanic*'s third-class passengers were held back from escaping the sinking
ship; now, in a less deferent age, that alleged indifference to the lower orders
came to be seen as one of the defining elements of the tragedy.

Over the last fifty years, writers and filmmakers have investigated the
Titanic saga from every conceivable angle. To the student of the disaster,
intrigued by its many mysteries, it's a puzzle that can never be solved. To the
world at large, however, the essential myth of the *Titanic* is straightforward.
The story that everyone knows, the one that's told in James Cameron's 1997
movie, is of a ship that's doomed to crash. The iceberg cannot be avoided;
the *Titanic* is in the grip of inexorable fate. Audiences experience a delicious
thrill in knowing that her passengers and crew remain blithely ignorant of
their impending doom, and can do nothing to prevent it. Cameron is just
one of many story-tellers to have placed invented "everyman" characters
aboard the *Titanic*, to find meaning, redemption and, above all, love in the
face of death.

A Night to Remember became a bestseller just as the heyday of the
great transatlantic liners was drawing to an end. James Cameron's *Titanic*
appeared as the last survivors of the disaster were about to fade out of
sight – indeed one such (fictional) survivor was integral to the plot. In
the meantime, however, the *Titanic* herself had returned to view. Her
re-discovery in 1985 was as shocking as it was exciting; that ship, crew
and passengers alike had passed beyond the reach of this world was so
integral to the myth that it seemed almost blasphemous to disturb her
slumbers on the ocean floor. Since then, millions of devotees have admired
the relics that have been raised from the deep, such as the captain's brass

THE *TITANIC* IN HISTORY

The sinking of the *Titanic* was not so much a major historic event as a cultural landmark, a tragic prologue to a century of cataclysmic wars and Earth-shaking revolutions. Even at the time, it was not the worst shipwreck ever, and the death toll has been far surpassed since then.

In fact, the *Titanic* was not as exceptional as popular history suggests. Yes, when launched, she was the largest ship ever built, but she was the second of three all-but-identical ships; the maiden voyage of her elder sister, the *Olympic*, had taken place a year previously, amid much greater publicity. What's more, a German company was already building an even larger vessel, the *Imperator*, which was launched a mere five weeks after the *Titanic* sank.

Neither was the *Titanic* thought to be uniquely safe, although the public had indeed come to believe that the latest ships were virtually unsinkable. And while the victims of the disaster were famous at the time, none would otherwise be remembered now; both John Jacob Astor IV and Benjamin Guggenheim, for example, were the prosperous but otherwise unremarkable descendants of hugely wealthy families.

megaphone and the crow's-nest bell. The actual *Titanic* remains below in ghostly splendour, destined to be eaten away by rust and microbes until not a trace survives.

What we know ... and what we don't

It will never be possible to tell the complete story of the *Titanic*. The only **eyewitnesses** were the participants themselves. Each of the seven hundred survivors had their own version of the tragedy, and each saw only a small fraction of the night's events. Some told their stories repeatedly over the years to come, varying them perhaps each time; others never spoke of the disaster. All shaped their accounts, however implicitly, to suit some agenda – thus no man said he'd fought his way onto a lifeboat, no woman that she'd chosen to leave her husband even though she knew the ship was sinking.

The best sources of information are the official **inquiries** into the sinking. The American inquiry opened the morning after the *Carpathia* reached New York, the British equivalent less than two weeks later. Each took the testimony of dozens of witnesses, and cross-examined them as to the details. For many of the *Titanic*'s crewmen, their evidence at the inquiries provides our only record of what they did and saw. Both inquiries were flawed, however; even when they managed to ask the right man the right question, they weren't necessarily given a truthful answer. Central figures like **Robert Hichens**, who was at the helm of the *Titanic* when she hit the iceberg, and **Charles Lightoller**, her senior surviving officer, were among many unreliable witnesses.

In addition, two survivors – with pleasing symmetry, an American first-class passenger, **Colonel Archibald Gracie**, and an English second-class passenger, **Lawrence Beesley** – wrote books about the disaster. Others sold their stories to the press, or gave interviews either at the time or in their later years. From the 1950s onwards, writers and researchers sought out and interviewed the dwindling band of survivors, hoping to garner yet more details before their voices fell silent forever.

The story of the *Titanic*'s maiden voyage, as it unfolds in Chapters 3 to 7 of this book, is based entirely on the personal testimonies of the survivors. Assembling all those individual stories into a coherent narrative has involved repeatedly choosing one witness against another, and at times opting for one out of several possible conclusions. Not every detail can be guaranteed with cast-iron certainty, but historians are in broad agreement on the main thrust of events.

Certain issues, however, remain deeply controversial, with powerful arguments on both sides and no definitive solution. Did Captain Smith race the *Titanic* towards the iceberg at reckless speed, perhaps under pressure from White Star chairman J. Bruce Ismay? What was the so-called "Mystery Ship", seen from the decks of the sinking *Titanic*? Was it the Leyland liner *Californian*? Was the sinking of the *Titanic* a vast insurance fraud? To avoid breaking the flow of the story, the most important such debates are considered separately, and at length, in Chapter 9.

Part I

TRIUMPH

Chapter 1
1912 Overture

Knowing that the Great War was just two years away, it's conventional in hindsight to depict the world of 1912 as peopled solely by pampered plutocrats and downtrodden workers, all sailing obliviously towards disaster. In truth, however, the world was already changing, faster than it ever had before, amid a ferment of social, political, cultural and technological innovation.

The greatest nations on Earth, Great Britain and the United States, were home to its two largest cities, London and New York. Given the ever-increasing urgency of trade, transportation and communications between the two, connections across the north Atlantic were the very lifeblood of the planet.

At the start of the twentieth century, the **British Empire** held dominion over a quarter of the globe, in terms of both population and area. As arch-imperialist Cecil Rhodes put it, "If there be a God, I think that what he would like me to do is to paint as much of Africa British-red as possible." His philosophy was simple: "I contend that we are the first race in the world, and that the more of the world we inhabit the better it is for the human race."

The **United States** was embarking on its own imperialist adventure. In 1898, it had conquered the Philippines, taken over Cuba, and annexed Hawaii. Three years later, after President William McKinley was assassinated in Buffalo, New York, the 42-year-old **Theodore Roosevelt** became the youngest US president in history. Having risen to prominence in the Spanish-American War, personally leading the "Rough Riders" in Cuba, he epitomized bullish American self-confidence and expansionism.

Also in 1901, the Victorian era finally drew to a close, when Queen Victoria died after 64 years on the British throne. Largely absent from London for forty years, the old queen had predicted that the monarchy might not long survive her death. Her son and heir, **Edward VII**, however – a bluff and bumptious character widely known as "Bertie" – proved hugely popular. His extended family ruled much of Europe. Both Kaiser Wilhelm of Germany and Tsar Nicholas of Russia were his nephews, while other relatives included the kings of Norway, Denmark, Greece, Belgium and Portugal.

On both sides of the Atlantic, however, political currents were shifting towards a new sense of **social equality**. In the United Kingdom, which still incorporated Ireland, a Liberal government came to power in 1906. The austere Herbert Asquith became prime minister in 1908, with the charismatic David Lloyd George as chancellor. They introduced Britain's first old age pension in 1909, paying five shillings per week to men aged seventy or over; the country's first unemployment benefit followed in 1911. The Liberals faced down Conservative threats to derail their programme in the House of Lords with a threat of their own, to create hundreds of new peerages and steamroller the legislation through; a huge constitutional crisis ensued.

Meanwhile, in the US, President Roosevelt became the defining figure of the **Progressive Era**, a reaction against the so-called Gilded Age, when industrialists and financiers had seemed able to manipulate the national economy at will. These "robber barons" included the likes of John D. Rockefeller, who controlled seventy percent of the world's oil almost before anyone else had realized it was worth controlling; Andrew Carnegie, who made his fortune manufacturing steel; and J. Pierpoint Morgan, who went for the most basic commodity of all – money. The three men combined forces in 1901 to end competition in the steel industry, by chartering the United States Steel Corporation, the first billion-dollar corporation.

The *Titanic* disaster is often depicted as a devastating shock to a world grown complacent on affluence and technical wizardry. In fact, the Progressive Era was all too familiar with **preventable tragedies**. An astonishing 35,000 Americans died each year in industrial accidents. Eight of the ten worst mining disasters in US history occurred between 1900 and 1914, while at least six hundred people died in the Iroquois Theater fire in Chicago in 1903. In 1904, over a thousand people, mostly women and children, were killed in New York, when the steamboat *General Slocum* caught fire in the East River. Spearheaded by Roosevelt, who fulminated against the "law-defying wealth" of the robber barons, the mood grew that it was the business of government to regulate industry, establish safety standards, and hold corporations to account.

Even though its frontier days were over, the US was continuing to grow. Between 1900 and 1910, **immigration** from Europe reached its peak. Over two million arrived from Italy alone, while more than a million new immigrants passed through Ellis Island in a single year, 1907. The last two states of what later became known as the "lower 48", New Mexico and Arizona, were admitted to the Union early in 1912.

Immigrants awaiting transfer from Ellis Island to Manhattan, 1912.

After Roosevelt declined to stand for re-election in 1908, he was succeeded by his preferred candidate, William Howard Taft. By 1912, however, the two former friends had fallen out, and were competing for the Republican nomination for that November's presidential election. The day before the *Titanic* went down, Roosevelt won a resounding victory in the Pennsylvania primary. Writer Henry Adams reacted to what he saw as a double blow by proclaiming, "The *Titanic* is wrecked; so is Taft; so is the Republican Party; all in one brief hour."

In both the US and Britain, the campaign to win **votes for women** was approaching its peak. At 5.30pm on 1 March 1912, just a month before the *Titanic* sailed, suffragettes on London's main commercial streets suddenly produced hidden hammers from their muffs and handbags, and smashed the nearest shop windows; 124 were arrested. At the same time, Mrs Emmeline Pankhurst was in Downing Street, throwing a stone at the window of the prime minister's house.

Elsewhere, France too controlled an extensive empire, dominating much of north and central Africa as well as Indochina. Belgium, Germany, Spain and Italy also had colonies in Africa. Change was afoot, however. South Africa was granted self-government in 1909, despite complaints from Labour MPs in Britain that its new constitution failed to acknowledge its black population. Three years later, January 1912 saw the founding of the African National

THE BIRTH OF MODERNISM

Virginia Woolf famously wrote that "on or about December 1910 human character changed". Her immediate point of reference was an exhibition at London's Grafton Galleries, "Manet and the Post-Impressionists", which marked the first showing in England for such artists as Matisse, Picasso and van Gogh. More generally, she was speaking of the arrival of **modernism**, which she suggested marked a shift in relations between "masters and servants, husbands and wives, parents and children".

The next summer saw another triumphant arrival from Paris, with the London debut of the dazzlingly innovative **Ballets Russes**. The Edwardian era had now ended, with the death of Edward VII, and Diaghilev's company made its first sensational appearance as part of the coronation celebrations for George V. Their return visit in the winter before the *Titanic* sailed was the highlight of London's social season. It marked the last time Anna Pavlova danced with Vaslav Nijinsky, who was soon to shock Paris with *L'après-midi d'un faune*.

Congress. That same month, the Republic of China was established under President Sun Yat-Sen; the last emperor abdicated at the start of February.

In retrospect, perhaps the most important development during the first decade of the twentieth century was the escalation of the **naval arms race** between Britain and Germany. Competition to produce ever mightier battleships reached a crescendo in 1906, with the launch of HMS *Dreadnought* by the Royal Navy. Her two crucial innovations – being armed exclusively with massive 12-inch guns, and powered by steam turbines – rendered all previous battleships obsolete. Having long boasted the biggest navy in the world, Britain now fought to stay ahead as Germany rushed to build her own rival fleet. Many in both countries came to feel that war was inevitable.

Technology and innovation

The arrival of the twentieth century triggered an astonishing **technological transformation**. In 1900, the first motorized omnibus ventured onto the muddy streets of London, where most people still walked to work, and crossing sweepers had to clear a way through the horse droppings. The Métro opened in Paris that same year, followed by the New York subway four years later. Wilbur and Orville Wright flew the first powered **airplane** in December 1903, and achieved sustained flight within five years.

At the start of the century, **motor cars** were the playthings of a tiny elite. Just over eight thousand cars shared the roads of Britain in 1904, when a maximum speed limit of 20mph was introduced. In the US, future president Woodrow Wilson observed in 1906 that "nothing has spread socialistic feeling in this country more than the use of the automobile, a picture of the arrogance of wealth". Fewer than ten percent of the American population at the time had electricity in their homes. By 1908, only nine cars had ever crossed the United States, and only one of those in winter. That year, however, Henry Ford built his first Model T in Detroit, instigating the world's first system of mass production to meet the demand.

Culturally too, a new era was dawning. Kodak introduced its first Brownie camera in 1900, making it possible for anyone to take what soon became known as "snapshots". The first purpose-built **movie theatre**, the Nickelodeon, opened in Pittsburgh, Pennsylvania, in 1905, and the **phonograph** began to spread into private homes, although as yet the sound quality was too poor for listening to music to be a pleasure. Sigmund Freud, who published *The Psychopathology of Everyday Life* in 1901, paid his only visit to the United States in 1909, the year after Buffalo Bill's touring Wild West show made its final appearance. Charlie Chaplin and Stan Laurel sailed to America with Fred Karno's Mumming Birds in 1910.

Tales of adventure and derring-do inspired millions. In November 1911, a British expedition led by **Captain Robert Scott** set out to become the first explorers to reach the South Pole. When they achieved their goal in January 1912, however, they discovered that a better equipped Norwegian party, under Roald Amundsen, had arrived there a month earlier. Amundsen announced his triumph in early March; another year was to go by, however, before the world learned what had become of Scott. It eventually transpired that he had frozen to death in his tent, the last of his group to perish, just two weeks before the *Titanic* sailed.

The first transatlantic liners

The story of the *Titanic* truly begins in 1858, with the launch of Isambard Kingdom Brunel's ***Great Eastern***. By then, steamships had been regularly crossing the Atlantic for twenty years, ever since Brunel's *Great Western* in 1838. The development of the first steam-powered ships dated back earlier still, to the late eighteenth century. The *Great Eastern*, however, was the first vessel ever to be made entirely of iron. Originally designed to travel to Australia and back without refuelling – it was believed there was no coal in Australia – she was equipped with masts and sails as well as twin paddle wheels and a screw propeller. It soon transpired, however, that she couldn't use sail power at the same time as steam. Brunel himself died in 1859, before the *Great Eastern* completed her first trip to America.

THE MIRACLE OF WIRELESS

Of all the new century's astonishing innovations, none seemed more miraculous than the transformation of **wireless** from a parlour trick to a means of instantaneous transatlantic communication. The man responsible, **Guglielmo Marconi**, was more of a practical genius than a scientist. Born in Italy in 1874, to an Italian father and an Irish mother, the young Marconi was a precocious self-taught amateur, who experimented endlessly with homemade electrical equipment in the grounds of the family estate. Moving to England in 1896, where he was aided by his mother's aristocratic connections, he attracted influential support from the British post office.

Long-distance telegraphy was already an established fact of life – Morse Code had been invented in 1844, and the first **transatlantic cable** completed in 1858. The development of wireless, therefore, was very much focused on aiding **navigation**. The idea of mass communication by radio had yet to occur to anyone. In 1897, Marconi established the first-ever wireless station in the Needles Hotel on the Isle of Wight, and entertained Queen Victoria by exchanging messages with the royal yacht anchored just offshore. Two years later, Marconi published a newspaper aboard the liner *St Paul* as it approached Southampton en route from New York, using wireless messages received from the Needles. Three years after that, aboard the *Philadelphia*, he demonstrated that ships could pick up messages throughout an entire Atlantic crossing.

Marconi was unable to explain why his signals travelled so much further at night than by day, but through trial and error he succeeded in establishing a dependable transatlantic wireless connection. The world's navies took note when superior use of wireless enabled the Japanese to wipe out almost the entire Russian Baltic fleet in 1905.

Wireless also began to demonstrate its potential to create sensational **news** stories. In January 1909, Marconi was acclaimed for saving almost four thousand lives, in the wireless-coordinated rescue operation that followed the collision off Nantucket between the White Star Line's *Republic* and the *Florida*. The next year, the captain of the transatlantic liner *Montrose* recognized a passenger aboard

Harland & Wolff and the White Star Line

Meanwhile, in September 1858, Edward Harland, who until then had managed Hickson's shipyard at Queen's Island, close to the mouth of the River Lagan in Belfast, Ireland, bought the yard outright for £5000. The money was borrowed from a German financier based in Liverpool, Gustav Schwabe. Three years later, Harland joined forces with Schwabe's nephew, Gustav Wolff, to form the company of **Harland & Wolff**.

Guglielmo Marconi in St John's, Newfoundland, in December 1901, when he received the first transatlantic radio signals from Cornwall, England.

his ship as fugitive wife-murderer **Dr Crippen**. The whole world followed the progress of the London detective, Walter Dew, who, summoned by wireless, took a faster ship to Canada and arrested Crippen before he could disembark.

As of early 1912, however, different countries and shipping companies operated different and not necessarily compatible wireless equipment and protocols. Ships were not legally obliged to maintain wireless connections at all, let alone around the clock. Marconi himself was living in a large country house in Fawley, Hampshire, with gardens that sloped down to Southampton Water, and a turreted tower that enjoyed views of the great liners as they sailed past. His family was invited to join the maiden voyage of the *Titanic*, but Marconi left for America on the *Lusitania* when the trip was delayed. After his young son fell ill, his wife cancelled as well; they contented themselves with waving as the *Titanic* steamed by.

At much the same time, in Liverpool, a young shipbroker named **Thomas Henry Ismay** was acquiring shares in the locally based **White Star Line**, established in 1845. The company promptly ran into trouble when it attempted to shift its focus from trade with Australia, while also upgrading its fleet. In 1864, its first steamship, the *Royal Standard*, sustained severe damage on her maiden voyage when she collided with an Antarctic iceberg. With the White Star Line on the brink of bankruptcy in 1867, Ismay bought its entire assets and goodwill for £1000. He then set about redefining the White Star Line, and equipping it with modern iron ships. Having started out by leasing whatever vessels he could, he soon decided he needed to build his own fleet. Determined to establish a regular passenger service between Liverpool and New York, he announced the formation of the Oceanic Steam Navigation Company in 1869.

With the encouragement of one of his principal investors, Gustav Schwabe, Ismay entered into partnership with Harland & Wolff, and commissioned the construction of four new steamships. The first to be completed was the *Oceanic*, launched in Belfast in 1870. The *Atlantic* followed later that same year, and the *Baltic* and *Republic* the next. Such was their success that Ismay swiftly ordered two more, even larger, ships, each weighing five thousand tons: the *Britannic*, launched in 1874, and the *Germanic*, in 1875. Each had a maximum speed of nineteen knots, and could thus cross the Atlantic in just over seven days.

The collaboration between Harland & Wolff and the White Star Line proved fruitful. Harland was among the first shipbuilders to realize that the new breed of steamship could dispense with the trappings and conventions of sailing ships. Superfluous features such as figureheads and bowsprits were stripped away, while the central superstructure too could now be built in sturdy iron. For his part, Ismay aimed to give passengers the most **comfortable** experience possible. His greatest innovation was to move the staterooms and saloon amidships, away from the noisy and juddering stern.

The race for supremacy

The White Star Line found itself at the forefront of a boom in transatlantic travel. The speed and reliability of the new steamships made it possible to operate to a fixed timetable, while their comfort and perceived safety enticed ever greater numbers to cross the ocean for pleasure rather than strict necessity. Not that the business was entirely dependent on wealthy travellers – other lucrative sources of revenue included carrying cargo, mail, and emigrants leaving the Old World for the New. **Emigrants** in particular, making the greatest investment of their lives on a journey into the unknown, showed a marked preference for the latest and largest liners.

Of the many German, American and British steamship lines who became locked in a fierce struggle for supremacy, it was the British and North American Royal Mail Steam Packet Company that became White Star's greatest rival. Established in Liverpool in 1840, after founder Samuel Cunard was awarded the contract to provide the first transatlantic steamship mail service, it was initially slow to follow White Star's example. In 1879, however, reorganized as the **Cunard Steamship Company**, the line began to commission its own sleek, steel liners. Starting with the *Servia* in 1881, each name was suffixed with *–ia*, in counterpoint to White Star's *–ic*.

Ever since 1838, the record holder for the fastest westbound Atlantic crossing had been said to hold the **Blue Riband**. The phrase was purely notional, derived from horse racing, but ownership of the Blue Riband became a point of huge honour. The *Germanic* held it for five years, until 1882, and the next generation of White Star Line vessels, the *Majestic* and *Teutonic*, recaptured it in 1891. After Cunard's *Campania* won the Blue Riband in 1893, however, the White Star Line never regained it. By now, Thomas Ismay was convinced that White Star should concentrate on what it did best – providing unparalleled elegance and comfort, while accepting slower speeds than Cunard or its major German competitor, **Hamburg-Amerika**. When Ismay died in 1899, a newspaper obituary appropriately credited him with being "the inventor of luxurious ocean travel".

The International Mercantile Marine

Thomas Ismay was succeeded at the helm of White Star by his son, **J. Bruce Ismay**. Born in 1862, the younger Ismay had spent all his working life with the company. Already a senior figure in the industry, he had chaired the 1898 international conference in London that specified fixed routes across the north Atlantic for all shipping lines to follow, in order to avoid seasonal ice and fog. Things had also changed at Harland & Wolff. Following the death of Edward Harland in 1895, the Canadian-born **William James Pirrie** was now managing director.

Around this time, American financier **J.P. Morgan** conceived the idea of creating a **monopoly** of all transatlantic freight and passenger traffic. His first purchase was the ailing Inman Line, a British steamship company squeezed dry by the struggle between White Star and Cunard. Morgan went on to snap up several lesser companies, including the Dominion, Red Star, and Leyland lines, but White Star and Cunard were his major targets.

Pirrie, who felt that the future of Harland & Wolff would be better assured in alliance with the giant conglomerate than by remaining dependent on the White Star Line, swiftly threw in his lot with Morgan. Despite Ismay's initial blustering – Pirrie called the prospective Morgan takeover "magnificent and ingenious", whereas to Ismay it was "a swindle and a humbug" – he soon capitulated. The White Star Line was sold for £10 million in 1901, and in 1902 the formation was announced of the International Mercantile Marine Company, or **IMM**. Both the principal German lines, Hamburg-Amerika and Norddeutscher-Lloyd, were included in the syndicate. Ismay became both its president and managing director, while Pirrie was one of the thirteen directors. In 1906, when the retirement of Gustav Wolff left him with complete authority over Harland & Wolff, he was elevated to the peerage as Viscount Pirrie.

Although now American-owned, the White Star Line continued to act as a separate entity. For the moment, Ismay carried on implementing the ambitious plans laid down by his father. The White Star's so-called "Big Four" were completed in steady succession: the *Celtic*, launched in 1901 and the first ship to be larger than the *Great Eastern*, was followed by the *Cedric* (1903), *Baltic* (1904) and *Adriatic* (1907).

Cunard, however, had managed to resist being drawn into the IMM, in part by cutting a deal in which the British government subsidized the construction of new ships in return for being able to requisition them as troop or cargo carriers in times of war. That agreement bore fruit when Cunard built the two largest ships the world had ever seen, the *Mauretania* and the *Lusitania*. Launched in 1906 and 1907 respectively, each attracted worldwide publicity, and went on to capture the Blue Riband. The *Mauretania* was to hold the Blue Riband for twenty years, from 1909 until 1929; the career of the *Lusitania*, however, proved to be much shorter.

Chapter 2
Building the *Titanic*

One London evening in July 1907, Lord William James Pirrie, the chairman of shipbuilders Harland & Wolff, entertained Joseph Bruce Ismay of the White Star Line to dinner in his Belgrave Square mansion. The pleasantries over, the two men set about addressing their great shared problem: how to compete with the latest generation of superliners then being constructed by Cunard, whose *Lusitania* and *Mauretania* were about to go into service.

Planning the Olympic class

In keeping with the tradition of their two companies, Pirrie and Ismay decided that rather than attempt to match the Cunard ships for speed, their primary aim should be to outclass the *Lusitania* and *Mauretania* in both **size** and **comfort**. While the White Star Line was already renowned for both qualities, there was still scope to build even bigger and better. The larger ships grew, the more passengers they could carry, and the more spacious their accommodation and dining rooms could be. As faster ships vibrated more, settling for a slower pace also enjoyed the pay-off of a generally smoother ride. It was essential to White Star's plans that they would in due course build **three** of these new behemoths, and thus be able to run them to a regular weekly timetable. Every week, one ship would cross in each direction, while the third could remain out of service to be re-stocked and refreshed.

This was the plan that resulted in the building of the *Titanic* and her sister ships. The longstanding trust between the two partners enabled Harland & Wolff simply go ahead and build the ships on the usual "cost plus" basis. They incurred such expenses as they deemed appropriate, and forwarded the bills to the White Star Line adding a fixed percentage, agreed in advance. In principle,

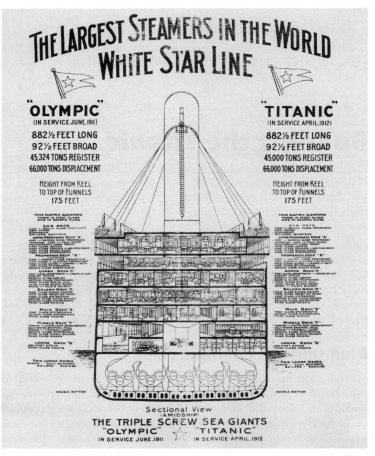

A White Star Line advertisement for the Olympic *and* Titanic *reveals their similarities.*

therefore, Harland & Wolff had no incentive to cut corners or trim costs, though naturally all design and pricing decisions were discussed as they arose. Besides Pirrie and Ismay, there was also a third, hidden party in the equation: American financier J. Pierpoint Morgan. As a subsidiary of the International Mercantile Marine or IMM (see p.11), the White Star Line formed part of Morgan's vast portfolio of investments, and Morgan ultimately footed the bills.

The ambitious new scheme was announced on 11 September 1907, in a bid to steal thunder from the *Lusitania*, then on her maiden voyage. On her second voyage a month later, the *Lusitania* broke the transatlantic speed record and reclaimed the so-called Blue Riband from the Hamburg Amerika Line

THOMAS ANDREWS

No figure aboard the *Titanic* seems to have been so universally loved as **Thomas Andrews**. Even if he didn't design the ship all by himself – something with which he's often credited – he certainly played the largest role. By all accounts he was a very charming man, as concerned with the well-being of employees and passengers as he was with the tiniest details of the ship itself. Very much the hero of Walter Lord's seminal account of the disaster, *A Night to Remember*, Andrews was later depicted in James Cameron's *Titanic* as the archetypal benign, twinkling Irishman.

Thomas Andrews was born in County Down, Ireland in 1873. His mother was the sister of William Pirrie, who in due course became chairman of Harland & Wolff. Following in his uncle's footsteps, young Thomas was apprenticed at the age of sixteen, and spent five years learning every aspect of work in the shipyards. By the time Pirrie and J. Bruce Ismay conceived the plan to build the *Olympic* and *Titanic*, Andrews was the managing director responsible for design at Harland & Wolff, and seemed destined to rise to the very top of the company.

An engineer who helped to build the *Titanic* later wrote that Andrews "hardly ever left this job until it was finished, in fact he would even come down in the middle of the night to see if there was any hold backs or any stuff going on. He was a very earnest and determined man, but at the same time most fair and considerate." Much like Ismay, Andrews would join the maiden voyage of each new ship to observe and iron out any problems that might occur. His experiences on the *Olympic*'s first transatlantic trip in 1911 prompted several modifications to her younger sister. Stewardess Violet Jessop, for example, credited him with having responded to her suggestions by making welcome adjustments to the layout and wardrobe space of her shared cabin.

Aboard the *Titanic*, Andrews led the so-called **Guarantee Group**, a nine-man team of Harland & Wolff specialists who nominally travelled as passengers. Shortly before sailing from Southampton, Andrews wrote to his wife of less than two years that "the *Titanic* is now about complete and will I think do the Old Firm credit tomorrow when we sail".

by reaching New York in under five days. In December of that same year, the *Mauretania* started her own record-breaking career; she was to capture the Blue Riband in 1909 and hold it for more than twenty years.

Names, design, and signing the dotted line

The White Star Line revealed the names of the first two of its new ships on 22 April 1908: *Olympic* and *Titanic*. The first was a reference to the Greek gods of Mount Olympus, the second to the mighty immortal Titans they subdued. Despite subsequent official denials, historians generally agree that the third ship was destined to be called the *Gigantic* – in Greek mythology, the Titans had after all previously defeated the Giants. That name was quietly dropped, however, most likely in the wake of the disaster, when with jingoism seeming a better bet than hubris it became the *Britannic*.

The two principal designers were Harland & Wolff's general manager **Alexander Carlisle**, who was Lord Pirrie's brother-in-law, and the company's chief draughtsman, **Thomas Andrews**, who as well as being a director was also Pirrie's nephew. These new ships did not represent any great advance in shipbuilding technology or design; they were simply scaled-up versions of proven models. At heart, they were enormous yachts, and the major decisions to be made centred more on their interior design than nautical matters.

Once Ismay had approved the plans, formal letters of agreement were signed for both the *Olympic* and the *Titanic* on 31 July 1908. Lord Pirrie had clearly been anticipating the need to construct larger ships for some time, as work on enlarging Harland & Wolff's facilities had started in 1906. Over the ensuing two years, two separate thousand-foot slipways took shape. Side by side, and surmounted by a single colossal gantry, they held cranes poised 214 feet above ground level.

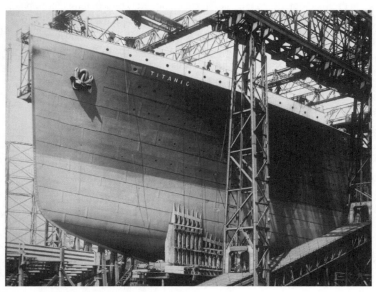

The prow of the Titanic *under construction.*

WHAT'S IN A NUMBER?

The claim has frequently been made that the hull of the *Titanic* bore the number 390904. Supposedly, workers were offended when they saw that number reflected, possibly in standing water in the shipyard, and read the words **"NO POPE"**. It has even been suggested that they deliberately sabotaged their own work, and thus contributed to the disaster.

That story falls down on almost every level. Most obviously, the *Titanic* had no such hull number. The only number relevant to her construction was her yard number, 401, which meant she was the 401st ship constructed by Harland & Wolff. She subsequently received the Board of Trade registration number 131428.

The one germ of truth stems from the shipyard's location in the Protestant heartland of Belfast, with an almost exclusively Protestant workforce. That, however, would make those workers more likely to write anti-Catholic slogans than be offended by them. Designer Thomas Andrews is said to have seen such slogans daubed on the *Titanic* both as she was being built and during her "positioning voyage" from Belfast to Southampton, and to have ordered them to be painted over.

Built in Belfast

The keel of the *Olympic* was laid at the Harland & Wolff shipyards on Queen's Island, Belfast, on 16 December 1908, and was completed within two weeks. Work on the *Titanic* began three months later, on 22 March 1909, and the keel itself laid nine days later. As author Filson Young, who visited the shipyards in 1911, later noted: "For months and months, in that monstrous iron enclosure there was nothing that had the faintest likeness to a ship". In due course, however, the "skeleton" of each vessel began to take shape, and piece after piece was placed in the appropriate spot on the vast scaffolding.

Welding techniques were not yet advanced enough to meet the demands of shipbuilding, so each steel plate of the hull was **riveted** to the next. Varying in thickness between an inch and an inch and a half, they typically measured six feet wide by thirty feet long, and weighed up to four tons. Where possible, new hydraulic riveting machines installed steel rivets, but in less accessible areas the time-honoured technique of hand hammering still persisted. One employee would use tongs to hold a red-hot iron rivet in the lined-up holes of two adjoining plates, then a second would brace a heavy hammer against one side, while the "basher" on the other side hammered the rivet into place. Each rivet on the hull was around three inches long by an inch thick; on the entire ship, a total of three million rivets were used.

Over **fifteen thousand men** worked to build the *Olympic* and the *Titanic*. At least two, and possibly as many as eight, **died** while working on the *Titanic*; with record-keeping as erratic as safety standards, it's impossible to establish an exact figure. The persistent myth that some unfortunate employee was trapped forever between the twin walls of the lower hull, however, is known to be untrue.

While Harland & Wolff were responsible for assembling the hull and superstructure of each ship, and for constructing its engines, boilers and machinery, many of the materials and components were manufactured elsewhere. The *Titanic*'s steel plates, for example, were produced to the highest standards of the day by David Colville & Sons, at the Dalzell Steel & Iron Works in Motherwell, Scotland. Her hundred-ton rudder, cast in six separate pieces, and her enormous stern frame, came from the Darlington Forge Company, in County Durham, England. Her anchors were shipped over from Netherton, Worcestershire. As a boy in Belfast, William MacQuitty, the producer of the 1958 movie *A Night to Remember*, saw a team of sixteen horses hauling one through the city in May 1911.

The launch of the *Olympic*

The *Olympic* was finally **launched** on 20 October 1910. Watched by well over a hundred thousand spectators, and painted a very light grey to show up well in press photos, she took just 62 seconds to slide down into the River Lagan. Within another minute, she was brought to a halt by assorted anchors and chains, ready for a team of tugs to tow her to a deep-water wharf in Belfast Harbour.

Such launches took place as soon as a ship's hull was watertight, and the basic internal structure of decks, bulkheads and the like was in place. The *Olympic* was incapable of moving under her own steam, however. Her engines, boilers, heavy machinery and funnels had yet to be installed, while all the passenger accommodation and other facilities had yet to be added. At around 24,000 tons, she was still only half her final weight. The world's largest dry dock, the **Thompson Graving Dock**, had been under simultaneous construction in Belfast, and was now ready to receive her. A two-hundred-ton floating crane was brought over from Germany to lift the colossal engines into place. It took until the end of the following May for the entire process to be completed.

The launch of the *Titanic*

The **launch** of the *Titanic*, on 31 May 1911, was timed to coincide with the start of the *Olympic*'s maiden voyage. Even if the crowd was a fraction smaller than for the *Olympic*'s launch, that still made for a gala day, which unfolded beneath "a sun of almost tropical heat". Lord and Lady Pirrie, who were celebrating their shared birthday, were joined by J.P. Morgan as well as J. Bruce Ismay.

Unlike Cunard, the White Star Line did not "christen" its ships by smashing champagne bottles; as one shipyard worker memorably explained to a journalist, "They just builds 'er and shoves 'er in". At the given signal, just after midday, a nudge from hydraulic rams sent the *Titanic* sliding down a slipway lubricated with 21 tons of soap and tallow. As she descended, one of the labourers hammering away the shoring timbers that held her up was fatally crushed by an unexpected collapse.

While the Pirries and their guests took a tour of the *Titanic*, out on the Lagan, a formal celebration dinner was held at Belfast's Grand Central Hotel. The *Titanic* was then towed away to be fitted out, and the spotlight shifted back to her elder sister.

The *Olympic* goes to sea

Late on the afternoon that the *Titanic* first floated out on the water, the *Olympic* set off on the first leg of her **maiden voyage**, carrying dignitaries including J.P. Morgan. Her first port of call was Liverpool, where she was opened for public visitation. The *Olympic* then continued to Southampton, where according to a medical officer aboard she "caused a sensation". Here too, on one of the final ten days before she sailed for New York, curious locals were allowed on board.

Her first transatlantic crossing began on 14 June. With **Captain E.J. Smith** in charge, and Thomas Andrews and J. Bruce Ismay among the passengers, she called at Cherbourg in France and Queenstown in Ireland, before arriving to a tumultuous reception in New York just under a week later. It took an hour, and the aid of twelve tugs, to nudge the *Olympic* into place alongside the newly extended Pier 59. Both pier and ship sustained superficial damage in the process.

The tug *Hallenbeck* was much more severely injured, however, when the *Olympic*'s starboard propeller was suddenly thrown into reverse. It's not known whether Captain Smith himself gave the order, but much of the stern and rudder of the *Hallenbeck* was sliced off. *The New York Times* dismissed the incident as "a playful touch", but it's now seen as the first evidence of Smith's overconfidence in handling the giant new ships.

The *Olympic* and the *Hawke*

Shortly after she sailed from Southampton on what was scheduled to be her fifth transatlantic voyage, on 20 September 1911, the *Olympic* was involved in a serious **collision** with an armoured Royal Navy cruiser, **HMS *Hawke***. The accident happened off the northernmost tip of the Isle of Wight, as the

THE *TITANIC*'S ENGINES

Both of the White Star Line's great Cunard rivals, the *Lusitania* and the *Mauretania*, had four propellers. However, following a successful 1909 experiment with a lesser White Star ship, the *Laurentic*, it was decided that each *Olympic* class liner would have **three propellers**.

The *Titanic*'s two main propellers, one on the port side and one starboard, were driven by separate four-cylinder, triple-expansion, inverted reciprocating steam engines. Those twin engines, the largest ever built, were almost forty feet tall, and boasted cylinders that measured almost nine feet across; they turned in opposite directions, to dampen vibrations. The propellers themselves had three blades, were twenty-three feet six inches across, and rotated up to eighty times per minute.

In addition, the *Titanic* had a smaller central propeller, powered by a Parson's low-pressure turbine, which used the exhaust steam from the other two to rotate a little more than twice as fast. This third propeller had four blades, and a diameter of sixteen feet six inches. While it greatly boosted the overall efficiency of the engines, its position forward of the rudder reduced the ship's manoeuvrability, and what's more this third propeller could not be thrown into reverse. Both factors may have contributed to the *Titanic*'s ultimate fate.

In operation, the engines required around 620 tons of **coal** per day, shovelled into 159 furnaces that fired 29 boilers, of which 24 were double-ended, in that they could be fed from both sides, and five were single-ended. They were located in six distinct **boiler rooms**, and fed into three of the *Titanic*'s four **funnels**, the aftmost of which was a dummy. Keeping the fires burning required the backbreaking labour of two hundred firemen, stokers and trimmers. The entire system was officially rated as producing 46,000 horsepower, but experience with the *Olympic* showed the actual figure to be well in excess of 50,000 horsepower.

Olympic was completing the intricate manoeuvre necessary to reach the open waters of the English Channel. Neither ship seems to have appreciated the danger caused by the *Olympic*'s overwhelming displacement until it was too late. The *Hawke* was sucked in, her helm jammed as she was trying to steer clear, and her sharply pointed, reinforced bow sliced head-on into the *Olympic*'s starboard quarter.

Holed both above and below the waterline, 86 feet from her stern, the *Olympic* limped back to Southampton. Two of her watertight compartments were flooded, but she was in no danger of sinking. However, all three blades of her starboard propeller, as well as the propeller shaft, were damaged

*Harland & Wolff workers pose beneath the **Titanic's** propellers.*

badly enough to need replacement. It took two weeks to patch her up at Southampton – with new steel plates below the waterline, and timber above – before she could sail back to Belfast to be repaired.

The White Star Line ultimately appealed the case all the way to the House of Lords, but was found responsible for the accident. The main cause was deemed to be displacement from the *Olympic*, exacerbated by faulty navigation. No blame was attached to Captain Smith, because he was not in formal command of his ship at the time. As remains true in many ports and waterways to this day, ships arriving in or departing from Southampton were required to take on board, and submit to the direction of, officially approved local **pilots**, in this instance George Bowyer. Neither Smith nor Bowyer seems to have learned from the experience; both were on the bridge of the *Titanic* six months later when she had a similar hair-raising encounter at the start of her maiden voyage (see p.47).

As well as putting the *Olympic* out of action, the incident delayed completion of the *Titanic*, as sections of her original propeller shaft were used for the *Olympic* instead. Its significance in *Titanic* lore goes deeper, however. This accident lies at the root of the much-vaunted **conspiracy theory** that the *Titanic* and the *Olympic* were somehow swapped over during the period when they were dry-docked side by side in Belfast. Supposedly the *Olympic* had been more gravely damaged than any outsider realized, and the inability of the White Star Line to claim insurance led to a fatal fraud; see p.214 for full details.

Lessons from the *Olympic*: fine-tuning the *Titanic*

Up to the moment of her launch, the *Titanic* was all but identical to the *Olympic*. As she was fitted out in the ten months that led up to her maiden voyage, however, **differences** crept in. Some were simply revisions prompted by the changing whims of the designers, others the result of lessons learned from the *Olympic*'s experiences at sea.

As was his habit with new additions to the White Star fleet, J. Bruce Ismay sailed on the *Olympic*'s maiden voyage. He returned determined to make the first-class facilities aboard the *Titanic* even more luxurious. Most of the huge promenade that ran along either side of B Deck was therefore removed, and the dining areas towards the stern, and the cabins towards the bow, were expanded to fill the space. In that process, each of the two sumptuous "parlour suites" on B-Deck acquired its own private fifty-foot promenade. Because passengers taking the air on the forward part of the *Olympic*'s A Deck had complained of sea spray blowing in their faces, the corresponding area on the *Titanic* was enclosed with sliding glass screens. As well as equipping the *Titanic* to carry 163 more passengers than the *Olympic*, these changes had the incidental long-term effect of making it possible to distinguish between photographs of the two ships.

The *Titanic* deck by deck

As tall as an eleven-storey building, as long as six city blocks, the *Titanic* was a bewildering multi-level maze. Its most fundamental dividing lines were **horizontal**, creating a stack of separate decks, from the Boat Deck, where the captain and his officers both lived and controlled the ship, down via seven further decks lettered A to G, to the engine and boiler rooms at the bottom. Those decks were not necessarily continuous, however, being interrupted by the ship's boiler casings rising up towards the funnels, as well as various features that rose through more than a single deck, including lounges, the Grand Staircase and even a squash court. Only the decks from C downwards were enclosed within the *Titanic*'s hull. The uppermost three decks – B, A and the Boat Deck – did not stretch all the way from bow to stern, but sat atop the hull, in the ship's central **superstructure**.

While the first-class passengers may have found the upper decks spacious and convenient, the ship's designers did not make ease of movement for anyone else a high priority. Crew and steerage passengers alike had to thread their way through a labyrinth of narrow corridors – known in shipboard parlance as "alleyways" – and staircases. Second Officer Lightoller later recalled that "it took me fourteen days before I could with confidence find my way from one part of that ship to another by the shortest route". The phrase has chilling implications; only a tiny handful of people ever spent fourteen days aboard the *Titanic*, which suggests that at the time of the disaster almost no one knew their way around the ship.

The Boat Deck

Known thanks to the presence of the ship's lifeboats as the **Boat Deck**, the *Titanic*'s uppermost deck was the nerve centre of the ship, with the wheelhouse and officers' quarters at its forward end. The **wireless room**, where the Marconi operators maintained radio communications with the outside world, was immediately aft, with half a dozen small first-class cabins nearby, of which only one was occupied on the *Titanic*'s only voyage. Otherwise the deck consisted largely of a broad open **promenade**, painted a dazzling white, which was divided fore to aft into three principal sections, reserved for officers, first-class and second-class passengers respectively. Also up here, the ship's **gymnasium** boasted all the latest equipment, including two exercise bicycles on which passengers could race against each other. As well as electrically operated horses there was even an "electric camel", also more prosaically described as a "trunk-rotating machine". As the one enclosed space that was accessible to passengers at the very highest level of the ship, close to the lifeboats, the gymnasium served as a gathering point during the disaster.

A Deck

A Deck, immediately below the Boat Deck, was also known as the **Promenade Deck**, on account of the long continuous first-class promenade, again painted white, which encircled it. Besides a handful of the less luxurious first-class cabins, which shared bathrooms and toilets, it held the main venues where first-class passengers could socialize. Amidships were the **First Class Lounge**, and the adjoining **Reading and Writing Room**, an innovation that had proved popular with the *Olympic*'s female passengers. Further aft, the **First Class Smoking Room** had all the heavy dignity of a London gentlemen's

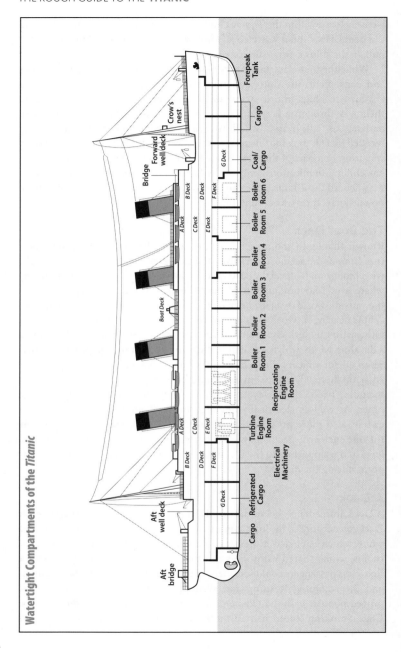

Watertight Compartments of the *Titanic*

TITANIC FACTS AND FIGURES

Length	882 feet 9 inches
Beam (width)	92 feet 6 inches
Height (keel to top of funnels)	175 feet
Draft (keel to waterline)	34 feet 7 inches
Height (waterline to Boat Deck)	62 feet 9 inches
Watertight compartments	16
Gross tonnage	46,328 tons
Coal (capacity)	8000 tons
Coal (per day)	825 tons
Horsepower	46,000
Max speed	24 knots
Passengers (capacity)	2439
Crew (capacity)	900
Passengers (actual)	1309
Crew (actual)	897

club. Reserved for the use of male passengers only, and fitted out with dark mahogany panelling, an imposing bar and stained-glass screens, it centred on a magnificent open fireplace.

Revolving doors on both the port and starboard side led aft into the two identical halves of the **Verandah Café**, each with dramatic bay windows. Much lighter than the Smoking Room, with its white wicker chairs and trellises of climbing plants, and modelled on a Parisian street café, it was also known as the Palm Court thanks to its palm trees.

B Deck

B Deck was almost entirely taken up with the grandest first-class staterooms, the largest of which, including the two promenade suites, were located amidships. Aft, however, the ship's **à la carte restaurant** offered first-class passengers an alternative to the main dining rooms, for all meals. It was decorated in Louis XVI style, with light walnut panelling and crystal chandeliers, and had its own small stretch of promenade. While controlled by the White Star Line, the restaurant was run by Luigi Gatti, who had been head-hunted from London's renowned *Oddenino's*; all its staff, who included ten of Gatti's cousins, counted as his personal employees. Beyond that stood the small **Second Class Smoking Room**, panelled in oak and featuring oak chairs upholstered in green leather, which was surrounded by another promenade area.

C Deck

C Deck too was very largely given over to first-class cabins, including two parlour suites, but also held the first-class barber's shop, the ship's telephone exchange and the purser's office. The stern held separate messes for seamen, greasers and firemen. The substantial and much appreciated **Second Class Library** was located aft, with a promenade to either side. Aft of that in turn was the **aft well deck**, an open deck area that was designated as the Third Class Promenade, and beyond it two small public areas for third-class passengers – one a general room, the other a smoking room.

D Deck

On **D Deck**, also known as the **Saloon Deck**, both the first- and second-class dining rooms stretched all the way from one side of the ship to the other. Boasting huge ocean-view windows, they were positioned here in the ship's most stable area, amidships and three decks down from the Boat Deck, to minimize any sense of motion from either the engines or the ocean. The **First Class Dining Room**, as befitted the world's largest ship, was the largest room

THE WORLD OF STEERAGE

Traditionally, the parts of a ship closest to the rudder, and thus known as **steerage**, would hold its lowest grade of accommodation. Steerage passengers, therefore, were those paying the lowest fare, which as a rule meant they were likely to be prospective immigrants to the US. Under British law, any ship carrying fifty or more such passengers, including the *Titanic*, was designated an **Emigrant Ship**, and subject to enforced standards of seaworthiness. American law went further, requiring all steerage passengers to be examined for communicable **diseases** such as typhoid and diphtheria before they could be admitted into the country. Whereas "cabin-class" passengers were free to disembark as soon as the ship docked in New York, before anyone could leave steerage, inspectors would come on board and individually check them all.

For that system to work, there had to be no possibility that the steerage passengers could infect their cabin-class counterparts during the voyage. Ship owners were therefore required to demonstrate that they had, and used, an efficient system to keep them apart. The obvious solution, as employed on the *Titanic*, was to have lockable gates.

Former president Theodore Roosevelt, crossing the Atlantic in 1910 on the German ship *Kaiserin Auguste Victoria*, told a journalist that he wished steerage could be abolished. He felt that immigrants should immediately "feel that they were entering into a new life of self-respect, with privacy and cleanliness".

ever set afloat. Capable of seating 550 diners, with secluded nooks available for private gatherings, it was entered via its own plushly carpeted Reception Room. The **Second Class Dining Room**, towards the stern, was significantly smaller, so it served its meals in separate sittings, holding a maximum of just under four hundred diners at a time. Meals for both dining rooms were prepared in the same galley, between the two. Just above the kitchens, on C Deck, was what the White Star Line proudly advertised as a "special Maids' and Valets' saloon, where servants may congregate and their meals be served".

The first-class passengers' entrance was also amidships on D Deck, while a handful of first-class cabins were located immediately forward of that. There was also a cluster of second-class cabins immediately aft of the Second Class Dining Room, and even a few third-class cabins crammed into the stern.

Forward of the *Titanic*'s central superstructure on D Deck was the **forward well deck**, another small open area to which third-class passengers had access. Indeed, it existed partly on their account; regulations stipulated that steerage passengers could not be accommodated more than two levels below

With the Olympic class of ship, the White Star Line made considerable steps in that direction. Most obviously, it replaced the term "steerage" with **Third Class**.

In fairness, the third-class accommodation on the *Titanic* was far above the normal standards. Instead of the usual large open dormitories, for example, the ship held individual cabins, albeit very plain, with exposed pipework and beams, and often uncomfortably close to the engines. Each had anything from two to ten berths, equipped with proper mattresses rather than straw. Single men were generally accommodated in the bow, at four to a room, and families in the stern, where family rooms were available. For a potential complement of over a thousand third-class passengers, there were just two bathtubs. Like every bathtub on the *Titanic*, they were fed with hot and cold seawater, which was seen as therapeutic, and equipped with specially adapted soap. Passengers could at least rinse the salt off with fresh water.

Though attention has always focused more on the *Titanic*'s first- and second-class passengers, the third-class contingent exceeded those two combined. As well as two separate areas of deck space, aft on C Deck and forward on D Deck, third-class passengers had the use of a general common room, a smoking room and two bars. The overall third-class experience was very different to that on the higher decks, however. With cabins and facilities squeezed into whatever spaces were free in the bow and stern, shipboard life required endless walking to and fro, along tortuous narrow corridors rather than wide-open decks and soaring staircases.

open deck, so such well decks were often incorporated into ship designs for a more efficient use of overall space. The bow of the ship here held the **firemen's quarters**, consisting of two open rooms each sleeping 54 men, plus communal washrooms and toilets.

E Deck

E Deck was the most cosmopolitan area of the ship, although the lack of open public spaces precluded much mingling. First-class cabins stretched along the starboard side amidships, with second-class cabins for the full width of the ship aft of that, and third-class cabins squeezed into the stern. The port side held accommodation for crew of all kinds, carefully segregated by class and status; thus there were separate quarters for first- and second-class stewards and waiters, for painters, for cooks, for the band musicians and so on. Seamen and trimmers had their quarters in the bow. The port-side "alleyway", nicknamed **Scotland Road** after one of Liverpool's busiest streets, was the ship's main thoroughfare for crew and third-class passengers alike.

F Deck

F Deck centred on the **Third Class Dining Room** and its associated kitchens and stores. Aft lay the engineers' quarters, and second- and third-class cabins, while further third-class cabins were located forward. Thanks to the watertight bulkheads, there were no alleyways on F Deck; to reach the dining room from a cabin on F or G decks, passengers had to climb up to E Deck and drop back down again.

F Deck was also home to the *Titanic*'s **swimming pool**. At just twenty feet long, this was really more of a plunge pool. It was only open to first-class passengers, with separate sessions for ladies and gentlemen. During the day, there was a charge of $1 per hour. Connected facilities immediately aft included an electrically heated bath, known as a **Turkish Bath**, with tiny rooms for shampooing, massage and the like.

G Deck

Because the huge engines and boilers down below reached so far up into the central part of the ship, **G Deck** did not stretch continuously from one end of the *Titanic* to the other, but consisted of two separate sections. As well as further crew and passenger accommodation, forward and aft, it held grocery stores, and some rooms devoted to refrigerated cargo, in the stern, and the **mail room** and baggage areas towards the bow.

Also near the bow was the **squash court**, the void of which extended upwards into F Deck as well. The sport of racquets, played in a larger court with a harder ball, was more popular at the time, but squash was spreading, and fit more comfortably into a ship. The *Titanic* had its own squash pro, Fred Wright, while the world champion, Charles Williams, happened to be among its passengers.

First-class accommodation

All of the **first-class accommodation** aboard the *Titanic* was located amidships, on every deck from the Boat Deck down to E Deck; the first-class elevators linked them all. The grandest cabins were the 28 staterooms that were created on B Deck in response to the early voyages of the *Olympic* (see p.22). Equipped with windows rather than portholes, as well as open fires, and massive wooden beds, these were individually decorated to suit a wide range of tastes and nationalities, in themes ranging from Regency to Early Dutch and Louis XVI. Many were linked by interconnecting doors, which could be unlocked to create suites.

The most luxurious of all were the four **parlour suites**, each consisting of two bedrooms plus a parlour and bathroom. Two of those were on C Deck, while the others, immediately above on B Deck, were **promenade suites**, featuring their own fifty-foot stretches of private deck, complete with mock-Tudor panelling. For the *Titanic*'s maiden voyage, one of those suites was occupied by White Star chairman J. Bruce Ismay, who naturally did not pay, while Mrs Charlotte Cardeza paid £512 6s for the other. Such fares were not all-inclusive; first-class passengers had to pay extra to use such facilities as the à la carte restaurant, the gymnasium, the squash court and the Turkish baths.

Second-class accommodation

The *Titanic*'s **second-class accommodation** was widely acknowledged to be as good as the first-class cabins on her rivals. Indeed, figures differ as to precisely how many first- and second-class cabins the *Titanic* had, because certain cabins could be reconfigured to suit either class, according to demand. Both the second- and third-class cabins were located on all decks from D down to G, but those in second-class were more closely concentrated together, just aft of amidships, and served by their own dedicated elevator that climbed all the way to the Boat Deck. As in first class, they had solid mahogany beds, and received natural light.

Crew accommodation

Contact between crew and passengers aboard the *Titanic* was kept to a minimum. The galleys and mess rooms for sailors and firemen alike were in the forecastle on C Deck, with their **dormitories** crammed into the bow on the four decks beneath. Where possible, an entire watch would sleep in one room, to avoid disturbing each other as they changed over; each of the firemen's rooms on D Deck thus held 54 berths, to correspond with the number of firemen on each watch. Spiral staircases led down to the boiler rooms.

Almost all the rest of the crew accommodation was along the port side of E Deck, accessed via the long open alleyway known as "Scotland Road". Clerks and waiters, printers and bakers all had their own separate dormitories, while the musicians shared a cabin that had another room to hold their instruments. Stewards were segregated by class, with 42 second-class stewards in one room and 34 third-class stewards in another. The eighteen stewardesses were elsewhere, however, in three-women cabins interspersed among the passengers on the upper decks. The engineers had their mess on E Deck too, with their cabins immediately below on D Deck.

The watertight compartments

Much the most famous and misunderstood design feature of the *Titanic* – and the reason why there was any question of her being considered "unsinkable" (see p.198) – was her system of distinct, self-contained **watertight compartments**. The theory was that a collision might pierce one, or at worst two, of those compartments, but that even if they then filled with water, the ship as a whole would not be threatened. Designer Thomas Andrews is said to have reassured a passenger that she could be "cut crosswise into three pieces and each piece would float".

It's seldom realized, however, that this system was neither new nor unique. Such compartments were in fact a legal requirement of the Board of Trade, and were closely monitored to meet agreed specifications. Far from advancing standards in safety, indeed, the *Titanic* reflected a **deterioration** that had been ongoing for the previous fifty years.

Completed in 1858, the very first all-iron ship, Isambard Kingdom Brunel's extraordinary *Great Eastern* (see p.7), was at 692 feet long by far the largest ship ever built. In addition to boasting two separate hulls, inner and outer, she was divided crossways by fifteen bulkheads, and lengthways by two more bulkheads that extended through her engine and boiler rooms. As a result, she held at least forty separate watertight compartments.

If anything, what was radical about the *Titanic* (and the *Olympic*) was not that she had watertight compartments, but that she did **not**. Instead of being truly watertight, her compartments were interrupted by open passageways that were designed to be closed in emergencies. On the *Great Eastern*, all the bulkheads rose to at least thirty feet above the waterline, and were entirely unbroken. The *Titanic*, on the other hand, was divided into sixteen side-to-side compartments, varying in length from 36 feet to 69 feet. Each was separated from the next by a **transverse bulkhead**, denoted from bow to stern by the letters A to P (there was no bulkhead I, to avoid potential confusion with the number 1).

None of those fifteen bulkheads, however, rose any higher than the underside of D Deck. Eight reached that high, and seven only as far as E Deck, the lowest point of which was a mere eleven feet above the waterline. Furthermore, only three of the *Titanic*'s bulkheads – A and B at the bow, and P closest to the stern – were solid and unbroken all the way up to D Deck. All the remaining twelve held openings of some kind, which were capable of being sealed by watertight doors if necessary.

Again unlike the *Great Eastern*, the *Titanic* did not have a double hull, just a **double bottom** that protected the first five feet up from its keel. Within this double wall, the *Titanic*'s lowest level consisted of a large watertight compartment that ran for almost the entire length of the ship. As well as being segmented by the transverse bulkheads, it was also further divided into three lengthwise segments. Somewhat counter-intuitively, water ballast as well as the ship's supply of fresh water was stored in large tanks at this level, so while watertight it was nonetheless largely filled with water.

The emergency doors

Immediately on top of the double bottom came the "tank top", which in the central portion of the ship served as the floor of the engine and boiler rooms. In ordinary conditions, the firemen and engineers down here made their way from one room to the next through open passageways, which could be closed off in emergencies by **watertight doors** that slid down vertically from above. Those doors simply fell under their own weight, like slow-motion guillotines, when a catch was released. When triggered electrically from the bridge, it took around 25 seconds for all to close simultaneously, accompanied by the continuous ringing of a warning bell. Each individual door would also close automatically, however, if water entered the compartment to either side, and could be closed by hand from below as well.

It's those twelve vertical doors at the level of the engine- and boiler-rooms – D to O inclusive – around which so much *Titanic* mythology swirls. Five of them – those that separated the six boiler rooms, in bulkheads E, F, G, H and J – were not in doorways, but in tunnel-like sealed passageways that lead through the coal bunkers. They were heavy enough to cut straight though any coal – or men – in their way.

None of the bulkheads held any openings on **G Deck**. Towards both bow and stern, G Deck consisted of separate watertight sections, as described on p.28, while amidships, it ceased to exist at all; there was simply an enormous gap, filled with the upper reaches of the engines and boilers.

On both **F** and **E Deck**, however, the bulkheads were pierced by doors that were usually left open, but could be slid closed horizontally by hand, either using a key in the door itself, or via a bolted floor hatch in the deck above. When the order to close all the watertight doors was issued, each of these doors had to be closed individually, which was a tricky procedure; during the disaster, several witnesses described seeing groups of seamen struggling to close them one by one.

Ten such doors were evenly distributed around F Deck, while nine were located in those parts of E Deck where the bulkheads extended, all of which were towards the stern. When open, their primary purpose was to allow ease of movement between the different areas of passenger accommodation. When closed, of course, they had the opposite effect, of confining small groups of passengers in sealed compartments from which they could only escape upwards – assuming the stairways weren't themselves locked.

Even in the best conditions, E Deck was the lowest deck on which it was at all easy to get from one end of the ship to the other. The crowded "glory holes" where the stewards slept, on its port side forward from the vertical bulkheads, opened onto the long uninterrupted "Scotland Road" alleyway, under ten feet wide. Once the emergency doors were closed, however, sealing the bulkheads below and making it impossible to use the passageways at that level, engineers and firemen who needed to get from one engine or boiler room to another were forced instead to climb up to E Deck, then drop down again.

Letting safety standards slip

The prime motivation for making the *Titanic* less safe than the *Great Eastern* was that stripping away safety precautions made it possible to increase the convenience and overall satisfaction of its passengers. Thus the huge dining rooms and saloons on the *Titanic* could only exist if there were no bulkheads to slice them up. Similarly, on the *Great Eastern* the decks themselves were substantially watertight, closed off by hatches, so water couldn't spill out onto higher decks, whereas *Titanic* features like the magnificent Grand Staircase effectively meant that the ship was riddled with open shafts.

The *Great Eastern*'s defences received their greatest test in August 1862, when she hit an unknown rock off Long Island. Despite sustaining a much larger gash than the one that sank the *Titanic*, she was protected by her inner hull, and continued safely to New York. Whether the *Titanic* would have fared better had she been fitted with longitudinal partitions like the *Great Eastern* – a British requirement for any vessel intended to carry troops – is a matter for debate. Such partitions did nothing to help the *Lusitania*, for example. When she was torpedoed in 1915, the rush of water into only one side caused such a list that she sank within twenty minutes.

Counting the lifeboats

Even though the *Titanic* was only equipped with enough **lifeboats** to save half the people aboard on its final, fatal night, that was still more than were required by law. The extraordinarily abstruse Board of Trade **regulations** specifying how many lifeboats a ship should carry depended on two main factors. The first, whether its weight exceeded ten thousand tons, had become ludicrously out of date since the figure was laid down in 1894. The second was whether it was adequately divided into watertight compartments. How many passengers and crew it might be carrying was not considered relevant.

The *Titanic* was thus obliged to carry **sixteen** lifeboats, plus rafts and floats equivalent to three quarters of the capacity of those lifeboats. That worked out at enough boats to hold 962 people. In fact she carried four more boats than she had to, capable of holding 1178 in total. That worked out at around a third of her potential complement of passengers and crew, or a barely more acceptable 53 percent of those who were actually on board at the time of the disaster.

Leaving aside the shortcomings of the *Titanic*'s own watertight subdivisions, as described above, the Board of Trade clearly placed too much confidence in such systems in general. Ships built without watertight compartments, such as typical cargo vessels, were obliged to have **double** the number of lifeboats necessary to accommodate everyone aboard, in order to have the full complement on both sides of the ship. The idea was that whichever way the ship might be listing in a disaster, enough boats could be launched to let everyone escape.

When Harland & Wolff were constructing the *Titanic* and the *Olympic* in Belfast, **Alexander Carlisle** was responsible for the "details and general arrangements" of their design. He successfully argued that each should be equipped with "double-acting" **davits** (the pairs of small cranes used to raise and lower each lifeboat). Each pair of these could in theory hold two boats at once, one inboard and one outboard, and launch two more in quick succession. The *Titanic* was therefore capable of carrying **sixty-four** lifeboats. Carlisle's motivation was not so much to ensure that the *Titanic* had enough lifeboats for everyone aboard, as to be prepared for any change in the regulations. His plans nonetheless specified three lifeboats for each pair of davits, making a total of forty-eight altogether.

Ultimately, however, it was the White Star Line that paid the bill, and made the decisions. Their priority was to leave as much deck space as possible free, for the passengers to enjoy. As detailed on p.79, therefore, when the *Titanic* sailed on her maiden voyage, each pair of davits was fitted with just one single lifeboat, and there were four additional "collapsible" boats. As Carlisle subsequently told the British inquiry into the disaster – run by that selfsame Board of Trade – two meetings, in 1909 and 1910, considered his proposals for "about five or ten minutes". The only White Star representative who spoke at the meetings was **J. Bruce Ismay**; he later professed not to remember anything about it.

In May 1911, a year before the *Titanic* sank, a Board of Trade committee did indeed meet to consider changing its lifeboat requirements. Alexander Carlisle, who by then had left Harland & Wolff, was called as an expert witness. He argued that the new breed of liners should carry far more lifeboats; dominated by ship owners, however, the committee actually recommended **fewer** lifeboats than before. Rather strangely, Carlisle signed the new recommendations. As he later put it, "I am not generally soft … but I must say I was very soft the day I signed that".

Sea trials of the *Titanic*

The *Titanic* was finally ready for her **sea trials** on 1 April 1912. That very day, **Captain Smith** took over control from **Herbert Haddock**, who had nominally been her master for the previous week and now in turn replaced Smith on the

The Titanic *sets off from Belfast for her sea trials, 2 April 1912.*

Olympic. However, the wind was considered too strong to take the *Titanic* out, so the trials were postponed until the following day, Tuesday 2 April.

Watched by a large crowd, and manned by a basic crew of around eighty who had been especially brought over from England, the *Titanic* was pulled out of her dock by tugs at 6am the next morning. Only once she was safely down the River Lagan and out onto Belfast Lough did she finally go under her own steam for the first time.

The morning was taken up with manoeuvres in the lough, performing various twists, turns and complete circles, and checking different propeller combinations. In the afternoon the *Titanic* ventured out onto the Irish Sea, sailing forty miles due south and then returning to Belfast. As Fifth Officer Lowe described the trials to the US inquiry, "she was not really put to it"; neither then, nor ever, did she attain her suggested maximum speed of 24 knots. However, at the 20 knots she did achieve, the *Titanic* conducted a "full speed astern" test, the equivalent of an emergency stop in a car. To bring the ship to a halt from that speed took just over three minutes, or around half a mile.

At around 6pm, without returning to the dock, she was awarded her **passenger certificate**, valid for one year, by Francis Carruthers of the Board of Trade. The trial process was later described by Walter Lord as "amazingly perfunctory", and many commentators at the time of the disaster felt the ship had not been adequately tested. In mitigation, it's worth mentioning that this was not the first time Carruthers had seen the *Titanic*; he had made repeated inspections during the ship's construction, and checked the blueprints at every stage.

At 8pm that same night, the *Titanic* sailed for Southampton.

Chapter 3
The *Titanic* sets sail

In the very early hours of Thursday, 4 April 1912, the *Titanic* arrived at **Southampton**. Workers at the city's Harland & Wolff plant – smaller than the Belfast yard, and devoted to internal features – now had six frantic days to apply the finishing touches before her departure. Although it was normal to invite the general public to visit a ship about to embark on its maiden voyage, too much remained to be done. Instead, as a goodwill gesture, the *Titanic* was "dressed" with flags and bunting on Good Friday, 5 April.

During the preceding weeks, Britain had been in the grip of a **National Coal Strike**, aimed at establishing the first-ever minimum wage for miners. As coal supplies dwindled, the entire economy was severely affected, with shipping among the hardest-hit industries. Even though the strike only reached its final messy resolution shortly before the *Titanic* sailed, however, the coal shortage never put her maiden voyage in jeopardy. The White Star Line had already cancelled crossings for its own *Adriatic* and *Oceanic*, and set about transferring their coal to the *Titanic*. Their prospective passengers were rebooked onto the *Titanic*, and coal was also bought from ships belonging to rival lines, including the *New York*. In the wake of the disaster, White Star representatives later attempted to prove that the *Titanic* could not have reached dangerously high speeds, because she had not been carrying enough fuel to do so. In fact, however, her bunkers at departure held 5892 tons of coal – a thousand more than the *Olympic* took on her own maiden voyage.

On Saturday 6 April, great **crowds** assembled for the recruitment of the *Titanic*'s crew. Thanks to the coal strike, at least seventeen thousand Southampton men who usually worked at sea had been idle during

March. Unemployment in the city was in any case rife, so their number was augmented by many thousands of men who entirely lacked skills or experience.

Despite the White Star Line's professed enthusiasm for keeping the same crews from one voyage to the next, the conditions were so poor that few workers felt any loyalty to the company. Instead, seamen would typically wait until they'd spent whatever money they'd made from their last trip, then sign up for the next available ship. Relations between White Star and its employees had reached rock bottom the previous year, when the *Olympic*'s coal porters went on strike after being refused payment for "standing by". They'd reported for work at the specified time, only to find that the ship was not ready. Since then, White Star had entrusted various newly recognized **unions** with recruiting specialist crew members. Would-be seamen and firemen therefore reported to the new Southampton-based British Seafarers' Union, while the White Star Line ran its own centre for potential stewards and stewardesses.

A total of 898 crew members signed up, of whom 246 had previously served on the *Olympic*. The majority were based in Southampton, although of the seven hundred who gave local addresses, many may simply have spent the preceding night in the town. Some, for example, joined from the laid-up *New York*.

In the final days before the voyage, the *Titanic*'s public and private spaces were systematically kitted out with all the necessities and conveniences of transatlantic travel. Crockery, cutlery and glassware were distributed in the cabins and dining rooms, as were almost two hundred thousand neatly folded items of linen. Carpets were laid, and painting continued until the last minute, including a final coat for her funnels. Fresh **provisions** of all kinds were also loaded in prodigious quantities, as the *Titanic*'s pantries needed to be stocked from scratch. Well over a hundred thousand pounds of meat and fish were supplemented by fruit and vegetables, ranging from forty tons of potatoes to eight hundred bundles of asparagus. There were 2200 pounds of coffee and 800 pounds of tea, 850 bottles of spirits and 8000 cigars. Specific refrigerated rooms on G Deck were dedicated to the storage of 40,000 eggs, 6000 pounds of butter, and even 1750 quarts of ice cream.

The officers of the *Titanic*

Captain Smith had seven officers – three senior, and four junior – beneath him on the *Titanic*. All had served their apprenticeships on sailing ships. Fifth Officer Lowe later drew a nice distinction between the duties of the junior and senior officers at the US inquiry: "We are there to do the navigating part so the senior officer can be and shall be in full charge of the bridge and have

SMITH OF THE *TITANIC*

"Shipbuilding is such a perfect art nowadays that absolute disaster, involving the passengers, is inconceivable. Whatever happens, there will be time enough before the vessel sinks to save the life of every person on board. I will go a bit further. I will say that I cannot imagine any condition that would cause the vessel to founder. Modern shipbuilding has gone beyond that."

Captain E.J. Smith, captain of the *Adriatic*,
interviewed by *The New York Times*, 1907

Remembered as the much-loved, softly spoken captain of the *Titanic*, **"E.J." Smith** has for so long belonged to the realm of myth that it comes as a shock to see the few seconds of genuine footage of the man that still survive. Filmed in 1911, and now online, it shows him in a crisp white uniform, pacing somewhat self-consciously on the deck of the *Olympic*.

Edward John Smith was born in the heart of industrial England, in Hanley, now part of Stoke-on-Trent, on 27 January 1850. His parents, then in their forties, had worked in the local potteries before setting up a grocery store in their Well Street home. Young "Ted" left school at fourteen to work in an iron foundry, but signed up as a seaman in Liverpool as soon as he reached seventeen. After two lengthy round-the-world voyages aboard the American-owned *Senator Weber* – whose captain was his own half-brother, Joseph Hancock – Smith rose quickly through the ranks on various other ships. He achieved his first command in 1876, becoming captain of the *Lizzie Fennell*.

In 1880, Smith succumbed to the lure and prestige of the **White Star Line**. Happy to work his way up again, he accepted a berth as fourth officer on the *Celtic*. Eight years had passed by the time he returned to the rank of captain, taking over the *Baltic* in 1888. In all, "E.J." was to command seventeen White Star liners. During his seven years as skipper of the *Majestic*, he sailed her twice to South Africa, carrying troops to and from the Boer War, and was awarded the Transport Medal. From the time a new incarnation of the *Baltic* was launched in 1904, it became a White Star Line tradition for Smith to skipper each new ship on her maiden voyage.

Having captained the *Olympic* in 1911, Smith naturally took charge of the *Titanic* in 1912. His annual salary of £1250 was more than twice the usual rate for

nothing to worry his head about. We have all that, the junior officers; there are four of us. The three seniors are in absolute charge of the boat. They have nothing to worry themselves about. They simply have to walk backward and forward and look after the ship, and we do all the figuring and all that sort of thing in our chart room."

Captain E.J. Smith (right) and Purser Hugh Walter McElroy pose aboard the **Titanic** *for photographer Francis M. Browne, who left the ship at Queenstown.*

captains with the rival Cunard line, and he was also eligible for a bonus of £200 for a collision-free year. Although it was widely believed that he would retire after the *Titanic's* first round-trip sailing, there were also reports that he planned to make his final crossing as captain of the *Gigantic*, when that came to be launched in 1915.

Despite his humble origins, Smith was on intimate terms with the Edwardian elite, so popular with his passengers that he was hailed in American society as the "millionaires' captain". His crews too revered him; Charles Lightoller, the *Titanic's* second officer, fondly recalled how they used to "flush with pride" as he'd bring the *Majestic* into New York at full speed, whisking her around treacherous corners with just a few feet to spare.

However, Smith and his entire generation, including all the *Titanic's* senior officers, had learned their craft not on steam-driven ships but in the days of sail. In retrospect it seems all too clear that he hadn't grasped quite how different – and difficult – the new breed of liners were to handle. Despite the *Olympic's* two collisions in 1911, in New York in June, and the Solent in September (see p.19), the *Titanic* had a dramatic near miss within moments of starting her maiden voyage (see p.47).

For an account of Captain Smith's conduct on the night of the sinking, and his ultimate fate, see p.112. To what extent he should bear or share responsibility for the disaster itself is discussed on p.180 onwards.

Born in Yorkshire in 1872, **Chief Officer Henry Tingle Wilde** had served on several White Star Line ships, and been Captain Smith's chief officer on the *Olympic* since the previous August. To his surprise, he was transferred to the *Titanic* at the last minute, the day before she sailed. He was expecting his own command, so his appointment was understood to be for the maiden voyage

THE CREW RESHUFFLE

On Tuesday 9 April, the day before the *Titanic* sailed, the White Star Line announced an unexpected **reshuffle** of her senior officers. The decision may have been prompted by Captain Smith's feeling that Chief Officer **William M. Murdoch** lacked experience of the new breed of large ships. **Henry Tingle Wilde**, Smith's chief officer aboard the *Olympic*, therefore raced to join the ship at the last minute, while Murdoch dropped down from chief to first officer, and **Charles Lightoller** from first to second officer; both felt understandably wounded. With the rest of the officers remaining unchanged, the *Titanic*'s original second officer, **David Blair**, was asked to leave the ship altogether. He expressed his regret in a private letter: "This is a marvellous ship, and I feel very disappointed I am not to make the first voyage."

That decision had an unexpected consequence. One of Blair's duties on the crossing from Belfast had been to take care of the **binoculars** in the crow's nest. In his haste to depart he locked them away (some say in the crow's nest itself, others in a locker in his cabin), forgot to tell anyone where they were, and accidentally walked away with the key in his pocket. For more about the controversy over the binoculars, and the ultimate fate of the missing key, see p.60.

only. In a letter to his sister, written while the *Titanic* was at sea and posted at Queenstown, he commented: "I still don't like this ship … I have a queer feeling about it."

Aged 39, like Wilde, **First Officer William McMaster Murdoch** was a Scotsman who had made his career with the White Star Line. Having previously been first officer aboard the *Oceanic*, *Adriatic* and *Olympic*, Murdoch was briefly chief officer of the *Titanic*, for its initial voyage from Belfast to Southampton. It came as a blow, therefore, when he was obliged by Wilde's appointment to step back to first officer.

Born in Lancashire in 1874, **Second Officer Charles Herbert Lightoller** had been at sea since he was thirteen. He had truly seen the world, including a stint as a gold prospector in the Yukon. A close friend of Murdoch since they'd served together on the Australia run a dozen years earlier, Lightoller was even more disappointed to be asked to shuffle down from first officer to second. After all, he'd been a first officer for several years, on the *Teutonic* and the *Oceanic*.

Third Officer Herbert John Pitman was born in 1877 to a farming family in Somerset. Although he had only been with the White Star Line since 1906, he'd moved rapidly up the ranks. His last appointment before the *Titanic* was as fourth officer on the *Oceanic*. After serving as an officer with the Wilson

Line of Hull, where he was born in 1884, **Fourth Officer Joseph Groves Boxhall** joined the White Star Line in 1907. Thanks to his skills as a navigator, Boxhall's duties included calculating the *Titanic*'s position.

Although the *Titanic* marked the first time **Fifth Officer Harold Godfrey Lowe** had crossed the Atlantic, and he had only been with the White Star Line for a year, the hot-blooded, 29-year-old Welshman was a highly experienced sailor, who had spent five years on West African steamships. Aged just 24, **Sixth Officer James Paul Moody**, the *Titanic*'s lowest-ranked officer, came from Scarborough in Yorkshire. He had also been with the White Star Line for a year, most recently serving aboard the *Oceanic*.

What the crew were paid

Rates of **pay** aboard the *Titanic* ranged from £105 per month for Captain Smith down to the £2 per month earned by each of the ship's three teenage bellboys. While Chief Engineer Joseph William Bell earned £35 per month, and Chief Baker Charles Joughin £12 per month, typical rates for able seamen, stokers and firemen were more like £5. The *Titanic*'s six full-time lookouts, for example, who worked in three two-man shifts for two hours on and four hours off, earned £5 5s per month. Male stewards were paid £3 15s, and stewardesses usually £3 10s, although the two stewardesses who worked in the Turkish Bath earned £4. Those who came into direct contact with passengers could expect to supplement their income with tips; for first-class cabin stewards, that was often their main incentive.

A NOTE ON MONEY AND PRICES

In Britain's pre-decimal currency system, each pound was divided into twenty shillings (abbreviated as "s"), and each shilling into twelve pence ("d"). £5 10s corresponds to £5.50 today, and 2s 6d to 12.5 pence.

Adjusted for inflation, Captain Smith's annual salary of £1260 would be the equivalent of £110,000 (or $180,000) today, while the figure of £5 per month for the stokers and firemen corresponds to £433 ($707) today.

The most expensive ticket bought by any Titanic passenger cost £512 6s. Charlotte Cardeza paid that for herself, her son and her maid to travel in a promenade suite on B Deck; the sum translates to more than £44,000 ($72,000) at today's prices.

Typical steerage fares ranged between £7 4s 7d and £9 7s, or between £625 and £800 ($1000–1300) at today's prices – somewhat more than you might now expect to pay for a transatlantic airfare.

Although the White Star Line expressed its pay in terms of monthly wages, rank and file employees were only paid for days spent actually at sea. As soon as a ship completed its voyage, all were laid off. Anyone working for £5 per month on the *Titanic* would have therefore expected to receive £1 for the six-day crossing. Notoriously, however, in keeping with the terms of their contracts, the White Star Line stopped the crew's pay at the precise moment the *Titanic* sank. Following widespread protests, they eventually relented and paid all the surviving crew members for the entire time they were away from England.

Certain workers aboard the ship were not employed by the White Star Line at all. The **musicians**, for example, were recruited and paid by an agency, and earned £4 per month, while the staff of the à la carte restaurant were employed directly by manager Luigi Gatti, for a notional wage of one shilling for the whole trip; naturally they hoped to earn much more from tips. Finally, two of the five **postal clerks** were employed by the British Post Office, and three by its US counterpart. It was because of her role carrying mail, incidentally, that the *Titanic* was officially known as **RMS Titanic**, standing for "Royal Mail Ship".

Wireless operators and equipment

The **wireless equipment** aboard the *Titanic* occupied three small adjoining rooms in the centre of the Boat Deck, around forty feet aft of the bridge, close to the officers' quarters. As well as the actual operating room, which lacked windows or portholes and had no direct phone link to the bridge, there was a shared sleeping cabin, and a dynamo room. Also known as the Silent Room, the latter held the spark transmitter, which used five kilowatts of power, drawn either from the main generator or emergency backup batteries. The *Titanic's* wireless range, estimated at 400 miles by day and 1200 at night, was matched only by that of the *Olympic*.

Installed by the Marconi Marine Company, the equipment was operated by two graduates of its training school in Liverpool. The senior of the two, **Jack Phillips**, celebrated his 25th birthday on the second day of the voyage; **Harold Bride** was three years younger. While theirs was regarded as a glamorous, cutting-edge job, and the operators criss-crossing the Atlantic saw themselves as members of an elite brotherhood, they were paid less than the lowliest firemen. Phillips earned £4 5s per month, and Bride half that. At £2 2s 6d per month, it would have taken Bride twenty years to earn enough to cross the Atlantic in one of the *Titanic's* costliest suites. The more experienced **Jack Binns**, the hero of the 1909 *Republic* incident (see p.84) who had sailed with Captain Smith many times, was originally due to join the *Titanic*, but took another job when the voyage was postponed. Bride was a late replacement,

Advertising poster for Vinolia Soap, as provided for the **Titanic's** *first-class passengers.*

recommended to Phillips by another of the Marconi coterie, **Harold Cottam**, who was currently sailing on the *Carpathia*.

While the Marconi operators were expected to facilitate necessary communication between ships, their primary day-to-day role was to provide a luxury service for the passengers. Wireless enabled passengers to keep in touch with their friends, family and work, and make further travel arrangements. Thus Mr and Mrs Isidor Straus, for example, exchanged greetings from the *Titanic* with their son and his wife, who were simultaneously sailing to Europe from New York aboard the *Amerika*. Sending such messages cost 12s 6d for the first ten words, and nine pence for each additional word.

Although their working hours were not fixed, the operators were expected to keep their equipment in action around the clock. That usually meant each could grab a few hours' sleep while the other took over, but they hit a crisis late on the night of Saturday 13 April, when the transmitter broke down altogether. It took the two men seven hours to dismantle the entire system, trace the problem to short-circuiting leads, and get it all working again – and they were then faced with a backlog of messages to transmit and transcribe. By the night of the disaster, both were exhausted.

Sailing Day

For Captain Smith, Wednesday 10 April – officially known as **Sailing Day** – began with an early-morning stroll down to the docks from his spacious home on Winn Road in the Southampton suburb of Portswood. All his officers had spent the night on the *Titanic*. As Second Officer Lightoller put it, the ship had all but completed its transformation from "a hive of bees" to "a nest about to swarm".

The entire crew was mustered at 8am for a **general inspection**. Because the *Titanic* was carrying emigrants from Britain, she was required to complement her Belfast sea trials with a final Board of Trade inspection in Southampton. Assistant Emigration Officer **Captain Maurice Clarke**, who had also visited the ship on the two previous days, now undertook his most thorough examination, which lasted for the four hours from 8am up to the moment of her departure.

As well as watching as three of the **watertight doors** were closed, Clarke instructed officers Lowe and Moody to swing out two of the **lifeboats**, and lower them into the water crewed by eight seamen. Second Officer Lightoller later complained that Clarke "certainly lived up to his reputation of being the best cursed B.O.T. representative in the South of England ... he must see everything, and himself check every item".

Clarke himself later told the British inquiry that he didn't feel that the procedure for checking the lifeboats was adequate; asked why he went ahead anyway, he replied: "Well, you will remember I am a civil servant. Custom guides us a good bit." The fact that there was a **fire** in the coal bunker (see p.180) was not brought to his attention, but when asked if it should have been, he responded, "Hardly, it is not an uncommon thing to have these small fires in the bunkers."

The passengers come aboard

Two separate **boat trains** carried passengers from London's Waterloo Station down to the quayside. Second- and third-class passengers reached Southampton at 9.30am, while the first-class train arrived at 11.30am, just half an hour before the ship sailed. The trains pulled in so close to the *Titanic* that many passengers were disappointed they couldn't get an overall view of the ship before they boarded.

Each class of passengers used its own separate entrance to board. The first-class entrance, amidships on D Deck, led immediately to the foot of the Grand Staircase. For ticket processing, cabin assignments and a general introduction to the ship, first-class passengers (or their servants) headed first to the Purser's Office, directly above on C Deck. That same office handled

Six-year old Douglas Spedden plays with a top aboard the **Titanic.** *He and his watching father survived the disaster, as did his mother Daisy, who wrote a book about Douglas's toy bear that was later published as* **Polar, The Titanic Bear.**

second-class passengers too, who threaded their way along there via the corridors from their own entrances, further aft on C Deck.

At the two third-class entrances – one further aft on C Deck, the other leading onto the forward well deck on D Deck – all prospective passengers had to submit to a quick **medical examination**. The doctors were especially looking for the eye disease trachoma; as no immigrant with an infectious condition would be allowed to disembark in the US, anyone with apparent symptoms was turned back at Southampton. At least one man, a Belgian baker, is known to have been turned away at this late stage, while his brother was allowed to board.

Once aboard, third-class passengers were channelled towards their cabins or berths by stewards stationed every few yards along the mystifying labyrinth of passageways. Although more than half of the third-class passengers did not speak English, there was only one official interpreter on board.

The cargo and crew

After the early-morning muster, many of the **crew** had seized the opportunity to go back ashore. Not all managed to return. One group of stewards and firemen remained in a nearby pub, The Grapes, until they heard the ship's whistle blow, ten minutes before departure. As they raced back, two dashed across a railway line in front of a train, and made it on board. The remaining

COUNTING THE PASSENGERS AND CREW

No sources agree as to exactly how many people were aboard the *Titanic*. The reasons they vary are too intricate to debate here; the figures given below are as good an estimate as it's possible to make. When the *Titanic* sailed from **Southampton**, she was carrying a total of 1842 people. Of those, 197 were first-class passengers, 254 second-class, and 493 third-class; the remaining 898 were crew.

At **Cherbourg**, fifteen first-class and seven second-class passengers, who had paid £1 10s and £1 respectively simply to cross the English Channel to France, disembarked, along with two dogs, four bicycles, and a canary. At the same time, an additional 142 first-class, 30 second-class, and 102 third-class passengers came aboard.

At **Queenstown**, a further seven first-class passengers, each of whom had paid £4 to reach Ireland, left the *Titanic*; one crewman deserted (see p.51); and seven second-class and 113 third-class passengers were ferried out to join her.

As the *Titanic* steamed out into the open Atlantic, therefore, she was carrying:

> First-class passengers: **324**
> Second-class passengers: **277**
> Third-class passengers: **708**
> Crew members and other employees: **897**

Little more than eighty of the crew were actually sailors, belonging to the **Deck Crew**. Around 320 more toiled down below as the **Engine Crew**, to make

four, who included the three Slade brothers, arrived just as the gangplank was being drawn up, and were refused access by an officious steward.

In between taking up their stations and making everything ready for departure, the rest of the crew had been finding their own accommodation. Captain Smith's personal steward, Arthur Paintin, was far from happy. He wrote to his parents that the *Titanic* was "much better than the *Olympic* as far as passengers are concerned, but my little room is not near so nice, no daylight, electric light on all day".

Meanwhile, the *Titanic*'s six **cargo** holds had been filling up. While the ship wasn't carrying the fortune in gold and jewels imagined by later treasure hunters, there were certainly a number of valuable items, including an edition of the *Rubáiyát of Omar Khayyám* encrusted with 1500 gemstones. The only **car** aboard was a 35-horsepower red Renault limousine, which belonged to Billy Carter from Philadelphia, and was carefully packed and swaddled in a crate. An estimated seven million items of **mail** were brought aboard, in more than 3400 sacks.

a total of 400 who were concerned with the operation of the ship itself. The remaining five hundred, known as the **Victualling Crew**, were devoted to the accommodation and catering of what was basically an enormous floating hotel.

While there's no precise breakdown of the various **nationalities** on board, we can safely say that the crew, from the officers down to the stokers and stewards, was very largely drawn from Britain and Ireland. The one exception would be the seventy-strong staff of the à la carte restaurant, almost all of whom were French or Italian.

As for the **passengers**, broadly speaking those in first class were American plutocrats with a smattering of British aristocrats, while second class was more evenly divided but rather more British than American. Those two classes included perhaps 20 honeymooning couples. Something over 40 percent of the third-class passengers spoke English as their first language, including the 113 from Ireland.

The remainder were drawn from all parts of Europe, plus a scattering from further afield. There was an especially strong Scandinavian contingent; over 100 came from Sweden, around 30 from Norway, and up to 70 from Finland. The eight Chinese men aboard, later widely assumed to have been stowaways, were in fact seamen travelling third class, en route to join another ship in New York; there was also one solitary Japanese person in second-class. Finally, it's thought that the *Titanic* was carrying just one black passenger, Joseph LaRoche, who was originally from Haiti and was travelling with his French wife and their two children.

An inauspicious start

Shortly after midday, the *Titanic* was cajoled out of her dock by five struggling tugs, and manoeuvred into position on the River Test, where she started her engines and set off at a stately six knots towards the sea. So many ships were still out of action due to the coal strike that in places they were tethered two abreast along the riverbank. Sightseers lined the decks of one such pair, consisting of the White Star Line's own *Oceanic* (the closest of the two to the shore), and the American liner *New York*.

As the *Titanic* passed the two ships, the **displacement** caused by her mighty bulk in the shallow, narrow channel created immense suction. One by one, the six cables that tethered the *New York* to the *Oceanic* snapped loudly; "as easily", according to one observer, "as a grocer snaps a piece of twine with his fingers". The *New York* swung free, and her stern appeared certain to crash into the *Titanic*. Captain Gale, of the tug *Vulcan*, secured two lines to the *New York* and pulled her back, while Captain Smith ordered the *Titanic*'s engines astern to create a backwash. Their quick thinking prevented a collision by a margin of just four feet. The *Titanic* had to stop her engines and wait while the *New York* was hauled safely away, however, causing a delay of one hour. Considering that Captain Smith, and the same Southampton pilot, **George Bowyer**, had been involved in a similar incident as they were guiding the *Olympic* through the same waters just a few months earlier (see p.19), the **near miss** with the *New York* provides further strong evidence of Smith's overconfidence in handling the demands of this new breed of enormous ships.

English schoolmaster **Lawrence Beesley**, watching fascinated from the *Titanic*, was reminded "of an experiment I had shown many times to a form of boys ... in which a small magnet is made to float on a cork in a bowl of water and small steel objects placed on neighbouring pieces of cork are drawn up to the floating magnet". He also noticed that a fellow passenger, a "young American kinematograph photographer", filmed the whole thing. Although neither filmmaker nor film was to survive, several photographers documented the entire incident.

Across the Channel to Cherbourg

When the *Titanic* finally resumed her progress, she passed from Southampton Water to the Solent, the strait that separates the British mainland from the Isle of Wight. Spectators along the shore included the family of radio pioneer Guglielmo Marconi (see p.9), who had at one stage expected to be on board as passengers, but were watching instead from the grounds of their home in Fawley on the mainland. Tracing a languid S-curve before the admiring gaze of the members of the Royal Yacht Squadron at Cowes, the *Titanic* circled the Isle of Wight and set off across the **English Channel**.

The passengers began to familiarize themselves with the ship. **Ida Straus**, sharing the Regency-style first-class "parlour suite" C55 with her husband Isidor, enthused "what a ship! So huge and so magnificently appointed." Of the two even grander "promenade suites" up on B Deck, the slightly larger B52 had originally been reserved by J.P. Morgan, but was occupied instead by **J. Bruce Ismay** of the White Star Line.

Second-class passenger Charlotte Collyer was similarly enthused; she later remembered: "the *Titanic* was wonderful, far more splendid and huge than I had dreamed of". Another second-class passenger, Imanita Shelley, however, offered a discordant tale of woe. She told the US inquiry she'd been sent to the wrong cabin "many decks down in the ship [and] so small that it could only be called a cell. It was impossible for a third person to enter said cabin unless both occupants first of all crawled into their bunks." Although she was subsequently reassigned to a larger cabin, she testified that the heating system was only working in three second-class cabins, while the rest were "like ice houses all of the voyage".

As the coast of northern France came into view, the sun was just starting to set. At **Cherbourg**, 82 miles out from Southampton, the actual port was not yet equipped to handle such colossal ships, so the *Titanic* anchored offshore in the roadstead. She remained there for something under two hours, while two White Star tenders, *Nomadic* and *Traffic*, ministered to her needs. As well as passengers and their luggage, the small steamers brought out the mail and huge crates of choice French provisions. A considerable swell kept the boats bobbing with alarming force; it took ten crew members to hold the gangplanks steady that led onto the *Titanic*.

Besides letting off her few cross-Channel passengers, the *Titanic* also welcomed an additional 374 passengers. Once again, the majority of the first-class passengers who boarded here were Americans, fresh from spending the winter social season in Europe and beyond. The contingent who had made the six-hour rail journey up from Paris to Cherbourg earlier that day, on the special *Train Transatlantique*, were even more opulent than those who were already aboard. Among them were **John Jacob Astor IV** and his wife Madeleine; another American millionaire, **Benjamin Guggenheim**, along with his valet, and his mistress "Ninette" Aubart, sharing a separate first-class stateroom with her maid; and **Margaret Brown**, known to history as "the unsinkable Molly Brown".

The two remaining luxury suites were now occupied. Down on the port side of C Deck, the Astors moved into the Louis XIV-style C62. **Charlotte Drake Cardeza** from Philadelphia, who also boarded at Cherbourg accompanied by her son and their respective servants, took up residence in the remaining "promenade suite", B51. Mrs Cardeza was hardly travelling light; her fourteen trunks, three suitcases and three crates contained seventy dresses, ten fur coats and ninety-one pairs of gloves.

Another couple who were destined to play a prominent role in the coming tragedy, **Sir Cosmo** and **Lady Duff Gordon**, had also joined the ship at Cherbourg. For the moment, for reasons known only to themselves, they were travelling in separate staterooms under the pseudonym of "Mr and Mrs Morgan". Lady Duff Gordon was entranced with her accommodation on A Deck: "My pretty little cabin with its electric heater and pink curtains delighted me."

Onwards to Queenstown

Once the *Titanic* had left Cherbourg shortly after 8pm, the passengers were free to settle down for the evening, and enjoy their first night aboard. The next morning, Thursday 11 April, as the ship approached **Ireland** in glorious

A FLOATING MENAGERIE

Much research has gone into establishing quite how many **dogs** sailed on the *Titanic*. The best guess is between twelve and fourteen, of which two simply crossed the Channel and left the ship at Cherbourg (along with a solitary canary). Of those aboard at the time of the disaster, the largest were confined to the kennels – no one knows quite where those were, but near the base of the dummy fourth funnel seems most likely. Smaller lapdogs were allowed to travel in their owners' cabins, and thus had a better chance of survival.

Three dogs are thought to have been carried from the sinking ship onto lifeboats. As well as a Pekinese puppy that belonged to Henry Sleeper Harper (named Sun Yat-Sen after China's new president), there were two Pomeranians, one belonging to Margaret Hays and the other to Elizabeth Rothschild. Among those that died were two dogs belonging to Billy Carter, who seems to have been no more solicitous of his pets than he was of his wife (see p.101), and Helen Bishop's Pekinese Frou Frou, which remained locked in her cabin. One survivor reported seeing Robert Daniel's French bulldog Gamin de Pycombe swimming after the ship went down, but the dog was never rescued. Daniel himself claimed that he ventured below to open the kennels at the last minute, while Madeleine Astor was reported as saying that her husband John Jacob Astor IV did much the same thing, and that she'd seen their Airedale Kitty running along the decks as the ship went down.

Early reports of the tragedy made much of a big black dog called Rigel, who supposedly swam close to the lifeboats in the open Atlantic for three hours, and whose loud barking alerted the approaching rescuers on the *Carpathia*. However, Rigel never existed, and neither did the pet pig that one passenger supposedly smuggled onto a lifeboat – it was in fact a clockwork musical pig, belonging to Edith Russell (see p.98).

While it would have been normal for the *Titanic* to have a **cat**, the only evidence that she did comes from stewardess Violet Jessop. She described a cat called Jenny, a veteran of other White Star ships, who "immediately picked herself a comfortable corner" and gave birth to a litter of kittens. Years later, a fireman who'd sailed with the *Titanic* from Belfast claimed that he saw the ship's cat disembark the morning she was due to leave Southampton, carrying each of her kittens down the gangplank one by one.

As the presence of a cat might suggest, the *Titanic* had its fair share of **rats**, which came scurrying up from the hold in her dying moments. There were also several **chickens**. Passenger Ella White had bought four in France to take home to America, and they too were stored somewhere below. Hence the early-morning crowing of a rooster that alarmed some superstitious travellers.

sunshine, Captain Smith ordered the *Titanic* into a sequence of successive sinuous curves and turns. Speed was clearly not an issue; the captain seems to have been experimenting with how the ship handled, as well perhaps as calibrating her compasses.

At around 11.30am, the *Titanic* anchored two miles off the coast of southern Ireland. She waited off Roche's Point, near the mouth of the large natural harbour that held the port then called **Queenstown**, and now known as Cobh. Two stocky side-wheel steamers chugged out to meet her, ferrying passengers and mail they'd picked up at the Queenstown railhead. This time, none of the 120 additional passengers they carried were first class; almost all were third-class emigrants, heading for a new life in the United States. Just as the tenders drew close to the *Titanic's* towering flanks, passengers on deck were alarmed to see the blackened face of a stoker suddenly emerge from the yawning hole atop her dummy fourth funnel. His harmless joke was later remembered as an omen of things to come.

Several smaller boats also made their way out to the *Titanic*. Among them were several so-called "bumboats", much like those that cluster around modern cruise ships, selling crafts, trinkets and souvenirs. During the brief moments they were allowed to display their wares aboard, one lucky vendor managed to persuade Colonel Astor to spend $800 on a lace shawl for his young bride.

Among the seven passengers who left the *Titanic* when the two tenders returned to Queenstown was a 32-year-old first-class passenger, **Francis M. Browne**, a trainee Jesuit priest who was also a keen amateur photographer and wireless enthusiast. Having spent his single day aboard the *Titanic* exploring the ship from top to bottom, he had captured a unique treasure trove of images, ranging from the gymnasium to the wireless room. Browne's ticket had been bought for him by his uncle, who as the bishop of Cloyne had his seat in Queenstown, and he had rushed from Ireland over to England specifically in order to sail back home again on the *Titanic*. His presence aboard, and fortuitous early disembarkation, have been enough to trigger wild conspiracy theories; search hard enough online, and you'll find him described as the lynchpin of a Jesuit scheme to destroy the *Titanic* and help the emergence of the New World Order. Browne did not, incidentally, take the famous final photo of Captain Smith that seems to show him peering down from the bridge as the *Titanic* departed; that was actually snapped by another passenger when the tender first approached.

The *Titanic* also picked up and dropped off mail during her brief Irish stopover. One of the many duties of the firemen and stokers was to carry the heavy mailbags to and from the mailroom deep in the bowels of the ship. One, **John Coffey**, took advantage of the toing and froing to desert. Having only

The final photo of the **Titanic,** *sailing west from Ireland on 11 April 1912.*

signed on as a fireman to get a free trip home to see his mother, he hid under some mailsacks when the mail tender went back ashore. Among the items in those mailbags was a letter from passenger Edith Russell, who complained: "I cannot get over my feeling of depression and premonition of trouble."

At 1.30pm, the *Titanic* raised her anchor and resumed her journey west, sailing parallel to, and in full view of, Ireland's southwestern shore. Few of the Irish emigrants who had just come aboard expected to see the mother country again. Many had said goodbye to their homes as guests of honour at their own "living wakes". Also known as "American wakes", such gatherings had become commonplace in the preceding centuries, as families bade farewell to those who were leaving Ireland forever. As night fell, the last peaks of southwest Ireland receded into the darkness, and the *Titanic* was alone on the Atlantic.

The final Sunday

Immediately after breakfast on Sunday 14 April, Captain Smith performed the traditional **captain's inspection** of his ship. Accompanied by the heads of all the departments aboard, including the chief officer, chief engineer, chief steward and purser, he made his stately progress from top to bottom, and bow to stern.

In theory, that should have been followed by a **boat drill**, in which crew members reported to their assigned lifeboats. Such a drill might have prevented the confusion that night, so the inquiries into the disaster devoted a lot of time to investigating why it never took place. Although no explanation was ever discovered, it became clear that Captain Smith had never bothered with drills at sea. One steward testified that "if we would all go to drill, meals would not be ready for the passengers", while a fireman revealed that the only drills he'd ever witnessed on the White Star Line had occurred on Sundays when his ship was in port, and empty of passengers. Instead, Smith led **Divine Service** in the First Class Dining Room at 11am, and then joined his officers on the bridge. An accurate position for the ship being agreed, the previous day's run was calculated as amounting to 546 miles.

Passengers re-emerging into the open air on deck after lunch were struck by how sharply the **temperature** had dropped. There was little genuine wind, but the cold blast created by the speed of the ship was enough to drive almost everyone inside for the afternoon. White Star chairman J. Bruce Ismay cut a prominent figure among the throng in the public areas, although precisely what he did and said over the course of the day is disputed, as discussed on p.183. The biggest excitement of the afternoon came when Irene Harris, wife of American theatrical impresario Henry Harris, fell on the Grand Staircase and broke her arm.

Among the diners in the à la carte restaurant that evening was Lady Duff Gordon, who many years later recalled the "warmth, lights, the hum of voices, the lilt of a German waltz – the unheeding sounds of a small world bent on pleasure". At a neighbouring table, George Widener was throwing a reception to mark Captain Smith's impending retirement. Smith, naturally, was the guest of honour, but made his excuses at 9pm to return to the bridge.

After dinner, several of the male first-class passengers settled down to play cards. Ordinarily, that would not have been permitted on a Sunday, but the captain appears to have made a special dispensation. Among them were a handful of the professional card-sharps who frequented the great ocean liners. They'd travel in disguise and under false names – yet another reason why the *Titanic*'s full passenger list will never be known.

The most detailed descriptions of the *Titanic*'s final day afloat come from the two passengers who wrote eyewitness books about the tragedy. The American **Colonel Gracie** began by playing squash for half an hour with the ship's professional, and then swam in the heated swimming pool. Clearly a social climber, he spoke with several of his wealthiest compatriots. He had a number of conversations with the Strauses who told him in the early evening that they'd just received a message from their son and his wife, who were aboard the *Amerika*.

Lawrence Beesley spent much of the day in and around the second-class library. He later ruefully remarked how few of the passengers he observed turned out to be aboard the *Carpathia* the following morning: not the two Catholic priests in eager discussion, the father playing with his sons in the corridor outside, nor the lone figure parading with his bagpipes down on the aft well deck. In the evening, Beesley joined a shipboard acquaintance, the Reverend Ernest Carter, from St Jude's parish in East London, who had been leading a session of hymn singing in the second-class saloon. The programme concluded at around 10pm with "For Those in Peril on the Sea". Carter introduced it with the words: "In this ship we're not in peril; but others may be. Let us sing the hymn for them."

Intimations of ice

Meanwhile, as the *Titanic* steamed west, her wireless operators had been picking up a steady stream of messages from ships approaching in the opposite direction, warning of **ice ahead**. Some were reporting their own observations, others relaying information received from yet more vessels. In retrospect, they can be seen to draw a cumulative picture of a massive swathe of ice that stretched for approximately eighty miles across the *Titanic*'s path. At the time, however, no one realized they formed pieces of a jigsaw.

The first intimation of ice came on Friday evening, when the French *Touraine* described crossing one thick ice field itself, and reported the sighting of another ice field by another ship. On Saturday, the *Rappahannock* came within signalling distance, and reported that it had sustained damage in a collision with pack ice. So many warnings were received during the *Titanic*'s final day that the approach of ice became common knowledge among the passengers. Among ships that sent out alerts were the *Caronia* at 9am; the *Noordam* at 11.40am; the *Baltic* at 1.42pm; the *Amerika* just three minutes later at 1.45pm; the *Californian* at 7.30pm; and the *Mesaba* at 9.40pm.

There's much debate among historians as to how many of those messages were taken seriously by Captain Smith, or even reached the bridge at all. Any message that was intended to be seen by a ship's captain was supposed to be prefixed with the letters **MSG** (standing for Master Service Gram). On receiving such a message, the *Titanic*'s operators had to physically carry it forty feet forward to the bridge. When they intercepted general wireless traffic between other ships, however, the prefix might not be there, while in other instances whoever was transmitting might simply have forgotten to add it. Assuming that the message itself, the piece of paper known as a **Marconigram**, did reach the bridge and was deemed important, it was then supposed to remain on display for all the officers to see.

The message from the *Baltic*

Two of Sunday's wireless messages have taken on special significance. The first, from the **Baltic**, passed on the news that the "Greek steamer *Athenai* reports passing icebergs and large quantities of field ice today in lat 41°51'N, long 49°52'W". It was taken straight to Captain Smith, who acknowledged its receipt before setting off for lunch. En route along A Deck, he ran into **J. Bruce Ismay** talking with some passengers. Without comment, Smith handed the Marconigram to Ismay, who glanced at it and put it in his pocket. Ismay kept the message for the rest of the afternoon, and several witnesses described him showing it to various passengers. Excited rumours of icebergs ahead began to circulate.

Why Smith gave the message to Ismay instead of leaving it on the bridge remains a mystery. He eventually asked for it back at 7.15pm. Some claim that he then did indeed post it up in the chart room, well before the time when the *Titanic* could expect to reach the specified area, but there's no proof. Be that as it may, it remains a crucial piece of evidence in the controversy that surrounds Ismay's role aboard the *Titanic*, and whether his insistence on speed was a major cause of the disaster (see p.180).

The message from the *Mesaba*

The message that arrived from the **Mesaba** at 9.40pm was unequivocal: "Lat 42°N to 41°25'N, Longitude 40°W to 50°30'W, saw much heavy pack ice and great number large icebergs, also field ice." By this point in the evening, Jack Phillips was working alone while Bride slept, and still trying to catch up with the heavy backlog of messages left by the previous night's breakdown (see p.43). He remained at his station, and did not take the message along to the bridge.

It's worth remembering that the wireless operators were neither integrated into the crew, nor trained in navigation. They weren't expected to keep track of the ship's position, and in any case the precise figures for latitude and longitude meant nothing to them. Even in the face of explicit ice warnings, they wouldn't have known how close the danger was. According to Second Officer Charles Lightoller, however, writing many years later, it was Phillips' failure to pass on the *Mesaba*'s warning that doomed the *Titanic*: "The position the ship gave was right ahead of us and not many miles distant. The wireless operator was not to know how close we were to this position, and therefore the extreme urgency of the message … he put the message under a paper weight at his elbow, just until he squared up what he was doing, and he would then have brought it to the bridge … that delay proved fatal and was the main contributory cause to the loss of that magnificent ship and hundreds of lives."

Whether Phillips literally "spiked" the message is not known. Lightoller did not mention the incident at either inquiry, and is the only source for the detail of the paperweight. He claimed to have spoken to Phillips aboard the upturned Collapsible Boat B, on which Phillips froze to death, although his fellow wireless operator Harold Bride was aboard the same boat and did not recall Phillips saying a word.

The final warning

Captain Smith made his last visit of the day to the bridge shortly after 9pm. **Second Officer Lightoller**, who was in charge, had been on duty since 6pm. The two men discussed the exceptional calm of the ocean, and agreed the rapidly lowering temperatures might indicate the presence of ice ahead. On Lightoller's instructions, the forward forecastle hatch had already been closed, so light from below would not make the task of the lookouts any more difficult. Smith retired to bed at 9.20pm with the words: "If it becomes at all doubtful, let me know at once. I shall be just inside."

Lightoller in turn handed the bridge over to **First Officer Murdoch** at 10pm. While they were waiting for Murdoch's eyes to become accustomed to the darkness of the bridge, the two commented that it was all but impossible to trace where the sea met the sky along the horizon. Any icebergs out there might be hard to spot.

One final ice warning reached the Titanic at around 11pm. It was an update from the *Californian*, announcing: "We are stopped and surrounded by ice". The captain of the *Californian*, Stanley Lord, had asked operator Cyril Evans to pass on the message. Rather than wait for Phillips to finish his endless stream of transmissions, Evans simply cut in on top of him, using a chatty, informal style, and creating a deafening racket. The weary Phillips snapped back with the letters "DDD", which by convention meant "Shut up!" or "Keep quiet!"

Rebuffed, Evans gave up his attempt to communicate, although for the remaining half hour or so before he decided to close down his equipment for the night, he could still hear Phillips transmitting. Because Evans had not prefixed the message with "MSG", Phillips did not take it to the bridge. Neither did he appreciate that the *Californian* lay just a few miles away, halted by an ice field towards which the *Titanic* was racing full tilt.

Part 2

TRAGEDY

Chapter 4
Collision

At 10pm on the night of Sunday 14 April, lookouts Frederick Fleet and Reginald Lee climbed twenty feet up inside the *Titanic*'s hollow forward mast to reach the crow's nest. The two men they were replacing on duty passed on the warning, "Keep a look out for small ice and growlers." Half an hour earlier, knowing that the lookouts regularly used the words "keep a look out for small ice" as a jokey greeting, Second Officer Lightoller had ordered that they be called and told specifically to watch for "growlers", or small icebergs.

The air had now hit **freezing** point; temperatures had been dropping for several hours, and had plummeted by 11°F since 7pm. The crow's nest was completely exposed to the biting onrush of wind. As he kept watch on the after bridge, Quartermaster George Rowe later recalled, "what we call Whiskers round the Light were noticeable, that is very minute splinters of ice like myriads of coloured light".

At the **speed** the *Titanic* was travelling, even large icebergs would have been exceptionally difficult to spot with sufficient time to react. The greatest danger was from a so-called "dark" or "blue" iceberg, one that had recently rolled over in the sea, exposing glassy transparent sides rather than the more familiar whitened face. In such calm conditions, however, without the slightest waves to foam against its base, even an ordinary iceberg might be all but invisible. When the sun finally rose the next morning, it revealed "dozens and dozens" of icebergs, including 25 that were more than 150 feet high, to which everyone had remained oblivious during the night.

The best way to see an iceberg on that cloudless and all but moonless night would have been in **silhouette**, as a black absence against the starlit sky. And the best place from which to do that would be low down, close to sea level, rather than from the crow's nest, which was almost a hundred feet above the ocean. Even the bridge was little better, being barely ten feet lower than the crow's nest.

At around 11.30pm, the lookouts began to make out a mysterious haze along the horizon. With hindsight, it's reasonable to assume this was the continuous ice shelf that lay directly in their path, several miles ahead. At 11.40pm, Frederick Fleet saw "a black thing looming up" straight in front of him, which he later described to the US inquiry as being "about the size of two tables". He rang the bell in the crow's nest three times, to warn of a sighting directly ahead; one ring would signal a sighting on the port side, while two would mean it was to starboard. He then telephoned the bridge, and gave Sixth Officer James P. Moody the verbal warning "**iceberg right ahead**".

Frantic manoeuvres

Officer Moody passed Fleet's message on to William Murdoch, the officer on watch. Murdoch in turn ordered Quartermaster Robert Hichens "**Hard a-starboard**", and instructed the engine room to "Stop. Full speed astern." He explained shortly afterwards that his intention was to "**port around**" the iceberg, following an S-shaped trajectory that would have required the further order "Hard a-port".

THE KEY TO THE MISSING BINOCULARS

It's often charged that the failure to spot the iceberg in time was due to the lack of **binoculars** in the crow's nest. Hardened seamen of the time, Lightoller of the *Titanic* and Captain Lord of the *Californian* among them, sniffed at the idea of lookouts using binoculars. That was partly because they limited the field of vision, and also because they might tempt the lookouts to delay reporting a sighting until they'd attempted to identify it. However, the fact is that the *Titanic* lookouts were supposed to have binoculars. Lookout Fleet, indeed, testified to the US inquiry that if he'd had binoculars to scan the horizon ahead, he would have seen the iceberg early enough for the *Titanic* to avoid it.

The only reason he didn't have any was because they had accidentally been **locked away**. When Second Officer David Blair was suddenly removed from the *Titanic*'s crew the day before she sailed for New York (see p.40) he secured the binoculars in a locker in the crow's nest, and absent-mindedly pocketed the key. Blair kept the locker key, complete with brass RMS *Titanic* tag, for the rest of his life. It was eventually auctioned for £70,000 in 2007, and is now on display in Nanjing, China.

As author Wyn Wade has pointed out, Murdoch's response ran completely contrary to accepted procedure. The then-current edition of *Knight's Modern Seamanship*, regarded to this day as the definitive manual, stated explicitly that: "The first impulse of many officers" in reaction to the danger of a head-on collision "is to turn away from the danger, and at the same time to reverse the engines with full power. This course is much more likely to cause collisions than to prevent them."

Even had the orders been appropriate, there's a further potential confusion, in that – as explained on p.185 – the instruction "Hard a-starboard" meant turn the ship itself to port. It has been suggested that Hichens may have mistakenly turned the wheel in the wrong direction, but most naval historians argue that no seaman would have made such an elementary error. Time ran out, in any case, before Murdoch's order to reverse the engines, which first required them to be stopped, could be completed. Any reduction of the *Titanic's* speed in those final moments would have been minimal. Murdoch had also activated the closure of the **watertight doors** on her lower decks, but that too required more time.

From the crow's nest, as the *Titanic* veered to port, it looked as though she would indeed avoid the looming iceberg. However, although she didn't visibly touch it, **blocks of ice** broke free and shattered on the forward well deck as she shaved close alongside. Those blocks were the only immediately

Was this the iceberg that sank the Titanic? Passengers on ships in the area took photos of many possible candidates in the days after the disaster.

Lookout Frederick Fleet, the man who spotted the iceberg.

apparent consequence of a long, scraping **collision** that could be heard deep beneath the surface of the sea.

Lookout Lee, who saw the whole thing in vivid close-up, later confirmed that the iceberg was indeed dark: "It was a dark mass that came through that haze and there was no white appearing until it was just close alongside the ship, and that was just a fringe at the top." The strike came moments later: "There was the sound of rending metal right away; it seemed to be running along the starboard side." Only once it passed by could he see that while the front of the iceberg was black, its other side was white. Still on the after bridge, Quartermaster Rowe saw the towering berg go by, and estimated its height to be around one hundred feet.

Exactly how much **time** elapsed between the initial sighting and the collision, and thus how far the iceberg was from the *Titanic*, remains unknowable. Frederick Fleet revealed fifty years later that before he rang the crow's nest bell, he asked his fellow lookout whether he could tell what the mysterious object looming ahead might be. He also said that he'd told Lee "there's no sense the two of us being up here, if we strike", and that Lee had time to descend to the deck, change his mind, and return to the crow's nest before the actual impact.

It's known that the *Titanic* succeeded in turning **22½ degrees** to port before she hit the iceberg. Subsequent tests on the *Olympic* showed that such a turn would have taken **37 seconds** from the moment Hichens turned the wheel. In that time, the *Titanic* would have travelled around a quarter of a mile. Add on the time it took for Fleet to ring the bell, and for his warning to be translated into action, and the original distance from the iceberg at the time it was sighted was probably between 600 yards and half a mile.

The moment of impact

The **collision** between the iceberg and the *Titanic* was very slight. There are no reliable reports that it knocked anyone over, or tipped anyone out of bed.

Fourth Officer Joseph Boxhall was walking on deck at that precise moment, approaching the bridge, and the impact didn't even break his stride.

In contrast, just three nights before, in the same ice field, the French liner **Niagara** had crashed straight into an iceberg. As *The New York Herald* reported, "Passengers were hurled headlong from their chairs and broken dishes and glass were scattered throughout the dining saloons. The next instant there was a panic among the passengers and they raced screaming and shouting to the decks." Despite those initial fears, the *Niagara* limped on, and reached New York under its own steam. One of the great ironies of the *Titanic* disaster is that the *Titanic* would quite possibly also have survived that kind of head-on collision. Instead, the glancing blow that she did receive – thanks to her failed last-minute bid to steer clear – was sufficient to sink her within a few hours.

The precise nature of the **damage** that destroyed the *Titanic* is still not known (see p.176). Those death wounds were inflicted underwater by the submerged portions of the iceberg. The estimated one ninth of the berg that stood free of the ocean did not strike the upper decks, above the waterline. However, the fact that chunks landed on the forward well deck indicates that it must have shaved very close by the ship, and towered significantly above the deck, and that the initial impact must have come somewhere forward of that point.

On the upper decks, few aboard were alarmed by the impact. Most of the passengers were in bed, and experienced it, if at all, as something dimly sensed in sleep. Even the officers on duty were not greatly concerned at first, while those who lay in their cabins knew from the nuances of noise that something was amiss, but saw no reason as yet to venture out into the freezing night. Only down in the engine rooms was it immediately apparent that things had gone very wrong indeed.

A rude awakening: how the passengers reacted

Many **passengers** reported having not so much heard the impact as felt it in their bones, as a shiver or a shudder rather than a crash. They were shaken awake, either by the slight nudge against the iceberg, or by the sudden cessation of the engines. Lady Lucy Duff Gordon gave *The Denver Post* a graphic description of the sensation in her first-class stateroom: "I was awakened by a long grinding sort of shock. It was not a tremendous crash, but more as though someone had drawn a giant finger all along the side of the boat."

Sylvia Caldwell was reminded of a large dog shaking a kitten in its mouth. Major Arthur Peuchen said it "felt as though a heavy wave had struck our ship". As an experienced yachtsman, however, he knew that couldn't be right: "it was an unusual thing to occur on a calm night." Meticulous as ever, **Lawrence Beesley**, author of the most precise and considered *Titanic* memoir, recalled two separate impacts. Shortly after "an extra heave of the engines and a more than usually obvious dancing motion of the mattress", came another, "the same thing repeated with about the same intensity". There was "no sense of shock, no jar that felt like one heavy body meeting another".

A handful of passengers managed to witness the culprit. First-class passenger George Rheims, who had left his stateroom on A Deck to go to the lavatory, felt a slight shock and turned just in time to see "something white" pass rapidly by. Following a "dull thump", George Harder heard "a sort of rumbling, scraping noise along the side of the boat. When I went to the porthole I saw this iceberg go by."

Few of those passengers who were awake and active on the upper decks at the time of the collision lived to tell the tale; mostly men, they subsequently stood aside as the women and children boarded the lifeboats. However, Hugh Woolner gave a rare eyewitness account of the scene in the First Class Smoking Room on A Deck: "We felt a sort of stopping, a sort of, not exactly shock, but a sort of slowing down; and then we sort of felt a rip that gave a sort of a slight twist to the whole room. Everybody, so far as I could see, stood up and a number of men walked out rapidly through the swinging doors on the port side, and ran along to the rail that was behind the mast … I stood hearing what the conjectures were. People were guessing what it might be, and one man called out, 'An iceberg has passed astern.'"

> **"…it was just as though we went over about a thousand marbles. There was nothing terrifying about it at all."**
>
> Ella White, a rescued first-class passenger

The lower you were in the ship, the louder and more obvious the collision was likely to be. Down in steerage, third-class passenger Daniel Buckley was never in any doubt: "I heard some terrible noise and I jumped out on the floor, and the first thing I knew my feet were getting wet."

The response of the crew

For the **crew**, less mystery surrounded the collision. Those who hadn't experienced it for themselves were soon told by their colleagues; while the passengers were undoubtedly shielded from the truth, the crew had to be kept informed. Even after a full survey was carried out below decks, however, few had any idea that the ship might actually sink.

Standing at the wheel, Quartermaster Hichens saw the immediate response in the wheelhouse. "During the time she was crushing the ice", he told the US

Portraits of noteworthy passengers, from **The Illustrated London News** *of 20 April 1912. Left to right, top to bottom: J. Bruce Ismay; Major Arthur Peuchen; Archie Butt; C.M. Hays; Madeleine Astor; John Jacob Astor IV; Lady Lucy Duff Gordon; Jack Phillips (wireless operator); the Countess of Rothes; Daniel Marvin; Mary Marvin; W.T. Stead; Benjamin Guggenheim; Karl Behr; Isidor Straus.*

inquiry, "we could hear the **grinding noise** along the ship's bottom. I heard the telegraph ring. The skipper came rushing out of his room … and asked, 'What is that?' Mr. Murdoch said, 'An iceberg.' He said, 'Close the emergency doors.'"

Murdoch told Fourth Officer **Joseph Boxhall**, who arrived in the wheelhouse seconds later, that he'd clearly seen the iceberg when the *Titanic* struck it. Captain Smith however had not, and joined Murdoch and Boxhall in walking to the corner of the bridge to look for it. Boxhall's evidence at the US inquiry contradicts other witnesses by describing a "very, very low growler" that did not reach as high as the rail on C Deck; Boxhall was so tentative, however, that it seems likely neither he nor Smith ever did see the iceberg. A somewhat more precise description of the collision came from Quartermaster Alfred Olliver, who hurried forward when he heard the three rings from the crow's nest bell, and reached the bridge "just as the shock came". Although he saw the iceberg pass by, just above the height of the Boat Deck, he was at pains to point out that "the grinding sound was before I saw the iceberg. The grinding sound was not when I saw the iceberg."

Both the *Titanic*'s second and third officers were in their cabins nearby, steps from the wheelhouse. **Charles Lightoller** was lying awake, "turning over my past sins and future punishments", and "just about ready for the land of nod", when he felt a "sudden vibrating jar". Third Officer **Herbert J. Pitman** was already asleep when that same "little vibration" woke him up. He drowsily wondered why he could hear the ship coming to anchor, with "the chain running out over the windlass". Lightoller stayed in bed, but Pitman went out on deck. Seeing nothing, he returned to his room, lit his pipe, and wondered if it had all been a dream. Boxhall came in search of both men a few minutes later, with the unequivocal news: "We've hit an iceberg … The water is up to F Deck in the mailroom".

On the after bridge, Quartermaster Rowe felt the impact as "similar to going alongside a dock wall rather heavy … I looked toward the starboard side of the ship and saw a mass of ice." Oblivious to its significance, he remained at his post awaiting orders. Indeed, he was still there almost an hour later, when he was amazed to see a loaded lifeboat go past, and called the bridge to see if they knew anything about it. Quartermaster Walter J. Perkis, who was asleep in the Quartermasters' quarters towards the stern on E Deck, told the US inquiry that he "did not feel anything at all". Even when the ship's joiner informed him that the *Titanic* had struck something, he "took no notice", and stayed in bed until midnight, when he was next due to go on duty.

The various able-bodied seamen who survived told similar stories. Thomas Jones, who was sitting in the forecastle, thought he heard the ship "going through a lot of loose ice". Everyone ran outside, to find the ice that had landed on the forward well deck. Assorted slumbering seamen reported being woken by "**crunching and jarring**"; the less fortunate were disturbed by their shipmates bursting in excitedly with armfuls of ice and even throwing it onto their bunks. Meanwhile, firemen had started to stream up out of the forecastle; one of them, seeing the ice on deck, reportedly exclaimed: "Oh, we have struck an iceberg, that's nothing." Going forward to investigate, Able-Bodied Seaman Johnson heard "a rush of water" down below.

Trimmer **Samuel Hemming** was asleep in his bunk when he was woken by the collision. Disturbed by an unusual **hissing sound**, he went out to investigate, and tracked down its source as air escaping from the forepeak tank. Although it was in fact being forced out by the inrush of water far below, Hemming felt reassured that nothing was seriously wrong. He was back in bed by the time the ship's boatswain, **Alfred Nichols**, burst into the room: "Turn out, you fellows. You haven't half an hour to live. That is from Mr Andrews. Keep it to yourselves and let no one know." In Nichols' own case, sadly, that proved to be true.

As for the many stewards and other employees aboard, most had far too much ocean-going experience to be alarmed by such a minor collision. Pantryman Albert V. Pearcey, for example, was standing and chatting on F Deck at the time, and felt nothing: "There was just a small motion, but nothing to speak of." On the higher decks, the passengers expected their personal stewards to know what was going on. Thus First-Class Bedroom Steward Alfred Crawford rushed outside when he heard the crash: "I went out on the outer deck and saw the iceberg floating alongside."

Lower down, however, the ordinary stewards, sleeping in dormitories that held around thirty men, were totally in the dark. The consensus when they were woken by the slight shock seems to have been that the *Titanic* had probably dropped a propeller, and would have to return to Belfast for a refit. After all, many had been aboard the *Olympic* just seven weeks earlier, on 24 February, when she lost a propeller blade in a collision with some unidentified underwater obstruction in the same area.

Thunder in the boiler rooms

The worst place to be at the moment of impact was on the starboard side of the closest boiler room to the front of the ship, **Boiler Room 6**. Fourteen men were hard at work there when a flashing red light warned them to close down the engines immediately. Leading Stoker **Frederick Barrett**, in charge of eight firemen, gave the order to "shut all dampers", and cut off the air to the fires. Before they could finish the job there came a tremendous noise, which Barrett likened to a "big gun" and his workmate George Beauchamp to the "roar of thunder". A horizontal sheet of water erupted from the side of the starboard stokehold, roughly two feet above the floor plates. Senator Smith of the US inquiry later asked Barrett where he thought it came from. "Well, out of the sea, I expect", was the laconic reply.

The watertight bulkheads were not yet closed. Before they slammed down, Barrett, along with an engineer and at least one other fireman, had time to leap backwards through the ship to reach Boiler Room 5. Matters there were little better, with water rushing in from a smaller gash that appeared to be the continuation of the same rupture. Meanwhile, the remaining men in Barrett's section were left behind in the rapidly flooding Boiler Room 6.

The engineer in charge of Boiler Room 5 then issued the order "**every man to his station**", which for Barrett meant returning to Boiler Room 6. Now that the bulkheads were down, the only way to get back was to climb the emergency ladders up as high as E Deck, then descend similar ladders on the other side. By the time Barrett reached Boiler Room 6, which he estimated as being ten minutes after the collision, the water had risen eight feet deep, and the room had been evacuated. He set off back to Boiler Room 5.

Trimmer **George Cavell** was alone at the time of the collision, inside one of the two bunkers on the starboard side of Boiler Room 4, slightly further back towards the stern. His job required him to keep the coal within the bunkers at an even level. With the shock of the impact, he suddenly found himself surrounded by falling coal, and had to dig his way out. Just as he succeeded in scrambling out to the stokehold, the lights failed, plunging the boiler room into darkness. In search of lamps, he climbed the ladders to E Deck, where he ran into a crowd of third-class passengers, soaking wet and running towards the back of the ship, with life belts in their hands.

Assessing the damage

Piecing together exactly what happened on the **bridge** in the aftermath of the collision is all but impossible. However, it's clear that within a few minutes, the *Titanic*'s engines had **stopped** for the last time. Thanks to First Officer Murdoch's initial order to throw the engines into reverse, they must have stopped shortly after the collision. **Captain Smith** then ordered for them to start up again, and for the *Titanic* to steam ahead at half-speed, before shutting them down completely. Quite how long that process lasted, or what exactly convinced the captain to stop again, is not known. With hindsight, of course, it's clear that the ship was in no fit state to continue, and the forward motion may have accelerated the flooding.

The captain's immediate priority was to establish just how badly the *Titanic* was damaged. Within moments of the collision, he despatched Fourth Officer Joseph Boxhall to make a quick inspection. Boxhall only descended as low as F Deck, before returning to announce that he'd seen no sign of damage, other than encountering a passenger carrying a block of ice. By now, however, alarming reports were reaching the bridge, and Boxhall was swiftly packed off again, to find the carpenter and "sound the ship", meaning to check the level of water in the hold. The carpenter himself, John Hutchinson, arrived seconds later, to report that the ship was "making water". A stewardess who happened to open her cabin door just as the carpenter went past described him as looking "absolutely bewildered".

At much the same time, White Star Line chairman **J. Bruce Ismay** came padding up to the bridge in his slippers, wearing his suit over his pyjamas. After the sinking, he was at pains to insist that he had sailed on the *Titanic* as an ordinary first-class passenger, with no involvement in the ship's navigation or speed. Shaken awake by the impact, however, he clearly felt entitled to demand an explanation from Captain Smith. Told that "we have struck ice", Ismay responded, "Do you think the ship is seriously damaged?" Smith replied, "I am afraid she is."

Smith and Andrews inspect the ship

The captain then set off on his own **tour of inspection**, taking designer **Thomas Andrews** along with him. Neither man survived – or indeed appears to have made any attempt to do so – so the exact details of where they went, and what they saw, are unknown. Wherever possible, they used the crew's stairway, in the hope of remaining inconspicuous and not spreading alarm. Down on E Deck, however, and up in the first-class foyer on A Deck, they had to make their way through crowds of anxious passengers. One passenger, standing at the foot of the Grand Staircase, described seeing "a look of terror" on Andrews' face as he "rushed by".

Boxhall, meanwhile, had seen for himself that icy water was gushing into the mailroom, in the forward hold of G Deck, forward of and higher than Boiler Room 6. The *Titanic*'s five **postal workers** had set about hauling the heavy bags of registered mail, one by one, to higher decks. Even though the mailroom floor was 24 feet above the keel, mailbags were already floating freely. By midnight, the mailroom was flooded. As the night progressed, several survivors noticed the mailmen persisting with their Sisyphean task. By the end, two hundred mailbags had been carried up to C Deck; all the men, however, perished.

Some open third-class berths stood close to the mailroom, so they too must have filled rapidly; what became of their occupants is not known. Also down this low were the squash court, where the lines on the wall made it easy to see how quickly the ship was flooding, and the rooms where the first-class passengers' luggage was stored. Huge trunks were soon floating free, and careering dangerously through the confined spaces.

As Smith and Andrews returned from their expedition, the captain dropped in on the **wireless room**. He told the operators that the *Titanic* had hit an iceberg, and they should stand by to send out distress signals if necessary. At midnight, Andrews delivered his grim verdict. With her six

THE LAST HOURS OF THOMAS ANDREWS

During the first few days of the voyage, chief designer **Thomas Andrews** roamed the *Titanic* inspecting every aspect of her operation. He filled notebooks with such observations as that too many screws had been used to fix the stateroom coat hooks, and that so few female passengers were using their designated Writing Room that it might as well be turned into more cabins.

Andrews was so hard at work in his cabin on A Deck that he didn't notice the collision with the iceberg. Alerted within minutes, however, he joined the captain on a tour of the stricken ship. He more than anyone knew the significance of the water that was already rising into the mailroom and squash court, and he pronounced the *Titanic*'s **death sentence**.

Andrews is curiously absent from accounts of the ship's final two hours. He seems to have been burdened not just by the awareness that the *Titanic* was carrying too few lifeboats, but by his own complicity in that fact, and his overconfidence in her safety features. The few glimpses that we have suggest that he walked the decks quietly taking those he could trust into his confidence, admonishing crew members to put on their life belts, and directing passengers towards the Boat Deck.

He did what little he could to delay the sinking, ensuring cabin doors were left open so that each deck took longer to flood. He was even seen methodically throwing deckchairs overboard, to give survivors something to cling to. In the very last sighting of all, however, a steward rushed into the First Class Smoking

forward watertight compartments breached, the *Titanic* was **doomed**. For Andrews, it was a matter of simple mathematics. As each compartment filled, it would drag the bow ever deeper, causing water to spill into the next. The obvious analogy is with what happens when you tilt an ice-cube tray filled with water. He gave her an hour, or an hour and a half at most, before she disappeared beneath the waters.

The midnight hour

Captain Smith's immediate response to Andrews' dire prediction was to order Boxhall, who had just arrived back at the bridge, to wake officers Lightoller and Pitman. All the officers and boat crew were to be mustered, and the lifeboats to be cleared, under the supervision of Chief Officer Wilde. At ten minutes after midnight, the captain reappeared in the wireless room, and told the incredulous operators to send the first **emergency message**.

As it turned out, the *Titanic* still had a little over two hours to live. While the valiant efforts of the engineers and firemen below decks may help to

Thomas Andrews, chief designer of the Titanic *and leader of the nine-man "Guarantee Group" of Harland & Wolff employees, all of whom died in the disaster.*

Room to find Andrews standing alone, his own life belt lying uselessly on a table nearby. **"Aren't you going to have a try for it, Mr Andrews?"** the steward asked. Lost in his thoughts, Andrews made no reply.

explain why she survived longer than Andrews anticipated, the response to the emergency on the bridge appears to have been strikingly disorganized. There's little evidence that Captain Smith had any overall plan.

The news spreads

Half an hour after the collision with the iceberg, only a small handful of those aboard knew that the *Titanic*'s fate was sealed. Awareness of the true gravity of the situation took a long time to spread, and reached the crew well before the passengers. Most obviously, no general order to **evacuate** the ship was ever issued, presumably because Smith was all too aware that the lack of lifeboat space meant it would be impossible to evacuate everyone anyway.

The desire to prevent a **panic** took precedence over keeping the passengers informed. The ship didn't have a PA system, so meal times, for example, were announced by the blowing of a bugle. During the disaster, therefore, information passed by **word of mouth**. As a result, who knew what, when, was a matter of luck, aided perhaps by social connections or sense of entitlement.

When passengers first emerged from their cabins, their desire to find out what was going on was prompted more by curiosity than any sense of alarm. The earliest to venture outside were intrigued by the ice that had fallen on the forward well deck – the only visible sign of the impact. Steerage passengers with easy access to the deck itself walked across it, played football with large chunks, and carried off pieces to show their friends. Several of those watching from the upper decks agreed to meet up for "snowballing matches" the next morning.

Some passengers heard reports that the ship had stopped to **avoid** hitting an iceberg, rather than because she had hit one. As the minutes went by, however, more and more **unsettling clues** suggested that something must be wrong. There was just too much activity for that time of night. Typically, among the first- and second-class passengers, the men would leave their wives in their cabins and head out to explore, only to return puzzled rather than reassured.

Along the ship's internal passageways, sailors were lifting mysterious floor hatches as they sought to close the manually operated watertight doors (see p.32). Up on the Boat Deck, the tarpaulins were being taken off the lifeboats. And the decks no longer seemed quite level; instead, one experienced a curious sensation of walking downhill.

On the upper decks, the stewards began to work their way from cabin to cabin. Each first-class steward was responsible for a mere eight or so cabins, and so had time to give their occupants personal attention. Passengers were advised to report to the Boat Deck, dressed warm and wearing their life belts, though most had the impression it was a precaution, not a necessity. There was less time for niceties on the lower decks. While third-class passengers seem to have received little information or advice during the disaster – whether they were actually held back from reaching the lifeboats is discussed on p.187 onwards – warnings certainly spread along the corridors. Daniel Buckley, for example, heard two sailors shouting, "All up on deck! Unless you want to get drowned."

Some steerage passengers, including Buckley, needed no such advice – the cabins nearest the bow were already awash. Bedraggled groups made their way to the forward well deck, clutching their possessions, where they made a disturbing spectacle for anyone looking down from above. Further aft, on decks E and F, passengers were surprised to find hallways that were usually left open had now been sealed off by the closure of the watertight doors.

During this earlier part of the night, crowds of steerage passengers appear to have gathered in such public areas as the Third Class Dining Saloon on F Deck, and the general and smoking rooms aft on C Deck. **Georges Youssef**, a seven-year-old Syrian boy travelling with his family in third class, later told how he and his eight-year-old sister had been spending their days aboard the *Titanic* playing in empty cabins. On the night of the disaster, his sister had fallen asleep in such a cabin, and it took a frantic search by his mother to find her.

Lady Duff Gordon had already put on all her thickest clothing when she was jokily warned by her steward to expect a "little trip of an hour or so" in a lifeboat. As she left her A Deck stateroom, she turned back for a last look. "It all looked so pretty, just like a bedroom on land, that it did not seem possible there could be any danger. But as if to give this reassuring thought the lie, a vase of flowers on the washstand slid off and fell with a crash to the floor."

On C Deck, **Elizabeth Shutes** was about to go back to sleep after being reassured that the "queer quivering" she'd detected was of no importance, when she overheard an officer in the next cabin revealing that "we can keep the water out for a while".

Charlotte Collyer, an English second-class passenger whose cabin was located on the lower decks, wrote that her husband went out to investigate the stopping of the engines. After he returned, they were just about to settle back to sleep when "suddenly we heard hundreds of people running along the passageway in front of our door. They did not cry out, but the patter of their feet reminded me of rats scurrying through an empty room." In her nightdress and dressing gown, Mrs Collyer went up on deck with her family. There, within moments, "we saw a stoker climbing up from below. All of the fingers of one hand had been cut off. Blood was running from the stumps and blood was spattered over his face and over his clothes ... I went over and spoke to him. I asked him if there was any danger. 'Danger', he screamed at the top of his voice, 'I should just say so! It's hell down below, look at me. This boat will sink like a stone in ten minutes.'"

Heading for the lifeboats

Passengers grappled with the issue of what was worth carrying from their cabins to the lifeboats. Their responses varied enormously. The Collyers took nothing at all; **Major Arthur Peuchen** chose to take three oranges rather than a box containing $300,000. Others took jewellery, treasured photographs or extra items of clothing, while at least one man made sure to retrieve his revolver. **Henry Widener** had just bought a hugely valuable second edition of Francis Bacon's essays in London, dating from 1598; saying goodbye to his mother as she boarded Boat 4, he told her: "I have placed the volume in my pocket – the little 'Bacon' goes with me." Edith Russell, on the other hand, had her own lucky bacon, in the form of a clockwork pig (see p.98).

Colonel Archibald Gracie was among several passengers who later reported having attempted to return to their cabins – usually to fetch blankets or warmer clothing – only to find them locked by stewards to prevent looting.

> **"...it would have been impossible, even in daylight, to have obtained a view of but a limited portion of this boat deck. We only knew what was going on within a radius of possibly forty feet."**
>
> First-class passenger Dr Washington Dodge, describing the moonless night of 14 April

There are even stories of passengers being locked into their cabins by mistake. The ship's designer Thomas Andrews, on the other hand, was seen by many witnesses to be going through the ship making sure that cabin doors were left wide open, presumably to delay the sinking. No one seems to have set about shutting all the portholes, however, which would have had a similar effect.

First-class passenger **Anna Warren**, who left the ship on one of the earliest lifeboats, said that until that point, just before 1am, "there was nothing which in any way resembled a panic ... There seemed to be a sort of aimless confusion and an utter lack of organized effort."

The battle in the boiler rooms

Once again, all we know of what went on in the *Titanic*'s engine and boiler rooms comes from the few witnesses who survived. That makes it exceptionally hard to piece together what actually happened; only a few searing glimpses illuminate the mystery.

For the **engineers**, the main priority was to get rid of the incoming water. While the actual pumps in the *Titanic*'s intricate, steam-driven pumping system were fixed in place, a network of pipes laid through the middle of the boiler rooms made it possible to attach hoses to remove water from any specific area. The trouble was, even after the initial rush died down, water was pouring in at a much faster rate than the pumps could remove it. All the crew could hope to achieve was to slow the rate of flooding. The **firemen** and **stokers**, meanwhile, concentrated on damping down the fires, to stop the pressure building in the boilers and prevent potential explosions.

The most detailed testimony at the inquiries came from Leading Stoker **Frederick Barrett**, who witnessed the impact from the unique vantage point of Boiler Room 6. Although Boiler Room 6 was swiftly abandoned, it seemed at first as though progress was being made in Boiler Room 5. Barrett organized a team of around fifteen stokers to draw the fires in all the boilers, which took twenty minutes.

The stokers then left, leaving Barrett to help two engineers with the pumps. He lifted off one of the heavy metal floor plates to give them access to the valves. Water having been sprayed on the boilers to cool them down, the room was filled with steam. Amid the chaos, Engineer **Jonathan**

Shepherd stumbled into the hole where the plate had been, and broke his leg. Barrett and the other engineer, Herbert Harvey, carried him to the nearby pump room.

A quarter of an hour later, a huge rush of water burst into Boiler Room 5. The most likely explanation, certainly in Barrett's view, was that the bulkhead between boiler rooms 6 and 5 had given way. His insistence that the flow was horizontal, not from above, is significant because the conventional model for explaining the sinking of the *Titanic* describes each watertight compartment as filling up and then overflowing into its neighbour. Here, however, it seems that the compartment that included Boiler Room 6 was not watertight at all. In view of the fact that the bulkhead at this point incorporated the bunker that was said to be on **fire** when the *Titanic* sailed, as described on p.180, some historians have suggested that the fire had weakened the bunker wall, and played a material role in the destruction of the ship.

As the water came in, Barrett managed to reach the escape ladder and climb out; he was lucky enough to leave the *Titanic* on Boat 13, at around 1.30am. Engineer Harvey, however, turned back to retrieve Shepherd from the pump room; both men were engulfed.

The battle to extinguish the furnaces lasted for just under an hour from the time of the collision. By now, all the fires had either been dampened by the firemen, or simply flooded with seawater. Fireman George Kemish, who later told Walter Lord, "we certainly had a Hell of a time putting those fires out", said the order came through from the captain for all hands to report to boat stations at 12.45am. Despite all they'd seen, the firemen still didn't think they were in any danger. When they found their sleeping quarters awash, "we thought this a huge joke and had a good laugh … The ship was as steady as if she had been in dry-dock, going down very steadily forward but even at that time it was hardly noticeable." Another fireman, Alfred Shiers, recalled that when he reached the Boat Deck at 1am, the crew was "all standing about … They did not think it was serious."

As for the *Titanic*'s engineers, who remained below decks after the firemen came up, persistent myth has it that they all died down there, doing their duty to the last. That duty is generally depicted as twofold: working the **pumps** to slow down the sinking, and keeping the ship's **electrical systems** functioning. In fact, however, it's clear that the engineers too had reached the upper decks well before the ship sank. Officer Lightoller explicitly stated in his memoirs that at about 1.45am, "I met all the engineers, as they came trooping up from below … They had all loyally stuck to their guns, long after they could be of any material assistance." He went on to mention that: "Much earlier on the engine-room telegraphs had been 'Rung off' … which conveys to the engine-room staff the final information that their services below can be of no further use."

Lightoller's assertion that the engineers had been released from their posts "much earlier on" suggests that the signal was given around the time that pumping became futile, and perhaps impossible. As for the electricity, it was indeed a small part of the engineers' responsibilities, but by the end of the night the *Titanic* was being powered by its standby battery, which was triggered in such an emergency without human intervention.

An infernal noise and a death-like silence

When the *Titanic*'s engines were first shut down, her furnaces were still blazing away. While the firemen battled to extinguish the fires, therefore, the boilers carried on producing immense quantities of steam. All that excess steam was forced out at high pressure through the ship's eight exhausts, creating an infernal **noise**. Officer Lightoller described it as "a row that would have dwarfed the row of a thousand railway engines thundering through a culvert".

That onslaught was all the more terrifying for the passengers because it coincided with something equally unexpected – the liner coming to a complete halt. As Lady Duff Gordon remembered it, "Then the boat stopped and immediately there was the frightful noise of escaping steam." The noise was so bad on the Boat Deck, according to Lightoller, that "it was an utter impossibility to convey an order by word of mouth". Instead he communicated with the crew via "a tap on the shoulder and an indication with the hand"; small wonder perhaps that confusion seems to have been so rife. Having so much background noise also created huge problems for wireless operator Jack Phillips during his initial attempts to summon help (see p.90).

Only when the firemen and stokers had completed their task, and began to appear on the Boat Deck – around the time the first lifeboats were being lowered – did the hideous roar of escaping steam finally die down. While the sudden cessation came as a relief in the wireless room, it filled many of those on board with dread. Lady Duff Gordon wrote of "an infinitely more frightening silence"; Officer Lightoller was struck by "a death-like silence a thousand times more exaggerated" than the appalling din that had preceded it. This sudden quiet also marked the moment when everyone became aware that the band was playing.

Chapter 5
Women and children first

Captain Smith's order to make the **lifeboats** ready, issued shortly after midnight, triggered a complicated and time-consuming operation. As well as stripping away the coverings from each boat, the crew had to untie the oars and mast that were lashed to the thwarts, find the plug for the drainage hole at the bottom, and attach cranks to the davits. Those basic preparations took something over twenty minutes; one seaman told the US inquiry that he and his colleagues were told to "turn them out as quietly as though nothing had happened".

Each boat was also supposed to hold certain **supplies**, including food and water, and some means of lighting. Whether they did so on the final night seems to have been entirely haphazard. It's known that the bakers brought up fresh bread for each boat, but several survivors reported there was nothing to eat or drink.

For most of the first hour, the deafening **roar** of steam made it all but impossible to hear a word out on deck, so everything had to be done with signals and gestures. Many of those passengers who did get the message to assemble on the Boat Deck quickly retreated inside as soon as they were exposed to the freezing cold and almighty racket.

The loading begins

Half an hour after giving his initial instructions, the captain still hadn't ordered the crew to start filling the lifeboats with people. **Second Officer Lightoller** had to prod him into giving his consent. From then on, the lifeboats were lowered in as quick a succession as Lightoller and his colleagues could manage. Broadly speaking, **First Officer Murdoch** was in charge of

The Boat Deck of the *Titanic*

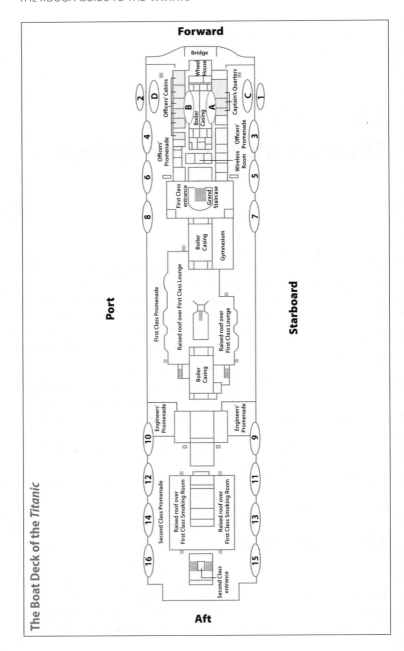

Forward

Bridge

Wheel House

Officers' Cabins

Captain's Quarters

B

Boiler Casing

A

Officers' Promenade

Officers' Promenade

Wireless Room

First Class entrance

Grand Staircase

Boiler Casing

Gymnasium

First Class Promenade

Raised roof over First Class Lounge

Raised roof over First Class Lounge

Boiler Casing

Port

Starboard

Engineers' Promenade

Engineers' Promenade

Second Class Promenade

Raised roof over First Class Smoking Room

Raised roof over First Class Smoking Room

Second Class entrance

Aft

WHERE THE LIFEBOATS WERE

Although the *Titanic* was equipped to carry sixty-four **lifeboats**, as explained on p.33, she had in fact just twenty, all of which were on the **Boat Deck**. Sixteen were solid wooden **rowing boats**, located in four groups of four, with four boats forward and four aft on each side. They were numbered 1 to 16, forward to aft, with the odd numbers on the starboard side and the even numbers on the port side.

The two furthest forward, boats 1 and 2, were cutters of slightly differing sizes, both smaller than the rest. Designated as **emergency boats**, they could hold forty people apiece, and were kept ready for immediate launch, should for example a passenger fall overboard. The remaining fourteen were larger, designed to carry sixty-five apiece, and protected by canvas coverings that had to be removed before use.

Each boat was suspended from two **davits** that resembled miniature cranes, by "**the falls**" – ropes threaded through a block and tackle at each end. The lifeboats were lowered by hand, ideally by teams of eight to ten men. Electric winches could only be used to lift them back out of the water.

In ordinary conditions, the lifeboats could be positioned either **inboard**, hanging over the deck, or **outboard**, hanging slightly outside; there was a gap in the railings at each relevant point on the Boat Deck. It's thought that once the *Titanic* was at sea, the four aftmost boats on each side were moved outboard, allowing the passengers more room to stroll on the promenade.

There were also four so-called **collapsible boats**, which had rounded wooden keels but canvas sides, and thus could be stowed relatively flat. Capable of holding up to 49 people, they were also known as Englehardt boats, on account of their manufacturer. Stored forward on the Boat Deck, they were intended to be lowered after the emergency boats, using the same davits. Two of the four, C and D, simply rested on the deck, below boats 1 and 2. The others, however, were kept on the roof of the officers' house. They were largely intended for show; there was no obvious way to get them down.

loading the lifeboats on the **starboard** side – the odd-numbered boats – while Lightoller was responsible for those on the **port** side. Neither was involved in the lowering of every single boat on "his" side, however. As the urgency increased, junior officers, crew members and passengers alike joined in the communal effort.

Murdoch and Lightoller followed their own variations on the rule of "**women and children first**". Lightoller interpreted it to mean "**women and children only**" – he proudly used the phrase as a chapter title in his

Four of the Titanic's *lifeboats, suspended from their davits.*

autobiography – and refused to let any men on board. For Murdoch, on the other hand, it was simply a question of priority; if any men were to hand once all the available women and children were aboard, then of course the men could board as well.

Within those general guidelines, each officer loaded the lifeboats with whomever happened to be nearby at the time. The lack of a systematic approach to the crisis was at its most apparent in the failure to shepherd passengers towards the boats in the first place. Several boats left **half-empty**, simply because there was no one around to fill them up. The controversy as to whether third-class passengers were deliberately prevented from reaching the lifeboats is explored in detail on p.187 onwards. Suffice it here to say that while one or two stewards fetched groups from the lower decks and guided them all the way to the boats, most did not.

Many accounts – and movies like *A Night to Remember* – depict Lightoller as the hero of the hour. In his autobiography, he congratulated himself on a job well done, claiming that he and his fellow officers "put up as fine a show as has ever been done in any sea tragedy in history. The final and conclusive proof lay in the fact that every single boat in the ship was cleared, swung out and safely lowered into the water and got away, without a hitch of any kind."

The sad truth, however, is that even though the *Titanic* was under-equipped with lifeboats, there was only just enough time to load and launch the few that it had. The final two hardly went off "without a hitch"; they were washed overboard, and one was upside down. It seems fair to conclude that even if the *Titanic* had been carrying enough lifeboats to accommodate everyone on board, her crew would not have managed to fill and dispatch any more of them safely.

Moreover, the fact that the lifeboats were on average only two-thirds full was partly due to the **ignorance** of Lightoller and his fellow officers. He explicitly told the US inquiry, "I knew that it was not practicable to lower them full of people", and "it seems hardly feasible that they would carry 65 people when suspended at each end". In fact, however, the boats were designed to be lowered full, and, as described on p.82, had been tested fully laden.

That said, to some extent the crew of the *Titanic* can be excused their caution. The official capacity of each lifeboat did not necessarily reflect the actual experience of loading it in emergency conditions with terrified passengers. As first-class passenger George Harder recalled, "They say those boats hold sixty people, but we had only 42, and, believe me, we did not have room to spare."

A precarious task

For passengers to get on board, each lifeboat had to be **lowered**, either a short distance to stand level with the edge of the Boat Deck, or further down to allow boarding from the lower decks, most obviously from A Deck, the Promenade Deck. However, the lower the boats were, the more difficult it became to coordinate the work of the men hauling the ropes with what was happening on the relevant deck.

As each boat was lowered, rocking precariously high above the ocean, it was essential to pay out the **ropes** at both ends simultaneously. With passengers tumbling in and shifting position, and the ropes either jamming in the never-used tackle, or tangling amid the mass of feet and limbs, there was a constant threat that the boat might tip over and spill everybody out. Especially as the **listing** of the *Titanic* increased, there was also the danger that the boats might hit obstructions, such as jutting spars, the rivets of the hull itself, or sudden spurts of water. Several boats saw a last-minute scurry to find the plug before the boat reached the water. And finally, once the boat was actually in the water, the ropes had to be detached before it could float free.

In theory, had each crew member known his assigned boat, and benefited from regular drills – as opposed to none whatsoever – the process would have been quicker and more efficient. However, the *Titanic* was notably short on seamen for a ship of its size, while only a small proportion of those it did have were capable of lowering the boats. What's more, of course, their number kept dwindling as more and more trained seamen departed with each boat that was launched. Not that there was any coherent system about that, either; some lifeboats were launched with just two crewmen, others with a dozen or more. To the huge indignation of the passengers, plenty of the crew members who were sent off with the boats turned out to have no expertise whatsoever. Several female survivors later complained that they'd been forced to leave their husbands behind, only to find themselves sharing a lifeboat with stewards who clearly didn't know how to row or hoist a sail.

Assignments and drills

Each of the **crewmen** responsible for lowering or manning the boats was assigned to a specific boat. Few however had checked, let alone remembered, their assignments. According to Officer Lightoller, in his memoirs, they seldom did, and the system was notional only, designed to reassure passengers but of no real worth – "just so much theory, concocted ashore with a keen eye to dividends".

Be that as it may, the *Titanic* had never staged a proper **lifeboat drill**. Her sea trials had simply required the lowering of two unloaded boats. A full boat drill was in theory scheduled for Sunday mornings, but on the only Sunday she was ever at sea, that drill was cancelled by Captain Smith (see p.53). Such a drill might have saved many lives that night, although on the other hand it would have allowed the passengers to see that there weren't enough places to go round. Many of the *Titanic's* officers and seamen had previously sailed on the *Olympic*, but that ship was not renowned for its safety drills either. On all White Star Line ships, firemen and other engine-room workers were notoriously reluctant to participate in drills, and Captain Smith seems also to have preferred not to alarm his passengers.

As a result, the crew of the *Titanic* were **woefully unprepared** when disaster hit. For example, several officers expressed the fear that when fully laden, the lifeboats might be too heavy for the davits to support. That helps to explain why the first lifeboats to leave carried so few passengers. Lightoller, testifying at the US inquiry, made a spurious distinction between each boat's "load at lowering" as opposed to its "load in the water", and claimed they were supposed to be lowered half empty. In fact, the *Olympic's* identical davits had been extensively tested in the Harland & Wolff shipyard, lowering lifeboats at their maximum capacity, but no one on the *Titanic* seems to have been informed.

Individual **passengers** were not assigned to particular boats, and neither were boats reserved for specific classes. During the tragedy, however, many of the crew and passengers alike seemed to have that impression. Lawrence

THE SINKING OF *LA BOURGOGNE*

One reason why the officers of the *Titanic* were so keen to avoid a panic may have been memories of another North Atlantic shipping disaster, just fourteen years earlier. In July 1898, the French liner **La Bourgogne**, carrying almost five hundred passengers and over two hundred crew, was crossing from New York to Le Havre. Early one morning, in thick fog off Nova Scotia, she collided at full speed with the sailing ship *Cromartyshire*.

While the *Cromartyshire* remained afloat, *La Bourgogne* passed from view, and sank within an hour. At daybreak, a motley assortment of lifeboats and rafts emerged from the fog. A total of 165 survivors from *La Bourgogne* were helped aboard the *Cromartyshire*; more than 500 people had drowned.

What alarmed the crew of the *Cromartyshire* was that there was only **one woman** among the survivors. The remainder were very largely crew, along with a few men from steerage. Lurid tales soon circulated that as *La Bourgogne* went down, her decks had been the scene of a **pitched battle**. Using knives, boat hooks, oars and whatever else came to hand, her crew had fought with passengers for places in the few lifeboats that survived the collision. They'd ignored all orders from their officers, of whom only three out of eighteen survived, and once the boats were in the water, they'd beaten off and stabbed swimming passengers who had tried to clamber aboard.

The entire incident was hushed up by the French maritime authorities, who refused to hold a proper investigation. That experience helped prompt the US Senate to stage its own inquiry into the *Titanic* disaster. During that inquiry, first-class passenger Charles E. Stengel testified that one of the *Titanic*'s officers had explained to him aboard the *Carpathia*: "Suppose we had reported the damage that was done to that vessel; there would not be one of you aboard. The stokers would have come up and taken every boat, and no one would have had a chance of getting aboard of those boats."

Beesley heard two female second-class passengers ask an officer, "May we pass to the boats?", and receive the reply, "No, madam, your boats are down on your own deck".

Reluctance to board the lifeboats

Not only were the *Titanic*'s twenty lifeboats too **few** to save all her passengers and crew, but they were not even used to their full **capacity**. Almost five hundred of those who died could have been saved had all the boats departed fully laden. Tragically, the lifeboats may not have been filled precisely *because* there weren't enough of them. In the early stages of loading, very few people knew that the *Titanic* was doomed to sink. Aware of the lifeboat shortage, the crew were so eager to avoid a panic that they lulled the passengers into a false sense of security. At first, the officers were not so much fighting off a mad scramble to get into the lifeboats as trying to persuade reluctant passengers to leave the apparent safety of the ship.

From the passengers' point of view, there were **good reasons** not to get into a lifeboat. So long as the *Titanic* was not visibly sinking, remaining on the warm, well-lit ship seemed preferable to clambering into a tiny and precarious lifeboat and being lowered eighty feet into the freezing Atlantic. John Jacob Astor IV, for example, was reported as scoffing at the very idea: "We are safer here than in that little boat", while a steward who tried to persuade third-class passengers to leave later recalled, "I heard two or three say they preferred to remain on the ship than be tossed about on the water like a cockle shell". Emily Ryerson later vividly described stepping into a lifeboat from the bright lights of A Deck: "as you went through the window it was as if you stepped out into the dark". As Boat 8 was being loaded, third-class passengers kept jumping out again, and going back inside the ship to get warm.

For anyone who didn't know that there weren't enough boats to save the men as well, the much-vaunted policy of "women and children first" lacked urgency, or even sense. Women thus chose instead to stay with their husbands or sons, in the hope of boarding a later boat together. For much of the night, it was more a question of forcing, or tricking, wives into boarding the boats and leaving their husbands behind, than of repelling husbands eager to board. As first-class passenger Eloise Smith put it, "I had not the least suspicion of the scarcity of lifeboats, or I never should have left my husband."

As an additional disincentive, everyone could see the so-called "**Mystery Ship**", not far away (see opposite). Officer Lightoller used its presence to reassure those passengers who "naturally kept coming up and asking, did I consider the situation serious. In all cases I tried to cheer them up, by telling them 'No' ... there was a ship not more than a few miles away."

Just three years earlier, in 1909, the White Star Line's *Republic* had been crippled in a collision in the North Atlantic. Rescue ships were summoned by wireless, and the *Republic*'s 1500 passengers and crew were ferried to safety in lifeboats before she sank. Many aboard the *Titanic* – particularly Captain Smith himself – seem to have envisaged a similar scenario; even if the "Mystery Ship" or some other saviour did not come alongside, the passengers could at least wait until she was close enough to set up a quick and orderly lifeboat shuttle service. No need to get into a lifeboat right away and hang around in the cold and dark.

What the passengers actually knew

The English schoolmaster **Lawrence Beesley**, a second-class passenger with an indefatigable curiosity, is the most reliable witness as to what the mass of passengers knew: "The great majority were never enlightened as to the amount of damage done, or even as to what had happened. We knew in a vague way that we had collided with an iceberg, but there our knowledge ended, and most of us drew no deductions from that fact alone." Instead, the passengers were left to draw their own conclusions from what they could see around them.

The lack of accurate information ensured that **rumours** spread instead. At one point, passengers believed that women were supposed to go to the port lifeboats, and men to the starboard ones. Then, when it was readily apparent that Murdoch was launching his boats more rapidly on the starboard side, the word went round that the boats for the men would be leaving later, from the port side.

> "... a ship that had come quietly to rest without any indication of disaster – no iceberg visible, no hole in the ship's side through which water was pouring in, nothing broken or out of place, no sound of alarm, no panic, no movement of any one except at a walking pace."
>
> Lawrence Beesley, from *The Loss of the S.S. Titanic*

The Mystery Ship

Perhaps the greatest of all the controversies that surround the sinking of the *Titanic* is whether her passengers could have been saved by some nearby ship. By far the most frequently mentioned possible rescuer is the ***Californian***. Amid all the debate as to how close the *Californian* may have been at the time of the disaster, however, it's easy to lose sight of the fact that another ship, whether or not it was the *Californian*, could definitely be seen from the deck of the *Titanic*. It's generally referred to as the **Mystery Ship**, although different historians have used the term in different ways. For those who believe it to have been the *Californian*, it's simply a convenient label; for those who do not, it denotes some as-yet unidentified third or even fourth vessel. That issue is discussed on p.204 onwards; that such a ship was visible, however, is not in doubt.

The most compelling witness to its presence has to be Fourth Officer **Joseph Boxhall**. He testified in detail at both the US and British inquiries that once it became clear that the *Titanic* was sinking, he spent over an hour "trying to signal a steamer that was almost ahead of us". This ship was first spotted at much the same time as the lifeboats were being uncovered. The lookouts

THE STORY OF THE STOKER

While wireless operator Jack Phillips stayed at the transmitter for all but a few minutes of the *Titanic*'s final night, his colleague Harold Bride occasionally ventured out onto the Boat Deck. Towards the very end, Bride returned from helping with the loading of Collapsible D to find "a **stoker**, or somebody from below decks", attempting to steal Phillips' life belt from him.

Bride later told various versions of a free-for-all **brawl**, all of which ended with the stoker lying motionless on the floor of the cabin. His account in *The New York Times* left the strong impression that he had beaten him to death. At the British inquiry, on the other hand, Bride appeared to pin the blame on Phillips; it was a **murder**, after all, so perhaps it seemed safer to pin the blame on his lost workmate. Asked "would you know the man again if you saw him?", Bride laconically replied, "I am not likely to see him".

The story was to grow in the telling. In subsequent books and newspaper reports, the shadowy figure became first "a grimy stoker of gigantic proportions", and then, in Logan Marshall's sensational 1912 *The Sinking of the Titanic*, "a negro stoker" armed with a knife. According to Marshall, Bride "pulled out his revolver and shot the negro dead", to which Phillips responded: "Thanks, old man".

who had relieved Fleet and Lee on schedule at midnight gave a single ring on the crow's nest bell to report something off the port bow. Boxhall went out on deck and could see it with the naked eye. Examining it more closely through binoculars (the bridge was equipped with binoculars, even if the lookouts were not), he thought it was roughly five miles away, only very slightly off the port bow, and coming closer. At first he saw two white masthead lights, and then green and red side lights as it grew nearer. He was certain it was a steamer rather than a fishing vessel, and had at least three masts.

When **Captain Smith** saw the steamer, he ordered Boxhall to contact it using the electric **Morse signal**: "Tell him to come at once, we are sinking." He did so in tandem with firing **distress rockets**, which seemed even more likely to attract the steamer's attention. Though Boxhall never discerned an answering flash, several passengers gathered around him were convinced they saw a light exposed aboard the steamer.

The presence of the Mystery Ship probably served to increase the death toll on the *Titanic*. Some passengers didn't board the lifeboats because they expected the ship to come over and pick them up anyway; some lifeboats were loaded less than full because it was assumed they would simply ferry passengers across to the ship then return to pick up another load. A number of witnesses described Captain Smith bellowing from the Boat Deck through a megaphone at the departing lifeboats, ordering them to head for the Mystery Ship and come back as soon as possible.

According to Boxhall, however, the Mystery Ship seemed to turn away shortly before 1.45am. When he was lowered in command of Boat 2 (see p.106), Boxhall could only see a single bright light, which he took to be the stern light. Several lifeboats did indeed head towards that enticing light, but it gradually faded from view, and when the sun rose the next morning there was no sign that it had ever existed.

The wireless room during the disaster

Only **Jack Phillips** was on duty in the *Titanic*'s **wireless room** at the time of the collision. He was steadily working his way through the huge backlog of passenger messages for North America that had accumulated while his equipment was out of action (see p.43). The most efficient way to transmit those was via the Cape Race wireless station on Newfoundland, which had only been within range for around two hours.

Harold Bride, asleep in their adjoining shared cabin, didn't notice the impact: "I didn't even feel the shock … There was no jolt whatever". Having

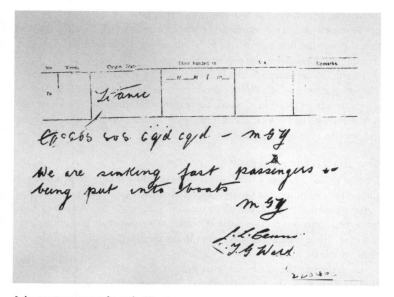

A desperate message from the **Titanic.**

agreed to take over at midnight, however, he poked his head out a few minutes later. Phillips handed over the headphones, and mentioned that he thought the ship might have hit something, so they might have to return to Belfast. At that moment, Captain Smith appeared, and told the two men that the *Titanic* had hit an iceberg. He didn't yet know how seriously she'd been damaged, but told Phillips and Bride they should get ready to call for help. He returned at ten past midnight, and tersely instructed Phillips, who now resumed his station, to "send the call for assistance".

In *The New York Times* a few days later, Bride described the mood in the wireless room as amazingly light-hearted. Phillips began by sending out the conventional emergency signal used by Marconi operators, "**CQD**". As Bride recalled, "He flashed away and we joked while he did so. We all made light of the disaster." A few years previously, the German government, resentful of Marconi's domination of the airwaves, had barred Marconi systems from its ships, and persuaded an international conference in 1906 to agree upon a new distress signal, **SOS**. The Marconi men, however, had persisted with the old signal, CQD. Prefixed by CQD, Phillips' first message read: "Have struck an iceberg. We are badly damaged. *Titanic*. 41° 46' N; 50° 24' W."

According to Bride, when Captain Smith later came back and asked what signal they were sending, "The **humour** of the situation appealed to me. I cut in with a little remark that made us all laugh, including the Captain. 'Send SOS', I said, 'it's the new call, and it may be your last chance to send it.'" Phillips duly started transmitting SOS as well as CQD. It's often claimed that this was the first-ever use of SOS, but several ships are known to have transmitted the signal in the preceding years.

Fourth Officer Joseph Boxhall quickly came up with a new estimate of the *Titanic*'s position, which Phillips used from then on – **41° 46' N; 50° 14' W.** Given the actual location in which the wreck was found, we now know that Boxhall was off by thirteen miles; fortunately, as described on p.130, his error did not affect the rescue operation.

The search for a saviour

Despite Bride's insistence that "we said lots of funny things to each other in the next few minutes", the situation rapidly acquired greater urgency. Phillips' initial signal had been picked up by the land station at Cape Race, as well as by several ships out on the North Atlantic. None was close enough to help, however. There was no response from the nearest ship of all – the "Mystery Ship", visible off the port bow (see p.85).

In retrospect it can be seen that even if the *Californian* was not itself the Mystery Ship, she still offered the best hope of rescue. Although the *Californian*'s wireless operator Cyril Evans had gone to bed, it's known that

ROCKETS IN THE NIGHT

Just as the *Titanic*'s first lifeboat was launched, at around 12.45am, Quartermaster George Rowe – who was still on the aft bridge, unaware anything was seriously wrong, and thus was astonished to see a lifeboat in the water – called up to the fore bridge to find out what was going on. Fourth Officer Joseph Boxhall asked him if he knew where the **distress rockets** were kept. Rowe located a box of twelve, and carried them up to the Boat Deck.

The first rocket hissed into the night sky around ten minutes later. Everyone on deck turned instinctively towards it, their faces lit by the sudden flash. According to Lawrence Beesley, its launch marked for many passengers the moment when they first realized the gravity of their plight: "Anybody knows what rockets at sea mean … Everybody knew without being told that we were calling for help from any one who was near enough to see."

Following Captain Smith's orders to fire one every five or six minutes, Boxhall and Rowe continued to launch them at steady intervals until around 1.25am. As outlined opposite, their main aim was to attract the attention of the "Mystery Ship". Why they didn't succeed in summoning help, even though they were definitely seen from the *Californian*, remains a matter of huge debate, considered in Chapter 9.

when the *Titanic*'s first distress signals went out, her third officer, Charles Groves, was idly attempting to pick up messages through his headphones. Unaware that the mechanism had to be wound up in order to work, however, he gave up for the night.

The first message that Phillips received was from a German ship, the **Frankfurt**. He immediately replied asking for her precise location, not realizing that the *Frankfurt* had not picked up the distress call, and was simply sending a routine greeting. He was therefore amazed that the *Frankfurt* did not get in touch again for almost twenty minutes. It took a further exchange before the *Frankfurt* responded that she'd changed her course and was coming to help.

In the interim, however, Phillips' friend Harold Cottam, aboard the **Carpathia**, had got in touch to say that he had transcribed several passenger messages for the *Titanic* from Cape Race. This too was just a friendly gesture; Cottam had not received the emergency signal either, and contacted Phillips on a whim, as he prepared for bed. When Phillips immediately responded with "struck a berg; come at once", the astonished Cottam double-checked whether he should disturb his captain. "Yes", replied Phillips, "it's a CQD, old man."

That exchange set in motion the rescue operation by the *Carpathia* described in detail on p.126 onwards. Meanwhile, Cottam and Phillips remained in close contact. Phillips complained that the dreadful rush of escaping steam on the *Titanic* was making it hard for him to hear incoming messages, so Cottam monitored all the traffic and filled him in on whatever he missed. The *Titanic* also established communication with the **Olympic**, which at five hundred miles was much too distant to arrive in time. The *Olympic* took a long time to appreciate how badly the *Titanic* was damaged, and was still enquiring at 1.25am, "Are you steering southerly to meet us?", but she did at least change her course.

Although the noise eventually ceased, the *Titanic*'s wireless room progressively lost power, which had a more severe impact on the ability to transmit messages than to receive them. At a very late stage of the evening, as Phillips was communicating with the *Olympic*, the *Frankfurt* got back in touch with the words, "What's up old man?" Phillips was infuriated by the sudden loud burst, and assumed that the *Frankfurt* had failed to grasp what was going on. He snapped back, "You fool, stand by and keep out". In fact, it seems likely that the *Frankfurt* had simply not heard his most recent, underpowered transmissions.

The very last message that the *Carpathia* picked up from the *Titanic* was at 1.45am: "Come as quickly as possible old man: our engine-room is filling up to the boilers".

The first lifeboats leave

From the moment Officer Lightoller set about launching the port-side lifeboats, he ran into difficulties. Mindful of the supposed danger of putting too many people aboard the lifeboats from the Boat Deck, he hoped to start proceedings by loading passengers onto **Boat 4** from A Deck. It swiftly turned out, however, that the glass screens along the A Deck promenade could not be opened; no one could find the key.

Deciding to load via the gangway down on C Deck instead, he ordered Boatswain **Alfred Nichols** to take six seamen below to open it up. It proved a fateful decision. Presumably cut off by a sudden inrush of water, none of the men was seen again. That left seven fewer sailors, out of the already inadequate supply, to lower and man the lifeboats.

The first lifeboat that was actually launched, therefore, was **Boat 7**, from the starboard side – and it set a similarly woeful example. When Officer Murdoch ordered it to be lowered, at 12.45pm, it was less than half full. Of the twenty-eight people aboard, three were crew, and the rest were first-class passengers, of whom more than half were men. The notion of "women and children first"

Boarding the lifeboats; a contemporary illustration.

had yet to become established; instead the cry went up that honeymooning couples should be given precedence. That later proved an embarrassment for the men who survived. D.H. Bishop insisted to the US inquiry that he "heard no order from any one for the men to stand back or 'women first' or 'women and children first'"; he claimed that he "fell into the boat", his wife that he was pushed in. Another American passenger, J.R. McGough, said that he wasn't even looking at the boat when an officer shoved him towards it, saying, "Here, you are a big fellow; get into that boat". Also aboard were **Dorothy Gibson**, an American actress who was soon to star, wearing the same clothes, in the first-ever *Titanic* movie (see p.221), and a dashing French airman, Pierre Maréchal, still sporting his monocle as he grabbed hold of an oar.

It took another ten minutes for boats 5 and 6 to be launched; they left at 12.55pm. **Boat 5**, on the starboard side, was made ready by Third Officer Pitman. As he worked, a man in a dressing gown and slippers kept urging him to lower the boat as soon as he could. Realizing that this was **J. Bruce Ismay**, Pitman went to the bridge to ask the captain whether he should obey Ismay's commands. Reassured that he should not, he swiftly loaded the boat with whatever women were to hand, making a special dispensation for two more honeymooning couples, and then allowed a few men to follow suit. As she was climbing in, Mrs F.M. Warren lost sight of her husband, who had been just behind her: "People came in so rapidly in the darkness that it was impossible to distinguish them, and I did not see him again".

At the last minute, one final woman appeared, and Ismay invited her to get on board. "I am only a stewardess", she said, to which Ismay responded, "Never mind, you are a woman; take your place." She was followed in quick succession by Dr Henry Frauenthal and his brother Isaac. Henry's wife Clara was already aboard, and the portly doctor either tumbled in as he was saying goodbye, or, more likely, jumped. Either way, he landed heavily on Annie Stengel, breaking two of her ribs.

With the boat half full, holding a total of around 36 people, and Officer Pitman in charge on board, Murdoch authorized its departure: "That is enough before lowering. We can get a lot more in after she's in the water." Epitomizing the desire of those who survived to convey that they had the blessing of those who did not, Pitman told the US inquiry, "Murdoch shook hands with me and said 'Goodbye; good luck.'"

Meanwhile, on the port side, Lightoller had turned his attentions to **Boat 6**. Of the couple of dozen female first-class passengers who climbed aboard, the best known was **Margaret Brown** of Denver, destined thanks to her night's activities to be remembered as "The Unsinkable Molly Brown". Also present were a couple of prominent English suffragettes, Edith Bowerman Chibnall, and her daughter Elsie Bowerman. Elsie subsequently witnessed the Russian Revolution first-hand in St Petersburg and became a barrister.

Boat 6 was even less full than Boat 5, with fewer than thirty aboard, when Lightoller gave the order to lower away, despite the fact that plenty of men were present on the Boat Deck, and he was running out of seamen to man the oars. When it began its precarious journey down to the sea, it held just two crew members: **Frederick Fleet**, the lookout who had spotted the iceberg, and Quartermaster **Robert Hichens**, who had been at the wheel at the time of the collision.

Alarmed by the shortage of men, a woman on Boat 6 called up to Lightoller, who asked the crowd on deck if any of them had nautical experience. A Canadian first-class passenger, **Major Arthur Peuchen**, responded that he was a keen yachtsman. Lightoller told him that if he was enough of a sailor to swing down the ropes to reach the boat, he could join it. Peuchen duly lowered himself hand over hand down into the darkness. The boat continued its descent, with a brief moment of jeopardy as it passed water gushing from a porthole on D Deck.

Hichens, who might justifiably be said to have had a bad night – recent revelations, detailed on p.184, suggest that the disaster may have been entirely his fault – was in a foul mood. He swiftly fell out with Peuchen and antagonized his fellow passengers by refusing to row. It soon transpired

A WORD ABOUT THE WITNESSES

The only **eyewitness accounts** of the *Titanic*'s final hours, of course, come from survivors. Keen to present themselves in a sympathetic light, almost all depicted the loading of the lifeboats as having taken place in orderly dignity, not violent chaos. In the aftermath of the tragedy, any male passenger who survived had to defend himself against the insinuation, or the explicit accusation, of **cowardice** or ignoble behaviour. The newspapers were filled with reports of fighting and even gunfire on the decks, and of men dressing as women to sneak off the ship. If to die was the act of a hero, then what did it mean to survive?

As a result, the men's stories tend to be remarkably similar, and follow certain set templates. In its ideal version, the man escorts one or more women to the Boat Deck and sees them safely aboard a lifeboat, then selflessly devotes himself to lowering the remaining lifeboats, ensuring that no unruly men climb aboard. When it comes to getting into a boat himself, however, he's much more passive. As a rule, he's either ordered in by an officer, perhaps to help with the rowing, or literally falls in by mistake.

There are two main exceptions. The men who left on the earliest lifeboats could claim that they were simply unaware of either the shortage of lifeboats or of the fact that the *Titanic* was going to sink. Those who remained on board until the very end, and went down with the *Titanic*, tended to describe their survival as purely miraculous. They just happened to surface near the drifting collapsible boats, and they certainly didn't fight their way onto them.

As for the **officers** and **crew**, those who left on the lifeboats did so simply because they were following orders. Even so, there's a revealing passage in Second Officer Lightoller's autobiography, when he mentions that "I was to thank my lucky stars" that he'd disobeyed an order to get into a lifeboat, adding that by taking his chances with the sinking ship, "I didn't have to take any old back-chat from anyone".

None of this should be taken as implying that any specific story or witness is unreliable. It's just striking how few of the men acknowledge wanting to escape the sinking ship, although in a moment of refreshing honesty, wireless man Harold Bride described helping to make the last of the collapsible boats ready, and admitted: "I looked at it longingly a few minutes".

Colonel Gracie attributed his survival to "mind over matter". In the ship's final moments, he wrote, "I questioned myself as to the performance of my religious duties". He then decided: "God helps those who help themselves; I should have only courted the fate of many hundreds of others had I supinely made no effort to supplement my prayers with all the strength and power which He has granted to me."

that there was a fourth man aboard, but he too was no help with the oars; accounts vary as to whether he was a stowaway with a broken arm, or a disabled boy.

Seven more lifeboats are launched

Far more crew members managed to board the next boat to leave, **Boat 3** on the starboard side. As well as thirteen crew, several of whom were firemen who hopped in at the last second, the boat held around twenty-five passengers, all first class, and evenly divided between men and women. Among them were American businessman Henry Sleeper Harper, along with his wife, his Egyptian dragoman or manservant Hammad, and his dog Sun Yat-Sen (see p.50).

Boat 3 was initially lowered only as far as A Deck. There was room for another thirty or so passengers to board from there, but the windows had still not been opened, so it continued on down. At one stage, problems with the ropes meant that all those aboard were nearly tipped into the sea.

Boat 1, the furthest forward on the starboard side, was one of the *Titanic*'s two small emergency cutters. Always kept swung out over the water, ready for action, it was known in shipboard parlance as the "Captain's Boat", but later achieved great notoriety as the so-called **Money Boat**. That was thanks to the controversy as to whether Sir Cosmo Duff Gordon's gift of £5 to each of its crewmen was in fact a bribe (see p.200 for the full story). The basic facts of its launching are not in dispute. Although Boat 1 was deemed capable of carrying forty people, when it was actually launched, at around 1.10am, it held just **twelve**: two sailors, five firemen and a mere five passengers, of whom three were men and two were women. Three of those passengers were Sir Cosmo, his wife, and her maid Miss Francatelli.

Strange as it may seem, when First Officer Murdoch turned his attention towards loading Boat 1, no passengers were to be seen on the Boat Deck. Having first ordered George Symons, who had been on lookout duty until 10pm, into the boat, Murdoch instructed Able Seaman Albert Horswell and five firemen who had been helping to lower the preceding lifeboats to climb in as well. Two women then came running up – Lady Duff Gordon and Miss Francatelli – and asked permission to board. With no further women around, Murdoch allowed three men who arrived just behind them, including Sir Cosmo, to follow them in. Then, with the boat less than half full, he gave the order to "lower away". Putting Symons in charge, he told him to remain close by in case he was called back.

Back on the port side, boats 8, 10 and 12 were loaded simultaneously. Between them, the three boats managed to depart with fewer than a hundred persons aboard, as against a combined capacity of a hundred and ninety-

THE STRAUSES

Mr. and Mrs. Isidor Straus

First-class passenger **Isidor Straus** was a hugely wealthy, self-made man, a German immigrant to the US whose investments ultimately included co-ownership of Macy's department store in New York. He had also briefly served as a Democratic Congressman for New York's 15th District. That he and his wife **Ida** are still remembered today, however, has more to do with their mutual devotion. They're usually described as an old couple, but he was aged 67, and she just 63. On the night of the disaster, Isidor and Ida were heard to agree that they would not be separated. After ensuring the safety of Ida's newly employed maid Ellen Bird, therefore, they sat side by side in deckchairs to await their fate.

The self-sacrifice of the Strauses was immortalized by Archibald Gracie, who implored each in turn to climb into a boat. Mrs Straus responded, "I will not be separated from my husband; **as we have lived, so will we die together.**" Isidor, offered consideration on account of his age, declared, "I do not wish any distinction in my favour which is not granted to others."

Only Isidor's body was recovered, and was buried at Woodlawn Cemetery in the Bronx. A joint memorial to the two stands in Straus Park, on West 106th Street in New York, inscribed with the words: "Lovely and pleasant they were in their lives, and in death they were not divided."

five. That was clearly a matter of policy; Second Officer Lightoller was still in charge here, but Captain Smith was present for much of the time, and lowered some of the ropes himself.

As not a single male passenger was allowed to board, the rigorous insistence on "women and children first" led to some heartbreaking situations. As Lightoller later described, "One young couple walked steadily up and down the boat deck throughout pretty well the whole proceedings … The girl … never made the slightest attempt to come towards the boats … although I looked towards her several times with a sort of silent invitation".

The assembled men on the Boat Deck parted to allow each woman through to the boats, then regrouped without a word. According to Lightoller, "They could not have stood quieter if they had been in church". In his evidence at the US inquiry, he also referred to having turned several stewardesses away, though it's not clear quite why, or whether it happened at this precise stage of the night.

It was at **Boat 8**, the first of the three to be lowered, that Mr and Mrs **Straus** declined to be separated. As detailed on p.95, the couple made sure Mrs Straus's maid Ellen went on board safely, wrapped in her mistress's fur coat, before retreating to face death together. Steward John Hart delivered a group of around thirty female steerage passengers to Boat 8, but it's believed that few actually got into the boat. Even of those who did, most promptly got out again and returned to the warmth of the ship.

Boat 8 was put under the command of a first-class steward, Alfred Crawford. His orders from Captain Smith were to row to the "Mystery Ship", and then return to the *Titanic* to pick up another load. However, it swiftly transpired that the four crew members aboard were not up to the job of manning a lifeboat. On Boat 8, as on several others, many women passengers were furious that stewards and firemen who had never handled an oar in their lives were allowed onto the boats while their husbands were left to their deaths. In this instance, a 33-year-old English aristocrat, the **Countess of Rothes**, was obliged to rise to the occasion, and remained at the tiller all night.

At first, Lightoller was able to help women into the boats by standing with one foot on the deck of the *Titanic* and the other on the lifeboat. As the ship listed increasingly to port, however, a terrifying gap began to open. Many of the women boarding **Boat 10**, which departed moments later, had to be forced to make the leap, while baker Charles Joughin, a substantial figure of a man, started simply throwing children from the deck into the boat. Estimates vary as to how many passengers were on board, but once again there was just one man – a third-class passenger, described by witnesses in the usual xenophobic terms as a "crazed Italian" who jumped from one of the lower decks as the boat went past.

Five minutes later, at 1.25am, **Boat 12** was lowered. Fifth Officer Harold Lowe had immediate responsibility, and ensured it held only women and children, apart from two crewmen.

THE COWARD

"Somewhere in the shadow of the appalling *Titanic* disaster slinks – still living by the inexplicable grace of God – a cur in human shape, today the most despicable human being in the world."

Thus Logan Marshall, in his 1912 book *The Sinking of the Titanic*, described one of the most enduring characters in the saga – a male passenger who had saved his life by **disguising himself** as a woman and sneaking onto a lifeboat. According to Marshall, "His identity is not yet known, though it will be in good time".

The so-called **Coward** had been a staple of sensational newspaper stories since day one. On 19 April, *The New York Journal* had identified first-class passenger William T. Sloper as the guilty party, probably out of simple spite after Sloper's refusal to give an exclusive interview. Wishing to avoid any further publicity, Sloper declined to sue the paper, and endured the gossip for the rest of his life.

While Sloper, who escaped in the very first lifeboat to be launched, may well have been innocent, the story itself is almost certainly true. There are at least two possible candidates for the real "Coward". One was **Daniel Buckley**, a 21-year-old third-class passenger from Ireland, who climbed into Boat 13 amid a large mixed group that included male passengers, sailors and firemen. He later told the US inquiry that when officers ordered all the men to get out, a woman in the boat – he claimed she was Mrs Astor, but she can't have been – saw him crying, and threw her shawl over him. He remained aboard, undetected.

Fifth Officer Lowe, also testifying at the US Inquiry, described a separate incident. As Boat 14 floated in the ocean after the ship had gone down, Lowe realized that there was a man aboard: "[he] was an Italian, and he sneaked in, and he was dressed like a woman … he had a shawl over his head, and everything else."

Officer Lowe had a habit of categorizing any passenger who behaved badly as being Italian; indeed, he had to make a formal apology to the Italian ambassador for his persistent slurs. It's quite likely, therefore, that his cross-dresser was in fact **Edward Ryan**, another Irish youth who was travelling third class. Shortly after the tragedy, Ryan wrote an account of his experiences in which he rescued both himself and an unknown woman by sliding down a rope from the deck of the *Titanic* into a conveniently passing lifeboat. A private letter to his parents, however, told a different story: "I had a towel round my neck. I just threw this over my head and left it hang in the back. I wore my waterproof overcoat. I then walked very stiff past the officers, who had declared they'd shoot the first man that dare pass out. They didn't notice me. They thought I was a woman."

At much the same time, two more boats left the starboard side. A team of stewards scoured both the Boat and A decks for waiting women of all passenger classes, then brought them together on A Deck for the actual loading. The stewards then stood in a double ring around each boat, only allowing women and children through.

Boat 9 was lowered at 1.20am, with Albert Haines, the boatswain's mate, in charge, and seven other crewmen. Also aboard was **Minnie Coutts**, a third-class passenger travelling with her two young sons. The family's escape was a matter of pure luck. Lost below decks, she happened to ask the right person for help at the right time. A sympathetic steward led her to safety, and handed over his own personal life belt, telling her, "There now, if the ship goes down, you'll remember me". American detective writer **Jacques Futrelle**, on the other hand, had to bid farewell to his wife as he hurried her aboard.

When **Boat 11** left five minutes later, every available space was taken. It probably held just over its recommended capacity of sixty-five, with nine crew members among the throng. One was steward James Witter, who claimed that he was standing on the rail helping to lower the boat when a "hysterical woman" tried to clamber in, and he fell in with her. Another, stewardess Anne Robinson, was no doubt experiencing a certain déjà vu; only three years previously, she had been aboard the Canadian steamer *Lake Champlain* when it too collided with an iceberg in the North Atlantic.

First-class passengers on Boat 11 included 22-year-old **Alice Cleaver**, a nursemaid who had recently been employed by the Canadian Allison family to look after their son, Trevor. In the general confusion, Alice had become separated from her employers; it's thought the Allisons failed to survive because they stayed on board looking for Trevor, unaware he was safe with Alice on Boat 11. A considerable myth has grown up around Alice, on the mistaken belief that she had been convicted of murdering her own child a few years earlier. Thus she's the central character in the justly forgotten 1997 movie *The Titanic*; in fact, however, the murderess was a different Alice Cleaver.

Another notorious story concerns fashion stylist **Edith Russell**. After surviving a car accident in France the previous year, she was given a fur-covered **china pig** by her mother as a good luck charm. Just before boarding Boat 11, she either raced back to her cabin, or sent a steward, to collect it. The pig was also a musical box that played a Brazilian dance tune called the "Maxixe" – a forerunner of the lambada – when you twisted its tail. Miss Russell did indeed twist its tail for much of the night, to entertain the children; early newspaper accounts, however, reported that she'd rescued a real live pig. When Edith died, aged 97, in 1975, she left the pig to Walter Lord, author of *A Night to Remember*. It can now be seen in the National Maritime Museum in Greenwich, London.

The last starboard lifeboats

Boat 13 followed from A Deck soon afterwards, also fully laden. Although it was largely filled with female passengers, including a sizeable third-class contingent, the men standing by were told to "tumble in" at the last moment, when no more women were to be seen.

These included **Paul Maugé**, a French secretary in the à la carte restaurant. He told the UK inquiry that all his fellow employees had been locked up in their cabins; that he only reached the Boat Deck because he was dressed like a passenger; and that one of the crew tried to pull him out of the lifeboat as it went past the lower decks. He also added an incongruous note of levity, when the inquiry erupted in laughter as he described attempting to persuade the chef to jump into the boat, only for him to decline because he was "too fat". Also among those who did brave the jump were an American, Dr Washington Dodge, and Lawrence Beesley, who wrote the most reliable eyewitness account of the sinking (see p.236).

Then Officer Murdoch gave the order, "Let no more in that boat; the falls will break", and the lowering began. At first, as Beesley breathlessly described, "it was a great adventure. It was exciting to feel the boat sink by jerks, foot by foot, as the ropes were paid out from above." By now, however, the **listing** of the *Titanic* was causing different problems here on the starboard side. As Boat 13 approached the waterline, it was uncomfortably close to the side of the ship. A powerful stream of water, measuring three feet across, was gushing from the condenser exhaust. The boat was almost **swamped**, but crew members used oars to stave it away from the flow. It landed in the ocean still tethered by its ropes, and found itself being pushed slightly aft, then held fast.

That, unfortunately, placed Boat 13 directly beneath **Boat 15**, which had also now started its descent. The sailors at the ropes on the Boat Deck, far above both boats, couldn't hear the frantic shouts from Boat 13. Had they let Boat 15 fall at that juncture, both might have been lost. In the event, the seamen aboard Boat 13 cut its ropes just in time, and it drifted clear moments before Boat 15 splashed into the water.

Boat 15 had been loaded on both the Boat Deck and A Deck. Officer Murdoch invited Steward Hart, who managed to return from the lower decks with a second batch of around 25 women and children steerage passengers, to climb in with them. Hart later testified that this group had been delayed by third-class men desperate to enter the lifeboats. It's not clear whether that delay happened below decks, or at the actual moment of departure; some reports suggest there was a scuffle on the Boat Deck when a group of third-class men attempted to rush the boat. (For the debate as to whether third-class passengers were deliberately impeded from accessing the boats, see p.187.)

Artist's rendition of the lowering of Boat 15, taken from The Graphic, *1912.*

There was still one final boat to load on the starboard side – not a lifeboat proper, but the first of the "collapsible" boats to leave, **Boat C**. Stored flat beneath Boat 1, it had been attached to the empty davits after that boat left. Like its predecessor, Boat C was to become the focus of considerable controversy.

Stories of scuffles and possible **shootings** surround the loading of Boat C, supervised by First Officer Murdoch. Some witnesses described a mixed group of stewards and third-class passengers attempting to rush it. As discussed on p.195, either Murdoch or the ship's purser, Herbert McElroy, may have fired his gun. First-class passenger Hugh Woolner told the US inquiry that he and a shipboard acquaintance, Hakan Steffanson, dragged several men out of the boat by their legs or whatever else they could grab. They then ushered "a bunch of women – I think Italians and foreigners" into it in their place. Amid the confusion, third-class pantry steward Albert Pearcey picked up two babies he found on the deck, and climbed into the boat with them.

At around 1.40am, Officer Murdoch made a final call for any women who remained on the Boat Deck to come forward. None did, so he ordered the boat to be lowered. At that point, two first-class male passengers quietly stepped into Boat C – **Billy Carter** and **J. Bruce Ismay**.

Carter, the owner of the shiny red Renault car now floating in its crate in the hold (see p.46), was clearly something of a cad. When his wife sued him for divorce three years later, she testified that "when the *Titanic* struck, my husband came to our stateroom and said, 'Get up and dress yourself and the children.' I never saw him again until I arrived on the *Carpathia* at 8 o'clock the next morning, when I saw him leaning on the rail. All he said was that he had had a jolly good breakfast, and that he never thought I would make it." Whether Ismay too was also a cad has been debated ever since (see p.184). The moment he climbed into the boat, he exposed himself to the contempt that would endure for the rest of his life.

According to Billy Carter, at least, the two men's conduct was above reproach. "We called for several minutes and got no answer," he later told newspaper reporters. "One of the officers then declared that, if we wanted to, we could get into the boat if we took the place of seamen. He gave us this preference because we were among the first-class passengers. Mr Ismay called again, and receiving no reply, we got into the lifeboat." Another first-class passenger, Jack Thayer, who was then aged seventeen, put it more bluntly in a private letter written after Ismay's death: "I saw Ismay, who had been assisting in the loading of the last boat, push his way into it." Ismay's own version was banal in the extreme. He explained that he'd climbed in "because there was room in the boat. She was being lowered away. I felt the ship was going down, and I got into the boat."

Due to the heavy listing of the *Titanic*, Boat C repeatedly caught against the rivets of the hull as it was lowered. Quartermaster George Thomas Rowe, who was in charge on the boat itself, later recalled that the forward well deck was awash when he arrived on the Boat Deck a few minutes earlier. By the time Boat C reached the water, it was completely submerged. Once the boat was out on the ocean, four **Chinese men** appeared from their hiding places. While they had clearly stowed away on the lifeboat, they were not stowaways on the *Titanic*, as was widely supposed, but seamen travelling second class to join another boat in New York.

JOHN JACOB ASTOR IV

Probably the wealthiest passenger aboard the *Titanic*, **Colonel John Jacob Astor IV** remains thanks to his famous name the best known victim of the disaster. He was not so much a "robber baron" in his own right, however, as one of the many beneficiaries of the colossal fortune that was left by his great-grandfather.

The original **John Jacob Astor** was born in Walldorf, Germany, in 1763, and emigrated to the newly independent United States in 1784. Over the next fifty years, he amassed vast riches in the fur trade, and bought huge tracts of Manhattan real estate. Since Astor died America's wealthiest man in 1848, his descendants had been property developers and speculators, renting out slum tenements while also constructing skyscrapers and hotels.

By the end of the nineteenth century, the sprawling Astor family stood at the centre of New York's social elite. The primary heir to the family fortune was **William Waldorf Astor**, who erected the Waldorf Hotel in 1890. After John Jacob Astor IV, who was William's cousin, built the neighbouring Astoria Hotel in 1897, the two hotels merged to become the **Waldorf-Astoria**. In his Fifth Avenue mansion, John Jacob also tinkered with such inventions as a bicycle brake, and even wrote a science-fiction novel, depicting life on Jupiter in 2088. He acquired the title of colonel when he financed and led a volunteer battalion in Cuba in 1898.

John Jacob Astor IV **divorced** his first wife in 1909, and married an eighteen-year-old debutante, Madeleine Force, two years later. The marriage was so controversial that several ministers refused to conduct the ceremony, while the one who finally did so was forced to resign shortly afterwards. The newlyweds weathered the storm by taking an extended **honeymoon** trip to Egypt and Italy. After four months away, they decided to return home on the *Titanic*.

The Astors sailed from Cherbourg, occupying a first-class "parlour suite" on C Deck. Besides his manservant, and her maid and private nurse, they were accompanied by their Airedale dog, Kitty. Many of their fellow passengers were close friends and acquaintances; they had for example passed part of the winter in Egypt with Margaret "Molly" Brown.

Madeleine Astor, who was pregnant, went to bed early on the night of the disaster. She and her husband were woken by the stopping of the engines. Colonel Astor sought a quiet word with Captain Smith, and was told that the ship was in serious trouble. Thereafter, he played little role in the general confusion, concentrating instead on his young bride. The pair was seen sitting side by side astride the mechanical horses in the gymnasium; Astor was slicing a life belt to show Madeleine what it was made of.

At first, Colonel Astor scoffed at the thought of getting into a lifeboat, stating: "we are safer here than in that little boat". Archibald Gracie pointed out the "Mystery Ship" to the couple, assuring them rescue would soon be at hand. Only as the end was clearly approaching did Madeleine finally step aboard Boat 4, the last lifeboat to be lowered. Colonel Astor asked if he might join her, on account of her "delicate condition", but Second Officer Lightoller refused: "No, sir. No men are allowed in these boats until the women are loaded first". Astor then asked for the boat's number, so he could find Madeleine when the crisis was over; Lightoller, who hadn't recognized him, thought it was so he could lodge a complaint.

John Jacob Astor IV, and his eighteen-year-old wife Madeleine at Newport, Rhode Island.

According to some witnesses, Astor actually got into the boat, and was asked to get out again; either way, as Gracie put it, he "bore the refusal bravely and resignedly". One story has it that he then went down to release Kitty and the other dogs from their kennels, and that Madeleine saw Kitty running across the decks as the ship went down. By the time the body of John Jacob Astor IV was found floating in the Atlantic a week later, the American inquiry into the tragedy had already opened in the Waldorf-Astoria hotel. The dead man's pockets contained $2440 and £125, as well as a gold pocket watch that his son Victor carried for the rest of his life.

That August, Madeleine Astor gave birth to a boy. Another branch of the family had already christened a John Jacob Astor V, so he took the name of John Jacob Astor VI. Five years later, Madeleine forfeited her $5 million inheritance by marrying a childhood friend. Both that marriage and her third, to Italian boxer and film star Enzo Fiermonte, ended in divorce. She died aged 46 in Florida in 1940.

Lightoller and the last port-side lifeboats

By the time the eight numbered lifeboats on the starboard side had been launched, there were still four to go on the port side. **Boat 16** was the first to leave. Partly perhaps because all the bustle on the starboard side of the Boat Deck distracted most passengers' attention, its loading was orderly and uneventful, supervised by Sixth Officer Moody. Almost all the first-class women and children had already left, so it held a considerable number of their third-class counterparts.

The ten or so crew members aboard included stewardesses Elizabeth Leather and **Violet Jessop**. The latter was cradling a baby that a fireman had found apparently abandoned, and thrown down to her; its mother reclaimed the child aboard the *Carpathia* the next morning. Trading on her unique claim to have survived accidents on all three of the Olympic class ships – the collision of the *Olympic* itself, the sinking of the *Titanic*, and the torpedoing of the *Brittanic* – Violet Jessop published her memoirs forty years later. There she described the sensation of being lowered down the side of the ship and passing six successive rows of bright portholes. Once in the water, she could see only five.

As each boat departed, Officer Lightoller made a quick dash to the long emergency spiral staircase that dropped all the way from the Boat Deck down to C Deck. A glance down the stairwell, to the ominous seawater swirling below, provided a ready gauge of how fast the ship was going down. As he later recalled, "that cold, green water, crawling its ghostly way up that staircase, was a sight that stamped itself indelibly on my memory". By now, he wrote, "It had become apparent that the ship was doomed, and in consequence I began to load the boats to the utmost capacity that I dared". It's an intriguing statement, first because it reveals that even he had not initially believed the *Titanic* would sink, and secondly because it acknowledges that he had deliberately been allowing the lifeboats to leave half-full.

For the **final half-hour** that the *Titanic* remained afloat, everyone on board must have shared Lightoller's awareness that she was going to sink. Ever since the collision, the ship had been sloping ominously forward, as she went down by the head, and she also seems to have listed to starboard before her alarming and ever-increasing roll to port. Until now, many passengers had nonetheless reassured themselves with the belief that the ship was just settling, and that in due course she'd stabilize at some new level in the water.

Various witnesses reported two separate incidents, late in the proceedings, in which first Chief Officer Wilde, and then Captain Smith, ordered: "Everyone on the starboard side to straighten her up". In both instances, hundreds of those assembled on the Boat Deck dutifully trooped over to

THE *TITANIC* ORPHANS

As the final lifeboat was about to leave the sinking *Titanic*, a second-class passenger, **Louis Hoffman**, approached the ring of men who were guarding access to Collapsible D. He handed over two angelic-looking young boys, who spoke French but not English, and asked for them to be placed in the boat. The two boys, aged two and three, became the only children to survive the disaster without a parent. When it transpired that Mr Hoffman had been travelling under an assumed name, and thus no one could identify either father or sons, the boys attracted worldwide publicity as the "*Titanic* Orphans", also known as the "*Titanic* waifs".

In due course, their mother, **Marcelle Navratil** from Nice in France, recognized them from a newspaper photograph as her sons **Michel** and **Edmond**. "Mr Hoffman" turned out to have been her estranged husband Michel, who had kidnapped the boys and was taking them to start a new life in America. Mme Navratil was reunited with the boys in New York in May and they sailed home to France.

The elder boy, Michel, eventually became a philosophy professor, though his reflections on the disaster remained bitter: "The people who came out alive often cheated and were aggressive, the honest didn't stand a chance". Having lived to become the *Titanic*'s last male survivor, he died in 2001.

*The so-called "*Titanic Orphans*", known to the press as "Lolo" and "Lump".*

starboard in the hope of righting the ship, perhaps delaying the sinking by a few more moments each time.

From the moment the ocean first washed over the forward well deck, at around 1.45am, and then swiftly submerged it, things definitely turned uglier on the Boat Deck. Not only was the *Titanic* obviously going down, but it was finally clear to all that there were not enough lifeboats to go round. The most persistent rumours and allegations that **shots** were fired centre on this portion of the evening (see p.195).

As for Lightoller himself, he turned his attention next to **Boat 2**, the port side's smaller "emergency boat". He was amazed to find that around twenty men had already climbed into it. One passenger claimed that they were stokers, while Lightoller wrote that "they come under the broad category known to sailors as 'Dagoes'". Between them, and possibly with the aid of firearms, Lightoller, Fourth Officer Joseph Boxhall and Captain Smith, who emerged from the bridge to join the effort, ordered the men out.

The captain then instructed Boxhall, who until now had been largely engaged with firing rockets and attempting to signal the "Mystery Ship" (see p.89), to take charge of Boat 2. Boxhall and Chief Officer Wilde loaded the boat with around fourteen women, plus four crew members; even at this late stage, it was still little more than half full. A solitary male third-class passenger leaped in at the last moment to join his wife and child. With Wilde supervising, Boxhall himself was lowered into the boat.

Next to leave was **Boat 14**. Its loading appears to have been utter chaos. Able Seaman Joseph Scarrott, who was assigned to this boat and was among the first to climb in, told the UK inquiry that "some men tried to rush the boats, foreigners they were, because they could not understand the order which I gave them, and I had to use a bit of persuasion. The only thing I could use was the boat's tiller." At least one of the men climbed straight back in and had to be thrown off again. Then Fifth Officer **Harold Lowe** arrived on the scene. The men whom Scarrott had driven off the boat presumably formed part of the crowd of "Latin people" Lowe later described as "glaring, more or less like **wild beasts**". Lowe himself freely acknowledged that he'd fired shots to warn them off (see p.196).

Female passengers, by contrast, were now being forcibly separated from their husbands and thrown into the boat. Passions were running high among the second-class men who submitted to being left behind; it's hardly surprising that a group of them grabbed hold of another steerage passenger who tried to jump into the boat, and beat him up. Lowe also used his gun to threaten an adolescent boy he found cowering in the bottom of the boat. Ignoring the pleas of the women to let him stay, he exhorted him to "for God's sake be a man!", and forced him back on deck. He failed however to spot a man who had sneaked aboard disguised as a woman, with a shawl over his head (see p.97).

After watching several boats depart without a single officer on board, Lowe suggested to Moody that it was about time an officer went. Moody responded that Lowe should go himself. He did, and was thus able to cope with a tricky situation when the aft rope tangled near the bottom of the descent. With the stern dangling five feet out of the water, while the boat tipped down at an alarming angle, Lowe moved quickly to slash the rope. Boat 14 smacked down into the Atlantic.

The final lifeboat to leave, **Boat 4** on the starboard side, had been among the very first to be made ready, only to suffer endless delay. Its core group of passengers first assembled at around 12.30pm. By the time it was finally lowered, almost an hour and a half later, the ocean was just fifteen feet below. The original idea, which may have been Captain Smith's, was to load Boat 4 from A Deck. First-class stewards had therefore rounded up many of the most prominent passengers – wealthy Americans like the Astors, the Wideners and the Thayers – and gathered them on the Promenade Deck to wait for Boat 4 to descend into view. When Second Officer Lightoller started to lower Boat 4 down from the Boat Deck, however, a snag became obvious: no one could open the windows on the glassed-in promenade. This was when Lightoller dispatched the Boatswain to open the gangway door on C Deck, as described on p.90. In the meantime, he decided to carry on loading the other boats from the Boat Deck. In the general confusion, he seems to have forgotten Boat 4 altogether.

Thus ensued a long, agonizing wait for the elite passengers, during which their mood passed from scepticism to awareness of their impending doom. They were briefly ordered up to the Boat Deck, and then sent back down again. Only after Boat 14 had been sent away did Lightoller at last remember Boat 4, and return to A Deck. The windows had finally been forced open, and deckchairs stacked up to provide an easy "stairway" up to the sills. To minimize the gap caused by the ship's listing, the crew used boat hooks to pull the boat as close to the rail as possible.

Six waiting husbands now had to bid farewell to their wives. Eleanor Widener left behind not only her husband but also her 27-year-old son Harry. Emily Ryerson boarded with her daughters Emily and Suzette, but her son Jack was denied entry until Mr Ryerson stepped forward and said, "Of course that boy goes with his mother; he is only thirteen." Lightoller reluctantly agreed, while also proclaiming "no more boys". However, Mrs Lucile Carter succeeded in getting her eleven-year-old son aboard, concealing his gender beneath a hat. She hadn't seen her husband since the first news of the collision, and was unaware that he had already left on Collapsible C (see

MAJOR ARCHIBALD BUTT

Among the most flamboyant victims of the *Titanic* tragedy was **Major Archibald Willingham de Graffenreid Butt**, chief military aide and confidante to presidents Roosevelt and Taft. A "Southern gentleman", gossipy but discreet, Butt was a stout, jovial man of 46, who was a journalist and social correspondent before going into the army. He was sailing home from a visit to Italy in the company of his friend, the artist **Francis D. Millet**. Although Taft had entrusted Butt to carry letters to both the king of Italy and the Pope, the real reason for his trip was that he was "completely tuckered out". Taft and Roosevelt had become estranged, and Butt, exhausted by the tensions, had begged for six weeks' leave from his White House post.

So renowned was Major Butt for his impeccable style that *The New York Times* itemized his outfit as he sailed for Europe: "a bright copper-colored Norfolk jacket fastened by big ball-shaped buttons of red porcelain, a lavender tie, tall baywing collar, trousers of the same material as the coat, a derby hat with broad, flat brim, and patent leather shoes with white tops".

After the disaster, *Harper's Weekly* eulogized Butt as having "saved the weak, beat back the craven; gentle and heroic, smiling and steadfast, he died the death of a soldier, the death of a gentleman". One unreliable account spoke of his punching out a panic-stricken man with the words, "Sorry, women will be attended to first or I'll break every damned bone in your body". A female first-class passenger described how he'd lowered her into a lifeboat, tucked her in with blankets, and tipped his hat in farewell.

In fact, Butt played little if any role during the *Titanic*'s final hours. A quiet, shadowy figure, he stood rapt in thought as the lifeboats were loaded. Another eminent Southerner, Archibald Gracie, saw Butt, Millet and two other men playing cards in the otherwise deserted smoking room at 2am, when the last lifeboat had gone and their doom was sealed. "All four seemed perfectly oblivious of what was going on on the decks outside."

President Taft – once felicitously compared by Butt to "a huge pan of sweet milk" – was so distressed by reports of the sinking that he dispatched USS *Chester* to seek news of his friend. When Butt proved not to have survived, the grieving president declared he was "like a member of my family, and I feel his loss as if he had been a younger brother." In truth, Butt may well have been about to transfer his loyalty back to Roosevelt, before death put an end to his dilemma.

Despite his protestations that "This bachelorhood is a miserable existence", Butt never married. He shared his bachelor quarters in Washington with Millet. President Taft dedicated a joint memorial to the two friends, near the White House, on the second anniversary of the disaster.

p.101). The most famous separation here parted **John Jacob Astor IV** from his young wife. No adult male passengers were aboard when Lightoller called out, "That's enough; lower away!"

As Boat 4 dropped down the side of the ship, Mrs Ryerson later recalled, "I could see all the portholes open and water washing in, and the decks still lighted". Lightoller then realized there were only two seamen aboard, too few to man the boat. Several more came swarming down the falls, and Quartermaster Walter Perkis was put in charge. Boat 4 remained so close to the sinking *Titanic* that not long afterwards, the crew was able to fish eight more crewmen out of the water.

After the lifeboats were gone

Heroic accounts of the tragedy later described a period after the lifeboats had gone during which those who were left quietly accepted their fate. Within a week, for example, London's *Daily Graphic* was stating: "there was nothing the passengers who remained could do but await death bravely and unflinchingly, which they did".

It's almost certainly more accurate to say that some did and some didn't. **Benjamin Guggenheim** was famously said to have re-emerged from his cabin alongside his valet, both wearing white tie and tails and without their life belts, and declared: "We've dressed in our best and are prepared to go down like gentlemen". For every such depiction of stoic acceptance, however, there's a rival report of panic and mayhem.

In any case, not everyone abandoned hope of rescue. Steerage passengers stranded on the aft well deck must have known for most of the final hour that they had no hope of a lifeboat. On the Boat Deck, on the other hand, the struggle to launch the collapsible lifeboats continued until the final seconds, so many of the men never had time to concede defeat.

By 2am, the only possibility of escape lay with the three remaining **collapsible boats**. As crew and passengers alike struggled to free the two that were stored on top of the wheelhouse, **Collapsible D** was attached to the port-side davits vacated by Boat 2. Although this was the very last boat to be lowered from the sinking ship, Lightoller could still tell the US inquiry that he had "great difficulty" finding women to fill it. Nonetheless, he allowed no men to board, linking arms with his fellow crewmen to form a ring through which only women could pass. Several Syrian women squeezed through with their children.

Yet more men said goodbye to their wives at this makeshift barrier; others, like the mysterious **Mr Hoffman** (see p.105), delivered their children into safe hands. One single woman, Winnie Troutt, was surprised to be presented by a stranger with a swaddled baby to take with her. When it appeared that no more women were to be found, men started to get into the boat, only to be ordered back out again as more women arrived. Only one seat remained to be filled when first-class passengers Edith Evans and Caroline Brown reached the boat. Miss Evans, who was single, turned to Mrs Brown and said, "You go first, you have children waiting at home." Miss Evans stayed aboard the *Titanic*, and did not survive.

The drop from the Boat Deck to the waiting ocean was by now a mere ten feet. Down on A Deck, water was lapping onto the promenade. First-class passenger Frederick Hoyt, who had gone down there after seeing his wife onto Collapsible D, could see her boat hanging from the davits. As he later wrote, "it occurred to me that if I swam out and waited for her to shove off they would pick me up, which was what happened". Guarding himself perhaps against charges of cowardice, he also said that Captain Smith had advised him to do so.

First-class passengers Hugh Woolner and Hakan Steffanson – last seen hauling men off Collapsible C (see p.101) – had also made their way down to A Deck. With the entire deck deserted, and the electric lights glowing an eerie red, Woolner told the US inquiry, they could see that they were in "rather a tight corner". They climbed onto the gunwales, ready to jump into the sea, only to find Collapsible D being lowered "right in front of our faces". So they both made a nine-foot leap, out and down, for the bow of the boat. Steffanson landed right inside, Woolner in the water, from where he was immediately dragged aboard.

The final moments

Many descriptions of the *Titanic*'s supposed **death throes** – including, as described on p.192, the story that the band kept playing until the last – are derived from witnesses who left on lifeboats well before the end, and were simply describing their own final impression. Ellen Mockler, for example, who later became a nun, described passengers as kneeling in prayer on the open decks, while two Catholic priests, including Father Thomas Byles from Yorkshire, led them in the rosary. That's no doubt true, but she left on Boat 16 at around 1.35am. As her lifeboat pulled away, she could hear the prayers continuing, but after a while she heard only screams. "We were told by the man who rowed our boat that we were mistaken as to the screams and that it was the people singing, but we knew otherwise", she recalled.

Some people chose not to remain on deck until the end. Thus Thomas Andrews was last seen standing quietly alone in the First Class Smoking Room; a foursome made up of Archibald Butt, Francis Millet, Clarence

Moore and Arthur Ryerson resumed the card game they'd left at the time of the collision; and Catherine Wallis, the third-class matron, retreated to her cabin and locked the door.

Colonel Archibald Gracie, who saw the card game as an empty performance designed "to show their entire indifference to the danger", left a vivid account of his own feelings as the climax of the night approached: "When I first saw and realized that every lifeboat had left the ship, the sensation felt was not an agreeable one. No thought of fear entered my head." Gracie's attitude that "God helps those who help themselves" (see p.93) was echoed by baker **Charles Joughin**. Fortified by strong liquor from the kitchens, he was down on B Deck, throwing deckchairs out of the windows in the hope that he might manage to cling to one when the ship went down.

At around 2.10am, according to Harold Bride, Captain Smith paid his final visit to the wireless room. He declared, "Men you have done your full duty. You can do no more. Abandon your cabin ... I release you. That's the way of it at this kind of a time. Now it's "."

The *Titanic* was now sinking with such a pronounced slope towards the bow that it was clear the forward end of the Boat Deck would soon be underwater. Any prospect of retreating aft, however, was precluded by the arrival of a vast crowd of steerage passengers. According to Gracie, "there arose before us from the decks below, a mass of humanity several lines deep, covering the Boat Deck, facing us, and completely blocking our passage towards the stern". As the first wave started to sweep along the Boat Deck, the crowd turned their backs and rushed for the stern. Officer Lightoller, still atop the wheelhouse, saw the wave "washing the people back in a dreadful huddled mass".

Baker Charles Joughin, who was by now on A Deck, heard the pounding of feet overhead, and then saw countless individuals clambering off the end of the Boat Deck. The *Titanic* was at such an angle that the Boat Deck was no longer higher than the rest. He joined them as they scrambled ever further aft, hoping to reach what could only be the temporary sanctuary of the poop deck, right at the stern on C Deck.

Meanwhile, Colonel Gracie had reacted to the oncoming wave with a move that sounds remarkably like bodysurfing: "I crouched down into it preparatory to jumping with it, and rose as if on the crest of a wave on the seashore", to join Lightoller on the roof of the officers' house. All his companions, he thought, were either smashed against the superstructure, or trapped and drowned as the *Titanic* rolled over them. Gracie himself, clinging to a railing, was then dragged below the waters. After holding his breath for what seemed an eternity, he eventually swam back to the surface, pushed up by air bubbles from deep within the ship.

CAPTAIN SMITH IN THE DISASTER

In the immediate aftermath of the *Titanic*'s sinking, **Captain Smith** was widely hailed as a **hero**, as though the very act of having gone down with his ship was enough to absolve him of any blame. That reputation grew despite the surprising lack of information as to what he actually did in the hours that followed the collision. After his initial inspection with Andrews, which confirmed how badly the ship was damaged, he rather recedes from the record. Apart from wireless operator Harold Bride, who described Smith keeping close track of the distress calls, few eyewitnesses remembered seeing him.

Smith certainly seems to have dithered as to when to start loading the lifeboats, and to have made the decision to minimize panic by deliberately keeping passengers in the dark as to what was going on. James Cameron's *Titanic* movie was probably unfair in depicting him as wandering the decks in a dazed stupor, however. He was clearly hopeful that rescue might be forthcoming from the "Mystery Ship" (see p.85), encouraging the use of rockets to attract its attention, and urging the lifeboats to ferry passengers across to it. He comes across as a sort of disembodied presence, a distant voice booming out occasional instructions through a brass megaphone, and occasionally manifesting himself to straighten a passenger's life belt or touch the cheek of a child. First-class passenger Frederick M. Hoyt offered a tantalizing glimpse in a letter, describing a snatched conversation with Smith on the sinking ship: "I simply sympathized

Lightoller too had the presence of mind not to retreat: "It came home to me how very fatal it would be to get amongst those hundreds and hundreds of people who would shortly be struggling for their lives in that deadly cold water. There was only one thing to do, and I might just as well do it and get it over, so, turning to the fore part of the bridge, I took a header."

At first Lightoller swam towards the crow's nest, which was still poking from the ocean ahead of him, but then he realized he should try to escape the ship altogether. Just then, he was drawn irresistibly downwards by an enormous flow of water into an air shaft just in front of the *Titanic*'s forward funnel. For a few moments, he found himself pinned against the thin grating that covered the top of the shaft, praying that it would not break beneath his weight; then a sudden uprush of hot air escaping from somewhere far below propelled him back towards the surface. Before he could reach it, he was trapped again: "Just how I got clear, I don't know, as I was rather losing interest in things.

According to his own dramatic account, even while he was still underwater, Gracie set about scooping up pieces of wreckage to put together a makeshift with him on the accident; but at that time, as I then never expected to be saved, I did not want to bother him with questions".

The notion of Captain Smith as a hero centred especially on his **death**, which in the absence of hard evidence acquired mythic overtones. All that's known for sure is that he remained on board, on or near the bridge, until the very end. Early reports that he'd shot himself became attached to other officers, and specifically Murdoch (see p.197). Stories circulated instead that Smith had dived from the bridge as the ship finally sank, and swum through the icy waters to the notorious "upturned boat" that floated free at the last second. One version had him carrying a child in his arms, which he handed over before swimming away.

A more haunting and slightly more plausible account came from Greaser Walter Hurst, a survivor on the upturned boat. He was convinced for the rest of his days that Smith was the swimmer he'd heard in the water nearby, who had "the voice of authority", and "kept cheering us with 'Good Boy, Good Lads'. I reached out the oar to help him but he was too far gone; as it touched him he turned about like a cork and was silent."

It also became widely believed that at the very end Smith had exhorted one and all to "Be British". Those stirring words were popularized in print and song, despite the lack of any first-hand testimony that they were ever spoken; indeed an article in *British Weekly* admitted that "'Be British,' was what we would have expected and wanted him to say". The memorial statue to Captain Smith that stands in Lichfield, Staffordshire, still bears those same words, "Be British".

raft. Understandably preoccupied with his own survival, it seems likely that he missed one of the crucial moments of the sinking. By the time he was able to take in his surroundings, the *Titanic* had disappeared altogether.

Gracie was later among the most vociferous of those who insisted that the *Titanic* did not **break apart** as she sank. He dismissed stories that the ship had split along the expansion joint just aft of its forward funnel, saying that he'd stepped across that very joint, and seen it to be intact, seconds before she went down. Lightoller, however – who surfaced after his own ordeal at much the same time as Gracie, into what he called "an utter nightmare of both sight and sound" – had a close-up view as that selfsame funnel toppled into the water. Falling just a few inches away from him, it crushed many of the others to death, but it served to save his life, by pushing him towards Collapsible B. The funnel may simply have fallen because the wire stays that tethered it were nowhere near strong enough to hold it at an angle, but Lightoller was convinced that the stays had snapped when the superstructure of the ship cracked at the expansion joint.

Washed away

Meanwhile, the battle to launch the last two collapsible boats had finally been lost. Teams of frantic men had managed to untie the ropes that bound both boats to the top of the wheelhouse, but in the attempt to slide them down a hastily assembled ramp of planks onto the deck, Collapsible B ended up **upside down**, while Collapsible A seems to have been damaged in such a way that its collapsible canvas sides could not be raised.

Attempts were made to fasten **Collapsible A** to a pair of davits, but time ran out long before the process of lifting it up, swinging it out and then lowering it over the side could be completed. Seeing that the bridge was about to be engulfed in water, a horde of men, and possibly a few women, climbed into the boat, and Steward Edward Brown cut through its ropes before it could be dragged down with the ship. In the end, therefore, Collapsible A was simply swept off the *Titanic* by the same final surge that carried away Gracie and Lightoller. In the process, however, all those who had managed to get aboard were washed straight back out again.

As for **Collapsible B**, known to posterity as the Upside Down Boat, there was no question of anyone getting on board before the sinking, or launching it properly. Instead it was pushed violently free of the wreck by the collapse of the forward funnel, and then served as a refuge for whoever could succeed in dragging, fighting or negotiating his way out of the maelstrom of desperate, drowning humanity.

Although neither boat was exactly suited for the rigours of a freezing night on the open Atlantic, they did at least have the minimal advantage of buoyancy tanks to help keep them afloat. B was no more than a convex raft, while A was little better. With its canvas sides down, A was filled over a foot deep with icy seawater. Those on board, who included one woman, had the choice of standing with the water well above their ankles, or sitting in it up to their waists. Exactly how many people ended up escaping on the two boats is unknown; probably fewer than twenty on A, a handful more than that on B. In each case, the survivors consisted of whoever managed to pull themselves up onto the boat from the seething mass of swimmers that were left behind after the *Titanic* went down.

Not surprisingly, few of the men who spent that appalling night on either boat later portrayed themselves as having fought their way to survival. Several accounts describe swimmers reaching the boats only to be **beaten off** and refused sanctuary, but no one acknowledges actually pushing anyone else away. Steward Brown, among those on Collapsible A, described a frenzied fight for survival in which they "tore my clothing away from me with struggling in the water". Norwegian steerage passenger Olaus Abelseth told a similar story, in which he'd had to fight off a man who grabbed him by the neck and pressed him under the water. When he reached Collapsible A, no one helped him aboard, but at least no one pushed him away.

Collapsible B turned out to be among the best documented of all the lifeboats. Two of those aboard, Gracie and Lightoller, later wrote books, while wireless operator **Harold Bride** also gave a thorough description. Lightoller said that following his terrifying immersion, he was among the very first to reach the collapsible boat. He steadfastly insisted that once he'd climbed up, "I did not see any effort made by others to get on board".

Bride recalled coming to his senses after being swept off the *Titanic* to realize that he was in the small enclosed space *under* Boat B. Ducking down beneath the surface to escape, he swam frantically away from the ship, desperate to escape the suction that never came. As it turned out, Boat B kept pace with him, and he was soon hauled aboard. In an unintentionally chilling phrase, he told the US inquiry, "I was the last man they **invited** on board". The obvious implication was that the crew were turning away passengers in favour of their friends; Bride said that there were "dozens" of swimmers around him.

Colonel Gracie, who reached Boat B a little later, wrote, "when I reached the side of the boat I met with a doubtful reception, and, as no extending hand was held out to me, I grabbed … a young member of the crew". Once aboard, he continued, "the situation was a desperate one, and was only saved by the refusal of the crew, especially at the stern of the boat, to take aboard another passenger". He himself, however, turned his head away and took no part in the grim proceedings. Gracie later consoled himself with the thought that "in no instance, I am happy to say, did I hear any word of rebuke uttered by a swimmer because of refusal to grant assistance".

Steward Thomas Whiteley, who clung for a while to an oak dresser and was among the last to approach Boat B, told the *Tribune* in New York that "somebody tried to hit me with an oar, but I scrambled on to her". Fireman Harry Senior told much the same tale, that "some chap hit me over the head with an oar" but that he'd gone to the other side and scrambled on there. Both Senior and chef Isaac Maynard were later reported as saying that **Captain Smith** was among those who swam up to the boat but did not get on board (see p.113).

The struggle at the stern

Many different hypotheses describe what happened to the sternward half of the ship in its dying moments. It seems likely that the *Titanic* started to break apart before she sank, and that in the immediate aftermath of the initial crack, the stern briefly moved back towards a more familiar horizontal position. Some suggest that even at that stage, those still aboard cherished a brief hope

*The **Titanic**'s last moments as reimagined by German marine artist Willy Stöwer.*

that perhaps the stern might float free. Instead, it swiftly started to climb again, quite possibly because it was still attached to the bow somewhere far below the surface.

To the very end, many hundreds of people were still gathered on the aft well deck. One by one, they dropped into the ocean, as author Filson Young memorably put it, "like mice shaken out of a trap into a bucket". Baker Charles Joughin told the UK inquiry that he was the last one left, clinging to the outside of the rail on the poop deck, when the ocean finally welled up under his life belt and lifted him off. "I do not believe my head went under the water at all", he claimed. "It may have been wetted, but no more." According to his own somewhat incredible account, he then floated in the open Atlantic until morning, warmed by his earlier intake of alcohol. Managing to make his way to Collapsible B, he said: "I tried to get on it, but I was pushed off it, and I what you call hung around it". He ended up clinging to the side in his life belt, clutching the arm of an acquaintance, chef Maynard.

As the bow sank, the stern was pulled up towards the vertical. Some of the witnesses in the lifeboats, powerless to help, later described it as having remained erect for as long as five minutes. Such an almighty cacophony boomed across the waters that many thought the boilers had exploded; in fact several may have torn free from the hull and crashed down towards the bow. That final shifting of weight pulled the *Titanic* inexorably beneath the waves, and she vanished from view.

Chapter 6
Plucked from the water

As the *Titanic*'s **lifeboats** dropped one by one into the ocean, each effectively became an independent entity. Attention on board the ship itself immediately shifted to the next lifeboat to be launched, leaving those already afloat free to determine their fate. Most lifeboats were given orders as they were lowered, often by Captain Smith himself, bellowing through a **megaphone** from the Boat Deck. Witnesses said they were either told to head for the "Mystery Ship", leave passengers there and return to fetch another load, or to remain close by the *Titanic*, ready to pick up more passengers from the lower decks.

In practice, however, once they were cut loose the lifeboats did whatever they – or rather, the strongest personalities aboard each boat – might decide. From their new sea-level vantage point, it was suddenly much more obvious that the *Titanic* was **sinking**; the slant of her illuminated portholes, and the steady disappearance of the lower decks, conveyed a grim message. The instinctive response was to row directly away from the sides of the ship, where leaping passengers, or even other lifeboats, might suddenly drop from above, or the boilers might explode. That impulse was further encouraged when the idea took hold that the sinking of the *Titanic* might create "**suction**" that dragged anything nearby down with it. All the lifeboats that were capable therefore pulled away to whatever they considered to be a safe distance, even though in the event little or no suction seems to have materialized.

Thus the general effect was for the lifeboats simply to **fan away** from the *Titanic*, ensuring that each quickly became separated from the rest. Many of those on the port side, who could see the lights of the Mystery Ship, did indeed start by rowing in that direction. They never seemed to get any closer, however, and within perhaps an hour the lights disappeared altogether.

*Boat 6 reaches the **Carpathia, with Quartermaster Robert Hichens huddled in the stern, and passengers including "Molly" Brown and Major Arthur Peuchen.***

But for the horror of the situation, conditions were ideal to be out on the water in an open boat. One of the stokers in Boat 13 with Lawrence Beesley "said he had been to sea for twenty-six years and never yet seen such a calm night", while another added, "it reminds me of a bloomin' picnic". As described on p.42, however, many of the crewmen who had secured places in the lifeboats turned out to have little idea of how to row. Fifth Officer Lowe later explained this apparent anomaly to the US inquiry with the words: "A sailor is not necessarily a boatman; neither is a boatman a sailor, because they are two very different callings". Several **women** ended up taking an oar themselves, not least to keep warm. In Boat 8, the Countess of Rothes stayed at the tiller throughout the night.

Many of those in the lifeboats did not expect to survive the night, adrift on the freezing sea. Few knew whether, let alone when, rescue might arrive. The earliest boats had left without knowing whether the *Titanic* had received any response to her distress calls. According to Beesley, the consensus on his boat was that the *Olympic* was on its way; another passenger, Bertha Watt, wrote to Walter Lord that: "We had been told before we left the ship that this was all precautionary measures & the *Olympic* would be along shortly to pick us all up".

According to passenger Karl Behr, an American tennis player who was with his fiancée in Boat 5, a fellow passenger discreetly showed him a small **revolver**, and whispered, "Should the worst come to the worst, you can use this revolver for your wife, after my wife and I have finished with it."

The *Titanic* goes down

Assuming they could bear to turn their heads, the survivors in the lifeboats were perfectly positioned to watch the *Titanic* finally go down. With their attention focused on the appalling spectacle, their stories are much more consistent than the jumbled impressions of the earlier part of the night.

As the ship sank by the head, all describe the **stern** as sloping up out of the water. Some saw her drop down towards the horizontal, then rise **perpendicular**, straight up from the ocean. And there she stayed, for what some witnesses considered to be a few seconds, others as long as five minutes. The *Titanic's* enormous **propellers** could be seen silhouetted against the night sky.

Lady Duff Gordon left an especially graphic account of the final moments: "The boat stood up like an **enormous black finger** against the sky. Little figures hung and dropped into the water. The screaming was agonizing. I never heard such a chorus of utter despair and agony". Similarly, First Class Bedroom Steward Henry Etches described the scene to the US inquiry: "I saw, when the ship rose – her stern rose – a thick mass of people on the after-end. I could not discern the faces, of course … She seemed to raise once as though she was going to take a violent dive, but sort of

> **"We heard a noise like an immense heap of gravel being tipped from a height, then she disappeared."**
>
> George Rowe, *Titanic* crew member

checked, as though she had scooped the water up and had leveled herself. She then seemed to settle very, very quiet, until the last, when she rose up, and she seemed to stand twenty seconds … and then she went down with an awful grating, like a small boat running off a shingley beach."

White Star chairman J. Bruce Ismay, on the other hand, chose not to watch: "I was sitting with my back to the ship. I was rowing all the time I was in the boat. We were pulling away … I did not wish to see her go down."

The most horrible sounds

As soon as the noise of the *Titanic* disintegrating died down, it was replaced by an ever more appalling chorus of despair. Fireman George Kemish described "a noise I shall never forget – **shouting, screaming and explosions**. A hundred thousand fans at a Cup Final could not make more noise."

DID THE *TITANIC* BREAK IN TWO?

The one major point of difference between the eyewitnesses was whether the *Titanic* **broke in two**. Since the discovery of the wreckage in 1986, we now know that she did, or at least into two large pieces and countless smaller ones. Despite much debate and investigation, no one knows exactly when and how that happened, and whether it was visible at the time or took place **underwater**.

The most likely scenario seems to be that as the stern began to lift clear of the water, at an angle of around fifteen degrees, it placed an **intolerable load** on the ship as a whole. A major crack seems to have opened up along the forward expansion joint on the Boat Deck, although that particular rupture did not necessarily extend any deeper than the superstructure itself. In any case, some sort of breakage allowed the stern to drop back down again, and simultaneously caused the bow to sink even more dramatically. As the two segments were still hinged together, that then dragged the stern back towards the vertical.

Depending on one's vantage point, anyone watching could easily fail to understand what was taking place. Those directly behind the stern, for example, might well have had the impression it was poking straight up from the water when it was in fact at more of an angle.

Amid all the upheaval, at a very late stage which to add to the drama coincided with the *Titanic*'s **lights** suddenly going out, a colossal **metallic roar** filled the night. Many of the spectators believed that the boilers were exploding. From the state of the wreckage, however, it's known for certain that the boilers remained intact. What witnesses were actually hearing was the ship's machinery, and anything else not bolted securely in place, being shaken loose as the *Titanic* shifted away from the horizontal. Lawrence Beesley wrote: "It was as if all the heavy things one could think of had been thrown downstairs from the top of a house, smashing each other and the stairs and everything in the way." That overwhelming onslaught of sound died away just before the *Titanic* finally went down.

Some survivors recalled that dreadful sound, carried across the still waters, as the greatest shock of the night. Lawrence Beesley insisted for the remainder of his life that until that moment he'd imagined everyone had managed to escape from the foundering ship: "Therefore the terrible nature of the cries, which reached us almost immediately after the *Titanic* sank, came upon us entirely unprepared for their terrible message", in which mingled "human fear, despair, agony, fierce resentment &

blind anger". Colonel Gracie told a similar story: "there arose to the sky the **most horrible sounds** ever heard by mortal man … the shrieks of the terror-stricken and the awful gaspings for breath". Individual voices could be picked out amid the general cacophony; Greaser Walter Hurst wrote forty years later, "I plainly heard screaming '**Save one Life**'. I've never forgotten that".

"Those heart-rending, never-to-be-forgotten sounds" also lingered with Officer Lightoller: "I have never allowed my thoughts to dwell on them, and there are some that would be alive and well to-day had they just determined to erase from their minds all memory of those ghastly moments".

The great dilemma

The desperate cries for help presented everyone in the lifeboats with a **moral dilemma**: whether to risk their own lives by attempting to save others from the icy ocean. This is perhaps the murkiest part of the entire night; almost **none** of the swimmers were saved, and no one on the lifeboats, who listened from a safe distance as their friends, families and shipmates died a dreadful death, ever quite explained why.

Instead the response to the pleas was in many cases far from heroic. On Boat 13, for example, Beesley reported that "we tried to sing to keep all from thinking of them". In other words, to block out the cries of the drowning. Everyone on Boat 11 "cheered and cheered to drown the screams". On Boat 1, the notorious **Money Boat** (see p.200), Sir Cosmo Duff Gordon offered the crew £5 each in what he always claimed was an attempt to compensate them for their loss, but was widely seen by others as a bribe for them not to endanger his life.

Lowe leaves it late

Out of all the lifeboats, only one returned to the scene of the wreck to pick up survivors – **Boat 14**, under Fifth Officer **Harold Lowe**. Shortly after his boat was lowered into the water, Lowe had decided the boats should try to stick together, to boost the chance of being spotted by rescuers. He therefore gathered up whatever lifeboats he could, which turned out to be three that had also been launched from the port side – boats 4, 10, 12 – and roped them together in a long line. Once the *Titanic* sank, he took charge as the only officer, and set about redistributing the passengers, in order to empty Boat 14 of all but the strongest oarsmen. That ultimately left him with seven men – five volunteers at the oars, a lookout, and himself at the tiller. By Lowe's own estimation, they were only ready to go back around an **hour** after the sinking. He was in no hurry, however; indeed he told both inquiries that he deliberately

MAGGIE BROWN

Thanks to her iconic status as the **"Unsinkable Molly Brown"**, as portrayed by actresses ranging from Debbie Reynolds to Kathy Bates, Margaret Brown is now remembered as the *Titanic*'s most famous passenger. Little of the legend, which depicts an uncouth country girl, scorned by society, is true. Not even the name is right – her intimates called her Maggie, while her *Denver Post* obituary claimed that "all the world knew her as 'The Unsinkable Mrs J.J. Brown'", which hardly has the same ring. Nonetheless, her real-life saga remains extraordinary.

Born to Irish immigrant parents in 1867, **Margaret Tobin** was raised in the definitive American small town of Hannibal, Missouri. The birthplace thirty years earlier of Mark Twain, it remains immortalized as the setting for *Tom Sawyer*. Not long after moving west to Leadville, Colorado, aged eighteen, she met and married engineer James Joseph Brown. Several years later, as a mining superintendent, he devised a method to extract previously unobtainable gold from the Little Johnny silver mine. That made him wealthy enough to set them up in a fine new home in Denver, though they continued to spend time in Leadville.

Maggie Brown became known in Denver as a supporter of votes for women, and of labour rights in general. Although she may have further alienated conservative citizens simply by being a Catholic, there's no evidence for the idea that she was ostracized by her new neighbours.

In January 1912, by now separated from her husband, Mrs Brown sailed to Europe on the *Olympic*. While visiting Egypt with her daughter, in the company of the honeymooning Astors (see p.102), she received news that her grandson was ill back home. She therefore hurried back to France, and boarded the *Titanic* at Cherbourg. On the night of the disaster, she was reading in her cabin when she felt the collision. Putting on a black and velvet two-piece suit, and grabbing her furs, she made her way to the Boat Deck, where she was roughly dropped into Boat 6 as it was being lowered.

How Maggie Brown stood up to Quartermaster Hichens in Boat 6, and helped steer the boat to safety, is described on p.126. Her conduct aboard the *Carpathia*

refrained from going sooner. In Washington, he said: "It was absolutely not safe. You could not do otherwise, because you would have hundreds of people around your boat, and the boat would go down just like that (*indicating*)." In London, he was more succinct: "it would have been suicide to go back there until the people had **thinned out**" – or, to put it more boldly, frozen to death.

It's clear from Lowe's testimony, in fact, that Boat 14 was very close to the wreck site all along. He guessed the distance as just 150 yards, but if anything it sounds closer still: "I was just on the margin. If anybody had struggled is less well known. By the time the ship reached New York, she was chair of the Survivors Committee and had already raised $10,000 for the survivors' welfare. When the *Carpathia* docked, she was so busy making arrangements for her fellow passengers that she was the last to disembark. And it was to the waiting reporters in New York that she made her immortal declaration: **"The ship can sink, but I can't; I'm unsinkable!"**

Mrs Brown continued to work on behalf of *Titanic* survivors for the rest of her life. She also made a short-lived run for the US Senate. During World War I, she became director of the American Committee for Devastated France, for which service the French government awarded her the Legion of Honour. She went on to study acting in Paris.

The flamboyant and unsinkable Margaret Brown, pictured in 1927.

Maggie only became **Molly** after her death in 1932. The name was popularized by writer Gene Fowler, whose largely fictitious account of her life incorporated such hackneyed Western myths as accidentally burning a fortune in a mining-shack stove. A Broadway **musical** eventually followed in 1960, which in turn became a 1964 **movie** starring Debbie Reynolds; it features nothing of interest to *Titanic* enthusiasts. Both Margaret Tobin's birthplace in Hannibal, and her former home in Denver, remain open as tourist attractions.

out of the mass, I was there to pick them up; but it was useless for me to go into the mass". The UK inquiry went into chilling detail as to whether Lowe seriously thought a freezing swimmer would have had the strength to grab the gunwales and haul himself aboard, but Lowe had no doubts: "a drowning man clings at anything".

When Lowe finally detached Boat 14 from its companions and went looking for survivors, it swiftly became apparent that he'd left it **too late**. Lawrence Beesley later said that the last of the harrowing cries had died out "nearly forty minutes after the *Titanic* sank". Arriving on the scene perhaps twenty minutes later, Lowe could only find three men alive. All had survived by dragging themselves up onto some piece of drifting wreckage; no one could live in the sub-zero ocean.

On that note, it's believed that few people immersed in icy water remain conscious for more than three or four minutes. The first thirty seconds are the most life-threatening of all, and those who attempt to swim lose their body heat much faster than those who simply float in a life belt. Very few of the *Titanic*'s victims drowned; most died of **suffocation**, when they became too cold to be able to breathe. In addition, slurred, raving speech is a common symptom of **hypothermia**, which may well explain why some survivors referred to crewmen as having been drunk.

In his truly horrendous evidence to the UK inquiry, seaman **Joseph Scarrott**, who was on Boat 14, described the lifeboat inching through "hundreds of dead bodies floating in life belts ... all hanging in one cluster". When they spotted a man kneeling atop what appeared to be a large staircase, a mere fifty feet away, "it took us a good half-hour to ... get through the bodies. We could not row the boat; we had to push them out of the way".

A **Japanese** man was spotted stretched out face down on a door. Lowe almost ignored him, assuming he was dead (and allegedly commenting, "if he isn't there's others better worth saving than a Jap!"). Once brought aboard, however, the man swiftly revived, and was soon manning an oar himself.

By the time Lowe lost hope of finding any more survivors, a slight wind had picked up. He therefore hoisted the sail in Boat 14 – making it the only boat to go under sail that night – and went in search of the other lifeboats. He soon had Collapsible D in tow.

As dawn broke, Collapsible B, the **Upside-Down Boat**, found itself in difficulties in the increasing swell. Officer Lightoller had organized everyone on board to stand in two parallel rows on her upturned hull with their feet in the water, and was frantically ordering them to lean this way or that to keep her stable. Already, some unknown number had given up the struggle, collapsed, and slipped into the ocean. Each body that departed lightened the overall load, allowing the boat that bit more time before it might be swamped altogether.

Fortunately, Lowe in Boat 14, and the three boats that were still roped together – 4, 10 and 12 – caught sight of Collapsible B just in time. Reaching it with moments to spare, boats 12 and 14 were able to take off all those left standing. Lowe then left the linked flotilla, and performed a similar rescue operation on **Collapsible A**, which he left to drift with three bodies still aboard.

The various **quiet deaths** in the dead of night, and the whole intricate process of swapping passengers from lifeboat to lifeboat in darkness –

desperately traumatic at the time, barely remembered later – are what makes it impossible for historians to be sure who left the *Titanic* on which lifeboat, and thus how many each lifeboat held.

Drama on Boat 6

The greatest clash of personalities occurred on **Boat 6**. By the time the *Titanic* sank, the boat had been in the water for an hour and a half, and tensions were already high. Quartermaster **Robert Hichens** had been placed in charge of the lifeboat little more than an hour after personally implementing the "hard a-starboard" order that doomed the *Titanic*. Three other men were aboard; **Lookout Frederick Fleet**, an unidentified male with a broken arm, and the Canadian **Major Arthur Peuchen**.

Hichens seems to have been in a state of **shock**, and concerned only with saving his skin. His insistence on remaining at the tiller – a simple task on such a still night – rather than taking an oar, had the double effect of giving him absolute control over where the lifeboat went, while also ensuring that it lacked the power to go anywhere very much. Peuchen, by contrast, felt he'd been allowed onto the lifeboat precisely because of his experience as a yachtsman (see p.92), and that Hichens was being obstructive and insubordinate. As on Boat 1, there was probably a **class** element to the conflict, in that first-class passengers who were used to being obeyed balked at deferring to ordinary seamen.

Boat 6 had originally started by heading towards the lights of the "Mystery Ship", which Hichens believed to be a small cod-fishing steamer, but made little progress. Very early on, according to Peuchen, Hichens heard a whistle from the *Titanic*, which he knew was a signal to return, but announced: "No, we are not going back to the boat … **It is our lives now, not theirs**." The crisis point came once the *Titanic* sank. Everyone aboard could hear the "frightful" sounds of the dying; a great many of the thirty or so women knew that their husbands were probably out there freezing to death, and begged Hichens to return. He refused, adding, according to Peuchen, that "there was **only a lot of stiffs** there".

Cross-examined on the issue at both inquiries, Hichens gave equally pitiful performances. In Washington, he claimed that the cries had lasted for three or four minutes; back in London, he revised that down to "a minute or two", and that even then they were only faintly audible. He also twice insisted that it was the lack of a compass that held him back; quizzed as to why he couldn't simply have headed for the sounds, or the spot where the *Titanic* had just gone down, he had no response.

The most active of the women on Boat 6 was **Margaret Brown**, known to posterity as the "Unsinkable Molly Brown" (see p.192). Having wielded an oar from the very start, as the night progressed she increasingly stood up to Hichens' sulks and tantrums. She later described him as "shivering like an aspen", and reported that after the bid to reach the "Mystery Ship" proved fruitless, he lost hope altogether. Hichens predicted that the boat would drift for days, and that they'd starve for lack of provisions. Even when the *Carpathia* appeared, he refused to make an effort to reach her. Long before then, Mrs Brown had had enough. Threatening to knock him overboard with her oar if he interfered any further, she encouraged all the women to carry on rowing, if only to stay warm enough to avoid freezing to death.

The *Carpathia* to the rescue

As described on p.89, it was pure chance that wireless operator **Harold Cottam**, aboard the Cunard liner ***Carpathia***, chose to get in touch with his friend and fellow operator Jack Phillips on the *Titanic* at around 12.25am on the night of the sinking. When Phillips replied "struck a berg; come at once", Cottam woke his captain, and the epic rescue began.

Displaying extraordinary presence of mind, the 42-year-old **Captain Arthur H. Rostron**, known on account of his remarkable energy as the "Electric Spark", issued an exemplary series of orders. His first priority was to reach the scene of the disaster as quickly as possible. Boxhall's position for the *Titanic* meant she was 58 miles northwest. At the *Carpathia*'s official maximum speed of fourteen knots, it would take just over four hours to reach her. That was too long; she'd have to do better. In Rostron's own words: "every ounce of power was got from the boilers and every particle of steam used for the engines, turning it from all other uses, such as heating". In the meantime, the ship was made ready to receive an unknown number of survivors.

The 13,600-ton *Carpathia* had sailed eastwards from New York, heading for Gibraltar and the Mediterranean, on 11 April. She was carrying slightly fewer than 750 passengers – 128 of them first class, 50 second class, and around 550 third class – making her just under three quarters full. **Stewards** were instructed to avoid disturbing those passengers, and to keep them out of the way as much as possible. Three **doctors** were delegated to examine and treat incoming survivors in each of the ship's three dining rooms. All spare berths, along with all public spaces and the officers' own cabins, were to be given over to the survivors, whose full names should be collected as they came on board. All the *Carpathia*'s **lifeboats** were made ready and swung out, and all the gangway doors were opened. Coffee, soup and tea were prepared, and oil brought up in case it was needed to soothe rough seas.

By the time the *Carpathia* received the *Titanic*'s last despairing message, at 1.45am – "**Come as quickly as possible, old man; engine room filled up to the**

boilers" – she had been steaming at full tilt for over an hour. She was heading, of course, straight into an ice field, taking the same risk that had just destroyed the *Titanic*. Captain Rostron posted extra lookouts to watch for ice, and an hour later the first **iceberg** was spotted. In all, the *Carpathia* had to steer around six large bergs.

At steady intervals from 2.45am onwards, the *Carpathia* fired her **rockets**, to alert anyone ahead that rescue was on the way. Fourth Officer Boxhall in Boat 2 had his own supply of green flares, which he too was setting off, and the watchers scanning the night sky from each vessel gradually began to believe that they were seeing distant flashes in response. Very few of the other lifeboats were carrying lights of any kind, so the survivors were resorting to more desperate measures to make themselves visible, brandishing flaming newspapers or simply striking matches.

Danger at dawn

As **dawn** broke over the North Atlantic, the wind was picking up, and the swell that had made Collapsible A so precarious grew to threaten the other lifeboats. According to Lady Duff Gordon in Boat 1, "we saw rows of 'white horses' racing towards us, beautiful but very alarming. Our little boat could never have lived long in a rough sea."

During the night, no one in the lifeboats had seen so much as a single iceberg, although Boxhall had heard the grinding of ice nearby, and the lap of waves against the base of a berg. Now, however, they were everywhere, in appalling, majestic splendour. Captain Rostron sent an officer to the top of the *Carpathia*'s wheelhouse to make a rough count: "he counted 25 large ones, 150 to 200 feet high, and stopped counting the smaller ones; there were dozens and dozens all over the place". What's more, an estimated two to three miles from where the *Titanic* had gone down, a **colossal unbroken ice field** stretched across the horizon, from northwest to southeast. Describing it as "nearly seventy miles long and twelve miles wide", Lawrence Beesley later commented to the effect that it was not so much a mystery that the *Titanic* hit an iceberg, as that the *Carpathia* did not.

The survivors come aboard

The *Carpathia* finally eased off its engines at 4am, when **Boat 2** became visible a few hundred yards ahead. Negotiating her way around one final iceberg, she slowed to a halt, and Boat 2 pulled alongside. The survivors now faced their final ordeal – ascending the *Carpathia*'s hull to safety. Those who had the strength climbed hand over hand up a flimsy rope ladder; those who did not were hauled up on a wooden "bosun's chair", or simply on canvas bags hanging from ropes as crude seats. Either way, the rocking of the boat was

Titanic *survivors on the deck of the* **Carpathia.**

liable to slam them against the sides. The smallest children were hoisted in hastily requisitioned mail sacks.

The very first survivor to climb aboard was **Elizabeth Allen**, from St Louis. As she later told Colonel Gracie, "I happened to be the first one up the ladder, as the others seemed afraid to start up, and when the officer who received me asked where the *Titanic* was, I told him she had gone down".

It was left to **Officer Boxhall**, the last to leave Boat 2, to give Rostron the first official report of the *Titanic*'s fate. At this stage, of course, Rostron had no idea how many lifeboats, let alone survivors, to expect. Boxhall was able to tell him that the *Titanic*'s full complement of boats had been launched, but also revealed that many hundreds of passengers and crew had been unable to escape.

From this point on, it was up to each lifeboat to make its own way to the *Carpathia*. With the exception of Boat 2, which had remained apart from the other port-side lifeboats, the **starboard** lifeboats were closer at hand. Lawrence Beesley described how, on Boat 13, "our crew rowed hard in friendly rivalry with other boats to be among the first home. But ... we had a heavy load aboard, and had to row round a huge iceberg on the way".

Lifeboats were soon arriving in quick succession. Boat 13 for example, which Beesley reckoned was "eighth or ninth at the side", reached the *Carpathia* around three quarters of an hour after Boat 2. Collapsible C, the only collapsible to survive the night unassisted, pulled alongside at around 6.30am. A shocked and shivering

J. Bruce Ismay climbed to the deck, but seemed barely able to function, querulously repeating: "I'm Ismay, I'm Ismay". When the *Carpathia*'s English doctor, Dr McGhee, suggested he have a hot drink in the saloon, Ismay at first turned him down, and asked to be left alone. Then he changed his mind: "If you can get me in some room where I can be quiet, I wish you would". And thus Ismay was spirited out of sight, into the doctor's own cabin, not to emerge until the *Carpathia* docked in New York.

Most of the port-side boats were considerably farther afield, and had to row several miles. Those that had set off towards the "Mystery Ship" were obliged to turn around and row back the way they'd come. That meant crossing the *Titanic* wreck site, amid what Beesley called "the debris of chairs and wreckage of all kinds". Presumably, although he forbore to mention it, that included bodies.

Despite the boost of knowing rescue was at hand, reaching the *Carpathia* proved for many survivors to be a long and exhausting struggle. Maggie Brown recalled that even when Boat 6 finally made it, it took three or four attempts to get close enough to make safe: "Each time they were dashed against the keel, and bounded off like a rubber ball".

The last lifeboat to arrive was **Boat 12**, at 8.30am. Its passengers included the indefatigable Colonel Gracie, who displayed his usual gung-ho spirit: "I mounted the ladder, and, for the purpose of testing my strength, I ran up as fast as I could and experienced no difficulty or feeling of exhaustion". Second Officer **Lightoller**, the *Titanic*'s senior surviving officer, was the last to come aboard. By one of those coincidences that characterized the night, he was greeted by the *Carpathia*'s first officer, Horace Dean, who had been the best man at his wedding. All in all, although the *Carpathia* reached the scene around an hour and forty minutes after the sinking, some survivors spent as long as **seven hours** in an open boat, out on the ocean.

As each new lifeboat drew close, survivors who had disembarked from the earlier boats thronged the decks to watch. Similarly, each fresh contingent scanned the *Carpathia* for familiar faces. Even at this late stage, many were unaware that most of those aboard the *Titanic* had gone down with the ship. According to Lady Duff Gordon, "we imagined most of our fellow passengers ... had been saved like us; not one of us guessed the appalling truth". As Elizabeth Shutes described, "Lifeboats kept coming in, and heart-rending was the sight as widow after widow was brought aboard. Each hoped some lifeboat ahead of hers might have brought her husband safely to this waiting vessel. But always no." Much of that dreadful waiting was conducted in silence. Only when no more lifeboats remained adrift did the grim realization hit home.

It's quite clear that the *Carpathia* never reached the spot where the *Titanic* actually went down. In Rostron's words, where the *Carpathia*

THE RIGHT COURSE TO THE WRONG POSITION

Fourth Officer **Joseph Boxhall**, in command of the first lifeboat to meet the *Carpathia*, happened also to have been responsible for calculating the latitude and longitude used in the *Titanic*'s distress calls. Captain Rostron therefore congratulated him on guiding the *Carpathia* to the scene, with the words: "What a splendid position that was you gave us".

Rostron always believed that the *Carpathia* had indeed managed to cover fifty-eight miles in three and a half hours to reach the wreck site, at an average speed of seventeen knots. Given the fact that Boxhall's position was out by around thirteen miles – as was proved by the discovery of the wreck in 1986 – it seems more likely, however, that she'd steamed a significantly shorter distance, at something close to her acknowledged maximum speed of fourteen knots. She had also had to slow down to avoid all those icebergs, and in any case she stopped when she reached the first lifeboats, rather than the actual wreck site. The great stroke of luck was that her course to Boxhall's erroneous position happened to take her through the right spot to cross paths with the lifeboats.

Officer Boxhall remained convinced for the rest of his life that his position had been correct. On 12 June 1967, in accordance with his final wishes, his cremated remains were scattered on that exact spot by the Cunard liner *Scotia*.

halted, "The sea was strangely empty. Hardly a bit of wreckage floated – just a deckchair or two, a few lifebelts, a good deal of cork; no more flotsam than one can often see on a seashore drifted in by the tide … I saw only one body in the water."

The *Carpathia* returns to New York

Shortly before 9am on the morning of Monday 15 April, less than half an hour after the final stragglers from Boat 12 had come aboard, the *Carpathia* set off back westwards across the Atlantic. Now that all the *Titanic*'s lifeboats were accounted for – as many as possible had actually been hauled up on deck – it was clear that there were no more survivors to be picked up.

Other boats had now reached the scene, and they could take over the unpleasant task of searching for bodies. Among them was the ***Californian***, which several of the *Carpathia*'s officers said they'd seen standing stationary about eight or ten miles to the north at the time they'd first spotted the lifeboats. Their evidence helps to explain why so many aboard the *Titanic* were convinced that the *Californian* was the Mystery Ship.

Although the *Carpathia* was originally bound for Gibraltar, Captain Rostron felt it best to get the survivors back to land as soon as possible. Continuing east would have taken him out of radio contact, and in any case he was carrying insufficient supplies to look after his newly increased load. The suggestion that the *Titanic* survivors might complete their voyage on the **Olympic**, which was due to arrive within a few hours, was quickly ruled out. For that to happen, they would have had to be lowered back into the sea on lifeboats for the transfer, which was clearly too traumatic to consider. Indeed, Rostron arranged for the *Olympic* to remain out of view altogether, to avoid distress.

The very nearest port was Halifax in Nova Scotia, but that would have involved heading into the ice field, so Rostron decided to return to **New York** instead. Ruth Blanchard later described the moment when the *Carpathia* set off as "the saddest time of all. That was the time when so many of the women who had been put into lifeboats by their husbands – and told they would meet each other later – realized that they would never see each other again."

A minister who was travelling on the *Carpathia* led a service of remembrance in the first-class dining saloon. As the day wore on, the crew set about compiling a definitive list of all those rescued, while the survivors made themselves comfortable wherever they could. All too often, and despite the many kindnesses of the *Carpathia*'s passengers, that simply meant huddling beneath a blanket on the open deck. The trip to New York took three and a half days, during part of which the *Carpathia* was engulfed in dense fog. Apart from a brief panic when she stopped her engines to allow for four victims of the tragedy to be buried at sea, the voyage was largely without incident. At one point, with typical insensitivity, the Duff Gordons arranged for a doctor aboard the *Carpathia* to take a photograph of them with their fellow survivors – once more wearing their life belts – from the "Money Boat".

In their different ways, everyone began to digest the ordeal they'd just endured. The *Titanic*'s passengers formed a Survivors Committee on the Tuesday morning, with the twin aims of rewarding Captain Rostron and his crew, and providing aid for those who had lost fortune or family.

Lawrence Beesley later described how appalled his fellow passengers were, when they learned aboard the *Carpathia* that the *Titanic* had received repeated radio warnings of ice ahead: "it was not then the unavoidable accident we had hitherto supposed". He devoted the Wednesday afternoon to that classic recourse of the indignant Englishman, writing an angry letter to *The Times*. Written in ignorance as to how or even whether the disaster was being reported, it's a fascinating reflection of the mood of the survivors. Beesley explicitly condemned the *Titanic* for ignoring its wireless messages, steaming into the ice field at reckless speed and carrying too few lifeboats.

Captain Arthur Rostron is presented with a silver "loving cup" by Margaret "Molly" Brown, on behalf of the Titanic Survivors' Committee, aboard the Carpathia *in New York, 29 May 1912.*

It doesn't take a conspiracy theorist to wonder whether the *Titanic's* surviving officers spent their time aboard the *Carpathia* getting their stories straight. A generous interpretation would be that they felt it important not to say anything that might jeopardize future official inquiries. Less charitably, they may have set in motion a cover-up designed to protect both their own careers and the reputation of the White Star Line.

The one area in which the conduct of Captain Rostron has been held up to question concerns his vessel's **radio contact** with the outside world. The two wireless men aboard the *Carpathia* – the ship's own Harold Cottam, and Harold Bride from the *Titanic* – gave exclusive priority to the personal messages of the survivors. That meant the *Carpathia* issued no bulletins to the press and ignored all enquiries, even when President Taft asked whether his friend Archie Butt was among those rescued. Although Rostron insisted the decision was his, it came to be widely believed that the two wireless men had withheld information in order to sell their stories to the newspapers. What's more, there's very strong evidence they were encouraged to do so by their employer, **Guglielmo Marconi**.

The strange behaviour of J. Bruce Ismay

Among the messages that Cottam and Bride did transmit was one to the White Star Line offices in New York, sent on Wednesday: "Most desirable *Titanic* crew aboard *Carpathia* should be returned home earliest moment possible. Suggest you hold *Cedric*, sailing her daylight Friday. YAMSI". Behind the transparent code name, **J. Bruce Ismay** was seeking to spend as little time as possible in the United States; it seems safe to assume that the request came from the *Titanic*'s officers as well as himself.

From the moment he disappeared behind the door of his appropriated cabin, Ismay's behaviour aboard the *Carpathia* attracted speculation and criticism. He failed to re-emerge during the entire voyage. For any number of reasons, from his responsibility for the *Titanic*'s paucity of lifeboats to his supposed obligation to go down with the ship, he was too ashamed to face his fellow survivors. Things went deeper than that, however; Ismay was in a state of utter collapse. Captain Rostron later described him as having been "mentally very ill", and there were widespread reports that he was under heavy sedation.

Unfortunately for Ismay, his attempt to arrange a quick passage home was intercepted by the US Navy ship *Chester*, dispatched by the anxious president in search of news of his friend Archie Butt. That same day it passed into the hands of Senator Smith, who had just been placed in charge of the official US inquiry (see p.146).

Recovering the bodies

One of the stranger anomalies about the *Titanic* disaster is that although over 1500 people died, a great number of whom were floating in the Atlantic wearing life belts, the boats that reached the scene soon afterwards encountered almost no **bodies**. Indeed, only **337** bodies were ever recovered; the remaining 1186 were never found.

As soon as news of the sinking was confirmed, the White Star Line chartered a cable-laying ship in **Halifax**, Nova Scotia, for the ghoulish job of gathering up the dead. The ***Mackay-Bennett*** sailed shortly after noon on Wednesday 17 April, before the survivors had even reached New York. Her usual crew was joined by a team of Canadian undertakers.

After putting out a call for other ships to report sightings of wreckage, the *Mackay-Bennett* reached the vicinity of the sinking late on Friday night. By now the bodies had become scattered, and the ship searched the area for several days, lowering her two small cutters to haul the victims in one by one. One of her engineers later described steaming "through a great quantity of wreckage, splintered woodwork, cabin fittings, mahogany parts of drawers, carvings, all wrenched away from their fastenings, deck chairs, and then bodies".

To aid with identification, a detailed description of each body was written as it was brought aboard. Each was assigned a unique **number**, and kept together with any associated clothing or possessions. An Anglican clergyman from Halifax Cathedral conducted **mass funerals** for those that held little prospect of being identified. As the ship pitched and rolled in dense fog, they were then buried at sea in weighted sacks. The mood aboard was "cold, wet, miserable and comfortless".

In death as in life, the *Titanic*'s passengers were segregated according to **class**. The hundred **coffins** that the *Mackay-Bennett* was carrying were reserved for the use of those bodies that could be identified as being first-class passengers, and kept on deck; those who remained were sewn up in **sacks** and stored below.

It soon became apparent that the *Mackay-Bennett* was filling up, and would need help. White Star therefore despatched another ship from Halifax, the *Minia*, on 22 April. The two vessels operated in tandem for several days, but the task grew increasingly fruitless. Wind and currents were dispersing the bodies ever more widely, while the life belts were disintegrating and allowing them to sink.

When the *Mackay-Bennett* returned to Halifax on 30 April, she was carrying 190 bodies, having buried 116 others at sea. The *Minia* came back six days later, having recovered seventeen bodies of which two were then buried at sea, while two more ships, the *Montmagny* and the *Algerine*, brought four bodies to Halifax, and buried one more at sea. The **final body count** also includes the five buried at sea by the *Carpathia*; the three still in Collapsible A when it was found by the *Oceanic* on 13 May; and Steward W. F. Cheverton, spotted by the *Ilford* on 8 June.

Various other stories circulated of bodies being sighted but not recovered. The German ship *Bremen* is said to have passed through a group of around a hundred floating corpses just a few days after the disaster, which may well have included those subsequently located by the *Mackay-Bennett*. However, reports that ten frozen men, still wearing their life belts, were seen huddled together on pack ice, having somehow found refuge there during the sinking, are almost certainly apocryphal.

Return to Halifax

A total of **209 bodies** were brought to Halifax, where a curling rink was converted into a temporary morgue. Fifty-nine of those that were identified were shipped elsewhere for burial, while the remaining one hundred and fifty were buried in the city. In theory each was allocated to one of three specific cemeteries according to religion, but that was often a matter of guesswork. Among those incorrectly assigned was **Michel Navratil**, the father of the as-yet-unidentified "*Titanic* Orphans" (see p.105), whose body, found with a loaded revolver in one pocket, was buried in Halifax's Jewish cemetery under his shipboard pseudonym of "Hoffman".

Only three **children's** bodies were retrieved. The youngest, a blond-haired boy taken from the water and designated as No. 4, could not be identified at the time, and was buried beneath a tombstone that read: "Erected to the memory of an unknown child". Only in 2006 did DNA analysis finally reveal him to be **Sidney Goodwin**, a nineteen-month-old English boy. Both his parents, and his five older siblings, who were travelling third class, died in the sinking; his was the only body recovered.

By contrast, the first and most famous body to be identified was No. 124. Thanks to a gold watch, a diamond ring, $2440 and £225 in cash and a collar monogrammed with the initials J.J.A., this was clearly **John Jacob Astor IV**. Suggestions that he had been crushed by the collapse of the *Titanic*'s foremost funnel were disproved by the body's pristine state. He was buried in New York on 4 May.

The *Carpathia* reaches New York

With steady rain falling, the *Carpathia* reached **New York** in the early evening of Thursday 18 April. Disdaining the flotilla of small boats that surrounded her, and the reporters who attempted to sneak on board with the harbour pilot and quarantine doctor, she steamed slowly past the Battery, where a crowd of ten thousand had gathered, at 7.45pm.

To everyone's surprise, the *Carpathia* continued past the thirty thousand spectators waiting at her own pier, and came to a halt just off the foot of West 20th Street, close to the spot where the *Titanic* had been scheduled to dock the previous day. There she solemnly dropped off the lost ship's lifeboats, which were tied up between piers 58 and 59.

Only then did the *Carpathia* double back and tie up at Pier 54, at around 9pm. When her gangways were lowered half an hour later, the first to disembark were her own passengers, who had set off from here a week earlier. The *Titanic*'s surviving first- and second-class passengers then followed, to battle through the throng of reporters and sightseers. Most were whisked away by friends or family; several even had private trains ready to take them home.

Meanwhile a select handful of interested parties were coming aboard the *Carpathia*. First to arrive was **Philip Franklin**, the New York-based vice president of the International Mercantile Marine, which owned the

White Star Line. He was soon closeted with IMM president J. Bruce Ismay. A few moments later, at 9.45pm, **Senator William Alden Smith**, chairman of the impending US Senate inquiry, arrived on the scene. His train from Washington had reached New York barely half an hour earlier.

Making his way to the cabin occupied by Ismay, Smith was confronted with a handwritten sign reading: "PLEASE DO NOT KNOCK". Franklin at first refused him entry, saying Ismay was far too ill to speak. Smith, who thanks to the "YAMSI" wireless message (see above) was well aware of Ismay's desire to go straight back to England, insisted. He made it clear that he expected Ismay to appear before his inquiry the very next morning, when the first session would open in the Waldorf-Astoria hotel. Smith then emerged to tell reporters that he and Ismay had had a "frank and courteous" meeting. Ismay himself left later, accompanied by two armed bodyguards hired for his protection.

At the same time, Smith's deputies were serving **warrants** on the *Titanic's* surviving officers, requiring them to testify before the inquiry. They too were suspected of hoping to escape without giving evidence. Second Officer Lightoller made it very clear in his autobiography, written 25 years later, that he still regarded being detained against his will in the US as a "colossal piece of impertinence".

Wireless pioneer **Guglielmo Marconi**, who was being hailed the world over as having made the entire rescue possible, also came unobtrusively aboard. With reporter Jim Speer from *The New York Times* in tow, he headed straight for the radio cabin, where the *Titanic's* **Harold Bride** was still at the transmitter, despite his injuries and days without sleep. The newspaper paid Bride $1000 for his exclusive story, and $500 to **Harold Cottam** of the *Carpathia* for his. Both official inquiries later attempted to investigate Marconi's behaviour and motivation, with little success.

The usual medical inspections having been cut back on compassionate grounds, the *Titanic's* 174 surviving third-class passengers were allowed to disembark at around 11pm. The great majority, who were without waiting relatives or worldly possessions, were escorted away by charities and welfare agencies.

Last of all to leave the *Carpathia*, at 11.30pm, were the remnants of the *Titanic's* crew. To avoid the eager newsmen, all 210 were kept together, and taken by barge to the Red Star liner *Lapland*, moored not far away at Pier 60.

Part 3

AFTERMATH

Chapter 7
Sensation and investigation

When the **first news** of the *Titanic* disaster was transmitted by the Cape Race wireless station in Newfoundland, it was still Sunday night in Canada: "At 10:25 o'clock tonight the White Star Line steamship *Titanic* called 'CQD' to the Marconi station here, and reported having struck an iceberg. The steamer said that immediate assistance was required."

The New York Times reacted faster than all its rivals. As soon as its newsroom picked up the message at 1.20am, managing editor **Carr Van Anda** called his contacts in Canada. Establishing that icebergs had been reported in the relevant area, and that nothing had been heard from the *Titanic* since an abruptly truncated exchange with the *Virginian*, Van Anda decided to trust his gut feeling that something was seriously wrong. His Monday-morning headline scooped the world: "NEW LINER *TITANIC* HITS AN ICEBERG; SINKING BY THE BOW AT MIDNIGHT; WOMEN PUT OFF IN LIFEBOATS; LAST WIRELESS AT 12.27AM BLURRED." Competing newspapers were either more circumspect, or just plain wrong. The *Evening Sun*, for example, announced, "All Saved From *Titanic* After Collision", and was among several that said the liner was being **towed to Halifax**.

Philip Franklin, the vice president of the International Mercantile Marine, the owners of the *Titanic*, was woken in his East 61st Street home by a call from a reporter, just after 2am. He found the story impossible to believe, but made a series of calls to White Star Line representatives, and arranged for a message to be sent to the *Olympic*. Speaking to the press the following morning, he declared: "We place absolute confidence in the *Titanic*. We believe that the boat is **unsinkable**". Countless reporters were to echo that word "unsinkable" in their stories, establishing a piece of *Titanic* lore that still endures a century later (see p.198).

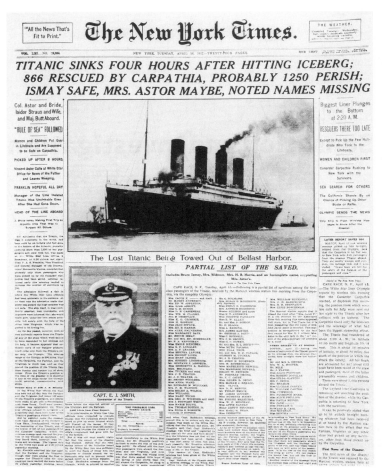

The New York Times *reports the disaster, 16 April 1912.*

Official confirmation of the sinking only reached the White Star Line at 6.16pm that evening, when a message arrived from Captain Haddock of the *Olympic*: "*Carpathia* reached *Titanic*'s position at daybreak. Found boats and wreckage only … About 675 souls saved, crew and passengers, latter nearly all women and children." A few minutes later, Franklin stepped out of his office to read a statement to the waiting reporters. In his own words, "I got off the first line and a half, where it said 'the *Titanic* sank at 2 o'clock am', and there was not a reporter left in the room – they were so anxious to get out to telephone the news."

A persistent legend soon grew up that the White Star Line **knew** that the *Titanic* had sunk for several hours before they announced the news. Supposedly they took advantage of the delay to re-insure the ship. It was also claimed that the family of **John Jacob Astor IV** knew about his death in time to hold a meeting that afternoon to discuss the future of his estate. The US inquiry found no evidence to support those charges, however. Such an obvious insurance fraud would have been detected immediately. It seems clear that White Star initially believed that the *Titanic* was being towed to Halifax. The company sent reassuring telegrams to relatives of those aboard, and even chartered a **train** to meet the passengers, which was already north of Boston by the time the tragic news arrived.

That said, the *Olympic*'s message did take its time to get through to the White Star Line. It had already been picked up in New York at 4.35pm, by a young wireless operator called David Sarnoff, in a radio station that had been installed for publicity services on the roof of Wanamaker's department store. Sarnoff remained at his post for the rest of the week, and became known as a primary conduit for information. Scores of **amateur radio** enthusiasts along the East Coast, on the other hand, added greatly to the confusion of the coming days by relaying inaccurate and unsourced reports.

No news is big news

During the **three days** between the announcement of the sinking and the arrival of the survivors in New York, newspapers all over the world filled their pages with **sensational stories** about the *Titanic*. The only trouble was, there was no actual news to report.

The *Carpathia* had a **wireless** range of just two hundred miles, and thus remained out of contact throughout Monday. As described on p.132, even when she did establish a connection, via other ships at sea, the two operators on board were under orders from Captain Rostron to do no more than transmit the names of the survivors. The *Titanic*'s rescued passengers were told they could write free messages to their relatives ashore, but the workload of the wireless men was so great that many were never sent. In the **absence of details** of the sinking, therefore, the newspapers printed every scrap of

> "When news of a shipwreck arrives without particulars, and journalists immediately begin to invent particulars, they are lying. It is nothing to the point that authentic news may arrive later on, and may confirm a scrap or two of their more obvious surmises."
>
> George Bernard Shaw, letter to the *Daily News and Leader*, May 1912

THE DISASTER IN FIGURES

	Survived	Died	Total	Survival rate
First class				
Men	57	116	173	32.9%
Women	140	4	144	97.2%
Children	6	1	7	85.7%
Second class				
Men	14	135	149	9.4%
Women	80	24	104	76.9%
Children	24	0	24	100%
Third class				
Men	72	385	457	15.8%
Women	74	88	162	45.7%
Children	32	57	89	36.0%
Adult males	143	636	779	18.4%
Adult females	294	116	410	71.7%
Children	62	58	120	51.7%
TOTAL	**499**	**810**	**1309**	**38.1%**
Crew & others	212	685	897	23.6%
All men aboard	335	1321	1656	20.2%
All women aboard	314	116	430	73.0%
TOTAL ABOARD	**711**	**1495**	**2206**	**32.2%**

information they could find about the *Titanic*. Reporters combing the archives for references to the ship swiftly established that she had been equipped with far too few lifeboats. Avid readers absorbed every intricacy of her layout – and especially her much-vaunted system of watertight compartments – as well as the biographies of her most distinguished passengers.

The tiniest snippets of fact were turned into extravagant **fictions**. The phrase in the *Olympic*'s message about the survivors being "nearly all women

There is no **definitive figure** for survivors or victims of the *Titanic* disaster; as explained on p.46, it's not known exactly how many people were aboard, and there are further discrepancies between the various lists of survivors. The tallies opposite are based on the official statistics published by the British inquiry, with minor adjustments for known errors.

Just over two thirds of all those aboard, passengers and crew, died in the disaster. The survival rate for **men** travelling first class was well over three times the rate for those travelling second class, and double that for men in steerage.

All those listed as **children** opposite were aged fourteen or younger, but some fourteen-year-olds have been counted as adults, including crew members and a newly wed Lebanese girl who was travelling with her husband. The youngest "adult" first- or second-class passenger to lose his life was farm labourer George Sweet, who died the day before his fifteenth birthday.

The only child travelling either first- or second-class who did not survive, two-year-old Loraine Allison, died because her parents remained aboard searching for their baby son Trevor, not realizing that he'd left with his nurse on Boat 11. More than half the **women**, and an even higher proportion of the children, travelling third class failed to find a place in the lifeboats. The death rate is thought to have been especially high among those passengers who did not speak English.

For **crew** as for passengers, survival rates largely correspond with their location on the ship. All seven of the *Titanic*'s quartermasters, and all six of her lookouts survived, as did two thirds of her Deck Crew, whereas only around twenty-two percent of those who worked in the engine rooms managed to escape. Out of the sixty-eight restaurant staff, three were rescued. All eight of the ship's musicians, and all five of her postal workers, died in the sinking. Twenty out of the ship's twenty-three female employees survived.

Several families travelling third class were entirely wiped out. John and Annie Sage from Peterborough perished alongside all nine of their children, aged from four up to twenty. Frederick and Augusta Goodwin, from Fulham in London, died with their six children, while two women with five children each also failed to survive, Maria Panula from Finland, and an Irish widow, Margaret Rice.

and children" prompted lengthy eulogies on how the men aboard must have behaved impeccably, in the finest traditions of their respective nationalities. As Americans became aware of the shortcomings of the *Titanic*'s safety features, the mood grew that the White Star Line, together with the British Board of Trade as the body responsible for regulating such ships, was to blame for the disaster. That the name of White Star Line president **J. Bruce Ismay** featured on the list of survivors gave public anger an obvious focus.

Londoners read about the tragedy, outside the White Star Line offices in Trafalgar Square. Author Gavin Murphy has identified the young newsboy as Ned Parfett, who died in the Great War.

Britain reacts

Although the first hints of the tragedy reached **Britain** shortly after North America, the time difference ensured that the bitter truth arrived too late to make the Tuesday-morning newspapers. As a result, readers of that day's *Daily Sketch*, for example, were informed that Captain Smith had "acted with commendable promptitude" in transferring all his passengers to the *Parisian*, *Carpathia* and *Virginian*, which were now carrying them towards Halifax and New York.

Within hours, however, everyone knew the *Titanic* had sunk. Prime Minister **Herbert Asquith** announced the loss to the House of Commons that afternoon, adding that: "the best traditions of the sea seemed to have been observed in the willing sacrifices which were offered to give the first chance of safety to those who were least able to help themselves".

While the major concern in the United States was the fate of the *Titanic*'s wealthiest passengers, attention in Britain was directed towards her lost **crew**. In **Southampton**, home to almost three quarters of the crew, wives would collect their absent husbands' pay from the White Star Line office on Canute Road. Many were therefore already gathered there that Monday morning when the message came that the *Titanic* was in trouble.

A week of agonizing uncertainty ensued, with overnight vigils as crowds awaited the latest news. Once the hopes raised by the misleading bulletins of Monday night had been dashed the next morning, the long wait for the names of survivors began. All too aware of the hierarchy of the ship, the relatives of the firemen and trimmers in particular expected the worst.

Although a full roster of first-class survivors reached London on Wednesday, it took until Friday for the complete list of surviving crew members to be posted outside the Southampton office. Even then, many of the names lacked initials, so families could not be sure which of their loved ones had died. The statistics were appalling. In the district of **Northam**, 20 families on a single street lost their breadwinner, as did 125 children in a single school. One woman was reported to have lost a husband, a son, two brothers and four cousins.

The first details emerge

The arrival of the *Carpathia* in New York on Thursday evening (see p.135) gave the newspapers something to sink their teeth into at last. The waiting newsmen were so frantic that long before the ship had docked they were shouting questions to anyone visible on deck, and even waving $50 bills to encourage them to jump overboard and be interviewed straight away.

Many of the surviving passengers were unwilling to talk to the press, while the crew was unable to, being whisked off en masse by the White Star Line. Reporters therefore badgered the *Carpathia*'s own passengers for gossip they'd heard on board, and survivors' relatives for second-hand accounts. Those passengers who were prepared to speak directly – like **Margaret "Molly" Brown**, who boasted "The ship can sink, but I can't; I'm unsinkable!" – became immediate stars. **Major Arthur Peuchen** was especially forthright. Asked about the cause of the disaster, he replied, "I say it was carelessness, gross carelessness".

Rumours took hold fast in that hysterical atmosphere. According to Lawrence Beesley, who was among the earliest *Titanic* passengers to disembark, "the first questions the excited crowds of reporters asked as they crowded round were whether it was true that officers shot passengers, and then themselves". The story got out that **Captain Smith** had been seen to shoot himself on the bridge as the ship was sinking. Countless newspapers passed on the tale the next day, only to withdraw it amid profuse apologies 24 hours later.

Several other enduring *Titanic* **legends** can be traced back to that first night. A seventeen-year-old Canadian first-class passenger, Vera Dick, told the *New York World* that: "As the steamship went down the band was up forward and we could faintly hear the start of 'Nearer My God to Thee.'" As discussed on p.194 onwards, that single questionable source is still widely believed a century later.

Over the coming weeks, the survivors told their individual tales to their home-town newspapers, friends and relatives. Repeated and embellished, they were passed on to a global audience. A more reliable flow of information became available with the opening of the Senate investigation into the tragedy, which took place the morning after the *Carpathia* reached New York.

The US inquiry

In setting up its inquiry into the *Titanic* disaster, the US Senate reacted with extraordinary speed. The *Titanic* sank early on Monday morning; the survivors, and with them the first details about the tragedy, reached New York late on Thursday evening; and the inquiry opened in the city's Waldorf-Astoria hotel the very next morning, on **Friday 19 April**.

Credit for that quick response is entirely due to a Republican senator from Michigan, **William Alden Smith**. As soon as he heard confirmation of the sinking, that Tuesday, he realized that Congress might be panicked into passing ill-conceived legislation. On Wednesday, therefore, he proposed to the Senate that its **Committee on Commerce**, of which he was a member, should launch a full investigation. The resolution was passed unanimously, and a subcommittee was set up with Smith himself as chairman. Its six additional members comprised three Republicans and three Democrats, carefully balanced to represent the liberal, moderate and conservative wings of each party.

On Thursday morning, Senator Smith was told that the Navy Department had picked up J. Bruce Ismay's notorious "**YAMSI**" wireless message from the *Carpathia* (see p.133). Ismay was clearly planning to thwart any investigation by returning immediately to England, along with the *Titanic*'s surviving crew. Smith went straight to the top, calling on **President Taft** in the White House to make sure that he had the right to subpoena even non-American witnesses. Already infuriated by the *Carpathia*'s failure to respond to his requests for news of Archie Butt, Taft gave Smith his blessing. The senator immediately left for New York, accompanied by a deputy with a stack of subpoenas. He arrived just in time to board the *Carpathia* as it docked (see p.136).

Born in Dowagiac, Michigan, in 1859, Senator Smith had started out selling popcorn on the streets of Grand Rapids. As a politician he refused to be intimidated by anyone. While not formally aligned with the Progressives (see p.4), he established a reputation as a champion of the common man, standing up against the wealthy trusts and corporations who seemed to regard themselves as being above the law. His great hope with the *Titanic*

White Star Line chairman J. Bruce Ismay (centre) gives evidence at the US Senate inquiry in the Waldorf-Astoria, New York.

inquiry was that if the IMM, the owners of the ship, proved to be responsible for the disaster, then they could be held accountable to its victims.

As described in the box on p.152, Smith was widely scorned as a nautical ignoramus. He had at least some relevant experience, however. In 1906, he had crossed the Atlantic aboard the *Baltic*, under the command of Captain E. J. Smith. He had dined at the captain's table, and Captain Smith had explained to him the ship's system of watertight compartments.

The New York hearings

Senator Smith's inquiry only held two days of hearings in **New York**, on Friday and Saturday. The scale of the task ahead was made immediately apparent by the first witness, **J. Bruce Ismay**. Although he began by insisting that the White Star Line welcomed the inquiry – "We have nothing to conceal; nothing to hide" – Ismay offered only the most minimal account of the disaster. "The accident took place on Sunday night. What the exact time was I do not know. I was in bed myself, asleep, when the accident happened. The ship sank, I am told, at 2.20. That, sir, I think is all I can tell you." Pressed to explain how he himself escaped, his story was similarly banal. Seeing a lifeboat being lowered with no one else around, he explained, "I got into it". Thanks to the very fact of his survival, Ismay was already attracting open contempt in the American press. He did himself no favours by protesting to a reporter that the inquiry was treating him "in a manner that seems unjust".

The *Titanic*'s senior surviving officer, Second Officer **Charles Lightoller**, also testified on the first day. At first charming, he visibly bristled as soon as Smith's questioning turned probing. During an interrogation that lasted well over three hours, Smith returned again and again to Lightoller's role in loading the lifeboats, and especially the fact that those lifeboats had left the ship half empty. Both the committee members and the watching pressmen were left with the impression that Lightoller was concealing something, perhaps to protect his employers … and with little idea as to what that might be.

First-class bedroom steward **Alfred Crawford**, Friday's final witness, was less central to the tragedy, but his graphic description of the loading of the lifeboats filled the next day's newspapers. In particular, he confirmed the story already circulating, that Mrs Straus had chosen to die with her husband rather than leave him behind (see p.95).

Other witnesses called in New York included Captain Rostron of the *Carpathia*; Guglielmo Marconi; and the two heroic **wireless men**, Harold Cottam of the *Carpathia*, and Harold Bride from the *Titanic*. The latter's appearance in a wheelchair, all too visibly suffering from the effects of his ordeal, created a sensation. So too did his words, as he described the desperate melee in the water after the ship went down.

The White Star Line was still hoping that the inquiry would be brief, and intended to make it so by taking the *Titanic*'s crew back home to England aboard the *Lapland*, on Saturday. Meanwhile, however, Senator Smith had sent a special deputy to eavesdrop on the ordinary crewmen on Friday, and find any who might have interesting stories to tell. That mission resulted in the issue of a further **29 subpoenas**, aimed especially at those crew members who had taken command of the lifeboats.

News of five more crew members who were potentially useful as witnesses reached Senator Smith on Saturday. The *Lapland* had by now already sailed, but it was ordered to stop, and a tug was dispatched to bring the five back to New York. Among them was **Robert Hichens**, who had been at the wheel of the *Titanic* when it hit the iceberg. The *Lapland* continued on its way, now carrying 167 surviving crew members.

The inquiry moves to Washington

Committee, witnesses and spectators alike decamped to **Washington** on Sunday 21 April, where the hearings resumed on Monday morning. In total, the inquiry gathered the testimony of eighty-seven witnesses and interested parties, although fewer than forty of those actually appeared in front of the committee. The remainder were either interviewed separately or submitted their evidence in writing. All the important testimony is cited in the relevant sections throughout this book. Some of the major events of the ensuing weeks, however, are worth mentioning.

The first witness to tell the inquiry about the "**Mystery Ship**" that had been seen from the sinking *Titanic* was Fourth Officer **Joseph Boxhall**, on Monday 22 April. Speculation as to its identity was mounting when an assistant engineer (or "donkeyman") on the *Californian*, Ernest Gill, told the *Boston American* that Wednesday that his ship had seen the *Titanic*'s distress rockets, but **Captain Lord** had made no attempt to respond.

Gill, Lord and the *Californian*'s wireless operator, Cyril Evans, were summoned to Washington. All three appeared before the inquiry in the space of a single afternoon, Friday 26 April, before making their separate ways home to England. Faced with the obvious contradictions in the testimony of the three men, between each other as well as with the witnesses aboard the *Titanic*, Senator Smith asked a captain from the US Hydrographics Office to set about calculating the relative positions of the *Titanic* and the *Californian*.

An enforced stay

When they first arrived in the capital, the crewmen of the *Titanic* were billeted in the Continental Hotel. Second Officer Lightoller was furious that the officers were expected to stay in the same lodgings as the 34 seamen and stewards, however, and after one night the lesser members of the crew were moved to another hotel. With only the barest of living expenses to keep them going, several raised money by telling their stories from the stage of a **vaudeville theatre**.

Fifth Officer **Harold Lowe** was a star of the inquiry. A dashing young man, he seemed to enjoy his verbal sparring with Senator Smith, responding for example to Smith's query as to what an iceberg was made of with a laconic, "ice, I suppose, sir". His gripping testimony detailed the loading of the lifeboats and his own role in searching for survivors on Boat 14. When asked about the rumours that shots had been fired on the *Titanic*, he caused a huge stir by revealing that not only had he heard shots, he'd fired them (see p.196).

Lowe's description of "a lot of Italians ... all along the ship's rails ... glaring, more or less like wild beasts, ready to spring" offended the Italian ambassador, who was present. He was therefore obliged to write an official apology, which

Wireless operator Harold Bride, suffering from frostbite, is carried off the **Carpathia**.
After selling his story for $1000, he testified at both inquiries.

included the words: "I do hereby cancel the word 'Italian' and substitute the
words 'immigrants belonging to Latin races'".

J. Bruce Ismay was a much more reluctant witness. He pestered Senator
Smith so repeatedly to be allowed to return home to England that Smith made
a formal announcement on the Wednesday morning that "from the beginning

until now there has been a voluntary, gratuitous, meddlesome attempt upon the part of **certain persons** to influence the course of the committee and to shape its procedure". Only Ismay knew he was the target of Smith's remarks.

Senator Smith finally allowed the *Titanic*'s ordinary crew members to leave Washington on Monday 29 April. They sailed from New York, aboard the *Celtic*, that same evening. Ismay himself made his last appearance before the committee the next day, and left New York for Liverpool on the *Adriatic* on Thursday 2 May, along with the *Titanic*'s four surviving officers.

Senator Smith returns to New York

Once all the *Titanic*'s surviving crew members had left Washington, on Tuesday 30 April, Smith's full subcommittee held no further hearings. However, the senator felt that his task was not yet complete. His major concern was that he might have been too ready to believe the testimony of the *Titanic*'s officers, especially as to whether the **steerage** passengers had been denied access to the lifeboats.

No third-class passengers had so far given evidence, but the final witness called, first-class passenger **Colonel Archibald Gracie**, had told an alarming tale. Gracie, who lived in Washington and was Smith's personal friend – and went on to write a book about the tragedy – had seen a vast number of steerage passengers suddenly emerge onto the Boat Deck, after the last lifeboats had gone. Where had they been until then?

Smith decided to go back to **New York**, and interview any third-class survivors who remained in the city. As he told the *New York World*, "the horrible impression remains on my mind that the people of the steerage did not get half a chance". The charitable agencies he asked for help managed to find three steerage passengers. None, however, complained of being held back – although of course the very fact of their survival made them the exception rather than the rule.

Staying once more at the Waldorf-Astoria, Smith also took statements from three first-class passengers, and continued to investigate the **wireless messages** sent from the *Carpathia* during her return voyage to New York. *Titanic* wireless operator **Harold Bride**, who had travelled to Washington to give additional evidence, was now back in New York trying to secure a passage home, and gave Smith yet more details about his own role.

Smith then returned to Washington, where he accepted evidence from a few more witnesses over the next couple of weeks, and set about writing his report. Even after finishing his first draft, however, some doubts remained. When he heard that the *Titanic*'s all-but-identical sister ship, the *Olympic*, had docked in New York on her first return to America since the sinking, he decided to pay her a visit.

THE PREPOSTEROUS SMITH

From the moment reports of the New York hearings reached London, **Senator Smith** attracted the hostility of the British press. The *Daily Express* referred to him as an "asinine American", while music hall comedians lampooned him with derisive songs. The basic charge, that Smith was **too ignorant** of nautical matters to conduct a proper inquiry, stuck to such an extent that it's still repeated by historians a century later.

The immediate criticism was triggered by Smith's inquisition of **Lightoller**. After Lightoller told him that the *Titanic* was equipped with "forty or fifty" watertight compartments – it actually had sixteen – Smith asked: "Are you able to say whether any of the crew or passengers took to these upper watertight compartments as a final, last resort; I mean as a place to die?" Smith later insisted that he knew the very idea of the compartments serving as a refuge to be absurd, but asked the question because many Americans imagined that there might still be survivors aboard the sunken ship.

Smith was also blamed for the perceived scapegoating of **J. Bruce Ismay**, even though Ismay was being similarly criticized in Britain. It seems clear that Smith's real offence in British eyes was what Lightoller called the "colossal piece of impertinence" of staging the inquiry at all, combined with the thankless duty of asking intrusive questions so soon after the tragedy. Lightoller later wrote that the inquiry was "nothing but a complete farce, wherein all the traditions and customs of the sea were continuously and persistently flouted".

In his superb study of Senator Smith, *The Titanic – End of a Dream*, **Wyn Wade** goes a long way towards redressing the balance. Wade depicts Smith as a diligent investigator who would probe an issue until he found a chink through which the truth might emerge, and an astonishingly hard worker who saw the inquiry through with incredible single-mindedness.

The notion of Smith as a "**nautical nincompoop**" was also spread by an American newspaper, *The New York Times*, which published an editorial condemning "The Preposterous Smith". However, Wade demonstrates that the paper had consistently praised Smith until his inquiry established that Guglielmo Marconi had conspired with the wireless operators aboard the *Carpathia* to withhold news of the tragedy in order to sell their story to… *The New York Times*.

Smith himself told the *New York World*: "I am no sailor and don't pretend to have any nautical knowledge … [but] … not a single detail it was possible to learn … escaped the attention of the committee. If I asked questions that seemed absurd to sailors, it did no harm."

On Saturday 25 May, Senator Smith arrived unannounced aboard the *Olympic*, and persuaded **Captain Haddock** to lower a fully loaded lifeboat, carrying sixty-five crew members. The *Olympic* was now equipped with **forty-three** lifeboats, as opposed to the *Titanic*'s twenty – indeed her voyage back to America had been delayed because her crew went on **strike** until she was provided with enough good-quality lifeboats.

The very last evidence gathered for the Senate inquiry came in extraordinary circumstances. When Captain Haddock told Smith, in passing, that a fireman on the *Olympic* had previously served on the *Titanic*, Smith immediately decided to go down to the boiler rooms and speak to him. There he found fireman **Frederick Barrett**, covered in grime, and back at the work that had all but cost him his life a few weeks earlier. Standing in **Boiler Room 6**, Barrett was able to point out exactly where he'd seen the water burst in, following the impact with the iceberg, and demonstrate the working of the notorious watertight doors. His graphic eyewitness account appears on p.67 onwards. Barrett also told Smith that on the day of the tragedy the firemen had been ordered to fire up three previously unused boilers. In other words, the *Titanic* had indeed been speeding faster than ever before – precisely the information Smith had been looking for all along.

Senator Smith makes his report

Three days after visiting the *Olympic* in New York, on Tuesday, 28 May 1912, Senator Smith presented his **report** to the US Senate. The passionate two-hour speech in which he announced his conclusions and recommendations was swiftly derided in England. The *Daily Mail* called it a "violent, unreasonable diatribe", while to the *Daily Express* it was a "grotesque oration … grandiloquent bosh". A century later, the senator's rhetoric seems typical of the era; what the British press really objected to was the **content**.

Senator Smith insisted that when the *Titanic* was designed and built "no sufficient tests were made of boilers or bulkheads or gearing or equipment, and no life-saving or signal devices were reviewed". As a result, "when the crisis came a state of **absolute unpreparedness** stupefied both passengers and crew".

The senator rejected the comfortable myth of the crew's heroic behaviour: "No general alarm was given, no ship's officers formally assembled, no orderly routine was attempted or organized system of safety begun. Haphazard, they rushed by one another on staircase and in hallway. If this is discipline, what would have been disorder?" As for his namesake, **Captain Smith**, the senator declared that "his indifference to danger was one of the direct and contributing causes of this unnecessary tragedy", and that his committee could find "no reasonable hypothesis in conjecture or speculation" to explain it.

Recognizing that those responsible for the disaster could only be held accountable under British rather than American law, Senator Smith added: "We shall leave to the honest judgment of England its painstaking chastisement of the British **Board of Trade**, to whose laxity of regulation and hasty inspection the world is largely indebted for this awful fatality."

On the controversial topic of the proximity of the *Californian* to the sinking *Titanic*, Smith expressed his opinion that "it was much nearer than the captain is willing to admit", and that therefore "the conduct of the captain of the *Californian* calls for drastic action by the Government of England". He also threw in a condemnation of the **Marconi Company**, saying that the paucity of wireless messages from the *Carpathia* had been a deliberate policy so they could sell the operators' stories to the press.

On the other hand, Smith did not believe that J. Bruce Ismay had ordered Captain Smith to put on dangerous speed, simply suggesting instead that Ismay's very presence may have acted as an unconscious spur for the captain to go faster. Neither, despite his earlier suspicions, did Smith find that third-class passengers had been prevented from reaching the lifeboats. He argued that those whose cabins were nearest the bow had been made instantly aware of the collision, by water entering their cabins, and had indeed succeeded in reaching the lifeboats. Those towards the stern, however, were several hundred yards from the crisis point. Because the stern was at first raised higher out of the water, they did not realize that the *Titanic* was sinking.

The senator rounded off his speech by introducing three pieces of **legislation**. One, to award Captain Rostron of the *Carpathia* a gold medal worth $1000, was passed immediately. Another was intended to set up a maritime commission to assess all current laws relating to building and equipping ships, and the third, which became known in due course as the **Smith Bill**, amounted to a comprehensive rewriting of all such laws. His specific recommendations ranged from making it compulsory for ships to carry enough lifeboats for all those aboard, with each person assigned to a specific boat, to specifying that ships should be required to carry two or more wireless operators, and maintain radio communications around the clock.

Memorials and fundraising

In the immediate aftermath of the tragedy, public grief found its expression in **memorial services**. Among the congregation of ten thousand at St Paul's Cathedral in London, on Friday 19 April, was **Alexander Carlisle**, who had designed the *Titanic* alongside Thomas Andrews, and was arguably responsible for its inadequate provision of lifeboats. Carlisle collapsed

BOATS FOR WOMEN

With the **suffragette** movement at its peak in 1912, much debate in North America focussed on whether the policy of **women and children first** could be reconciled with demands for female equality. A poem in the *St. Louis Post-Dispatch* expressed the matter succinctly.

> "Votes for women!" was the cry,
> Reaching upward to the Sky.
> Crashing glass and flashing eye –
> "Votes for Women!" was the cry.
>
> "Boats for women!" was the cry.
> When the brave were come to die.
> When the end was drawing nigh –
> "Boats for women!" was the cry.

Correspondents and editorials in many newspapers questioned whether it could really be right for America's leading industrialists to give up their lives for unknown immigrant women, or argued that their sacrifice was all the more noble precisely *because* the women were so unimportant. A prominent anarchist, **Emma Goldman**, said that if women really wanted to be considered as equals, then those aboard the *Titanic* should indeed have refused special treatment.

Alice Stone Blackwell countered such arguments in a powerful editorial in *Women's Journal*, the week after the sinking: "It is absurd to fancy that chivalry is a tribute rendered by a voter to a non-voter as a sort of offset for the lack of the ballot… The 'law of the sea' is quite different from the custom on land. The captain is expected to be the last man to leave his ship; all other lives must be saved before his. The captain of industry makes sure first of a comfortable living for himself, even if the workers in his employ die of tuberculosis through insufficient food and unsanitary conditions…"

The labour leader Mary Harris Jones, remembered as **"Mother" Jones**, made a similar point in a speech to striking Colorado miners that summer: "The papers came out and said those millionaires tried to save the women. Oh, Lord, why don't they give up their millions if they want to save the women and children? Why do they rob them of home, why do they rob millions of women to fill the hell-holes of capitalism?"

under the strain, and had to be taken home in an ambulance. The next day saw a similar commemoration at St Mary's Church in Southampton, while churches all over the world were filled that Sunday for solemn reflections on the disaster.

Few **funerals** attracted attention, however, as only around a quarter of the victims' bodies were retrieved from the ocean. Only 59 of those were returned to their home towns for burial, and many of those towns were far removed from the public eye. The most widely reported funeral in the US was that of John Jacob Astor IV, who was buried in New York on 4 May. Although the body of Ida Straus was never found, a service in memory of her and her husband Isidor took place at Carnegie Hall on Sunday 12 May, with speakers including Andrew Carnegie and the mayor of New York.

Of the select few British victims whose bodies were shipped home, the most prominent was violinist **Wallace Hartley**, hailed as having inspired the *Titanic*'s musicians to keep on playing as the ship was sinking. Over thirty thousand mourners watched as he was carried to his grave in Colne, Lancashire, on Saturday May 18. The site was later marked by a monument that depicted a hymn book open at "Nearer My God to Thee".

Many **memorials** and public occasions were intended not only to honour the victims of the disaster, but to raise money for their dependants. On both sides of the Atlantic, committees were formed to collect and distribute money. Efforts in the **United States** were directed largely at meeting the short-term needs of the surviving steerage passengers, enabling some to continue with their plans to build new lives in the New World, and others, like the many newly bereaved widows, to return to their families in the Old World. The **Women's Relief Committee**, in conjunction with the *New York American* newspaper, collected over $100,000 within a week of the sinking, while a fund instigated by the mayor of New York went on to raise over $161,000. Among the biggest events was a gala matinee at the Metropolitan Opera House in New York, on Monday 29 April, when performers included the tenor Enrico Caruso.

A separate fund, set up by First Lady Helen Herron Taft and largely prompted by anti-suffragette sentiments, invited women to donate a dollar each to erect a monument to the heroic menfolk of the *Titanic*. More than 25,000 contributions were received, though it wasn't until 1931 that the **Women's Titanic Memorial** was unveiled by Mrs Taft in Washington, DC.

In **Britain**, the prime concern was for the families of crew members. Fundraising events in aid of the **Titanic Relief Fund** included matinées at many leading theatres. On Tuesday 14 May – the same day that the Duff Gordons appeared before the British inquiry (see p.203) – the king and queen were at the Royal Opera House in Covent Garden to watch a bill that included dancer Anna Pavlova and actress Sarah Bernhardt. The official programme for the occasion included a new poem by Thomas Hardy, "The Convergence of the Twain". The **Titanic Band Memorial Concert**, at the Royal Albert Hall on Empire Day, 24 May, featured an orchestra of five hundred musicians performing "Nearer My God to Thee", conducted by Sir Henry Wood.

The Titanic Relief Fund eventually collected something over **£400,000**. Its activities were largely concentrated in **Southampton**, with the primary aim of paying the widows and dependants of the crew who died on the *Titanic* half of their lost husbands' wages. Further disasters caused its remit to be expanded in 1916, when it became the Titanic, Empress of Ireland and Lusitania Fund. During its early years the fund supported around 1400 claimants. A committee kept track of the recipients' lives, stopping the payments of women who remarried or reached pensionable age, or lapsed into disreputable conduct.

When the fund was eventually wound up in 1959, to ensure that it did not have an "embarrassing" amount of money left over when the last recipient died, 64 women were still receiving payments. The remaining money was converted into annuities for their benefit; it's said that one *Titanic* relative still derived a regular income into the twenty-first century.

Morals and meanings

Lawrence Beesley, in his eyewitness memoir, described his fellow *Titanic* survivors, as they sailed for New York aboard the *Carpathia*, discussing: **"What is the purpose of all this?** Why the disaster? Why this man saved and that man lost?" Beesley was no atheist, but he observed that: "I heard no one attribute all this to a Divine Power who ordains and arranges the lives of men, and as part of a definite scheme sends such calamity and misery in order to purify, to teach, to spiritualize."

By the following Sunday, priests and ministers the world over were preaching on those same topics. Author **Steven Biel** has catalogued many of that day's **sermons**. Choice examples include the Archbishop of Baltimore, who proclaimed that, "the remote cause of this unspeakable disaster is the excessive pursuit of luxury"; the New York Presbyterian minister who called it "a terrific and ghastly illustration of what things come to when men throw God out at the door"; and Reverend James O'May of Chicago, who commented: "It was a huge ocean joy ride, and it ended where joy rides generally stop". In England, meanwhile, the Bishop of Winchester was asking: "When has such a mighty lesson against our confidence and trust in power, machinery, and money been shot through the nation? The *Titanic* name and thing will stand for a monument and warning to human presumption."

Other commentators drew quite different conclusions. For some it prompted the age-old question of why an all-powerful God would permit such suffering. A popular saying of the time, **"God went down with the *Titanic*"**, echoed the notion that the disaster had caused many people to lose their faith. Others saw the lessons of the tragedy as being **political** rather than religious. As Victor Berger, a Socialist congressman from Wisconsin, put it:

"Greed and speed are the characteristics of the capitalist system. They caused the disaster and are causing disasters almost as appalling every day in the industrial world."

The pundits have their say

Many of Britain's most famous literary figures offered their reflections on the *Titanic* tragedy. **George Bernard Shaw** took a break from writing *Pygmalion* to condemn the "explosion of outrageous romantic lying" that surrounded the sinking of the *Titanic*. His most specific concern was that Captain Smith was being hailed as a hero, when: "The one thing positively known is that Captain Smith had lost his ship by deliberately and knowingly steaming into an ice field at the highest speed he had coal for. He paid the penalty, as did most of those for whose lives he was responsible."

Sir Arthur Conan Doyle, best known for his Sherlock Holmes stories, was outraged by Shaw's remarks. He sprang to defend Captain Smith as "an old and honoured sailor who has made one terrible mistake, and who deliberately gave his life in reparation, discarding his lifebelt, working to the last for those whom he had unwillingly injured, and finally swimming with a child to a boat into which he himself refused to enter."

G.K. Chesterton, the Christian philosopher and creator of amateur sleuth Father Brown, stood up for a different Smith. Denouncing English papers that were "sneering at Senator Smith for not knowing certain facts about shipping", Chesterton argued that: "it does not much matter whether Senator Smith knows the facts; what matters is whether he is really trying to find them out". He drew an explicit contrast between the US, where "Public Opinion … impatient, inquisitive, often ferocious" was determined to seek out the truth, and Britain, where "Our national evil … is to hush everything up; it is to damp everything down; it is to leave every great affair unfinished, to leave every enormous question unanswered".

As a former merchant seaman himself, the Polish-born novelist **Joseph Conrad** had a lot to say about the *Titanic*. He was aghast at the effrontery of the US inquiry: "Why an officer of the British merchant service should answer the questions of any king, emperor, autocrat, or senator of any foreign power (as to an event in which a British ship alone was concerned, and which did not even take place in the territorial waters of that power) passes my understanding." Senator Smith came in for special criticism, for "rushing to New York … to bully and badger the luckless 'Yamsi'" – a reference to the "code name" used by J. Bruce Ismay.

Conrad however also condemned almost every aspect of the tragedy and its reporting. He called the *Titanic* itself a "45,000 tons hotel of thin steel plates" built for the benefit of a "fatuous handful of individuals" and "about

as strong as a Huntley and Palmer biscuit-tin". The chief lesson of the sinking was that: "in the worst extremity, the majority of people, even of common people, will behave decently. It's a fact of which only the journalists don't seem aware." Heroism had played no part in it: "There is nothing more heroic in being drowned very much against your will, off a holed, helpless, big tank in which you bought your passage than in quietly dying of colic caused by the imperfect salmon in the tin you bought from your grocer". All in all, the disaster was "a perfect exhibition of the modern blind trust in mere material and appliances".

In the *Daily Mail*, **H.G. Wells** hailed the sinking as "the penetrating comment of chance upon our entire social system". As for Ismay himself, "his escape – with five and fifty third-class children waiting below to drown – was the abandonment of every noble pretension".

According to Steven Biel, American author **Henry Adams**, who had a ticket for the *Titanic*'s return voyage to Europe, was the most profoundly affected by the tragedy of all. He saw the simultaneous foundering of both the *Titanic* and the Republican Party in the same week (the latter being Adams' over-reaction to Roosevelt's defeat of Taft in the Pennsylvania primary) as a powerful metaphor: "Our society has politically run on an iceberg, and the confusion and darkness are fatal". Adams transferred his booking to the *Olympic*, which he claimed to hope would sink as well, but suffered a **stroke** (which he survived) just nine days after the sinking and was unable to travel.

The British inquiry

Much like their American counterparts, members of the British **House of Commons** were calling for an official investigation into the *Titanic* disaster even before the survivors had reached dry land. In Britain, however, the resultant inquiry was run by the very body that was arguably responsible for the tragedy – the government department that regulated shipping, the **Board of Trade**. Just a few weeks earlier, the board had certified the seaworthiness of the *Titanic*. For the inquiry to conclude that the *Titanic* had been unfit for service would amount to the board blaming itself for the disaster.

On Monday 22 April, the Lord Chancellor appointed a temporary **Wreck Commissioner** to examine the evidence on behalf of the Board of Trade. The man chosen, **Lord Mersey** of Toxteth, was a former judge who had been raised to the peerage two years earlier. He'd previously served on the committee that had investigated a notorious incident in South Africa, the Jameson Raid of 1895–96. Having exonerated the British government of all complicity, he was seen as a safe establishment figure. The Home Secretary added five "**assessors**" to aid Lord Mersey in his work, all of whom were naval experts.

Lord Mersey of Toxteth (right), the Wreck Commissioner who led the British inquiry, accompanied by his son, the Hon. Clive Bigham, who served as his secretary.

Although it had little interest in assigning blame to individuals, the British investigation was much more like a **court of law** than the rather ad hoc Senate proceedings. Lawyers were appointed to represent interested parties during all or part of the inquiry. Among the **unions** who employed counsels on behalf of their members – both living and dead – were those representing ordinary seamen, firemen, engineers, stewards and dockers. The **White Star Line** had four of its own lawyers, while the **Leyland Line**, owners of the *Californian*, had one. Another counsel spoke specifically for the third-class passengers. In a further conflict of interest, the two chief legal officers of the Crown, the **Attorney General** Sir Rufus Isaacs and the **Solicitor General** Sir John Simon, were instructed to represent not only the public interest at large, but also the specific interests of the Board of Trade.

The inquiry sets to work

The **Wreck Commissioner's Court** met for the first time on **Thursday 2 May** in the drill hall of the London Scottish Regiment at Buckingham Gate in London. The acoustics in the hall were dreadful, but it had at least been equipped with both a huge cross-sectional diagram and a twenty-foot scale model of the lost *Titanic*.

When the inquiry heard its first witnesses, the next day, those *Titanic* crew members who had testified to the Senate inquiry were still on their way home to England. However, SS *Lapland*, carrying the remaining 167 crew members who had been allowed to leave the US earlier (see p.148), had docked at **Plymouth** on Sunday 28 April. To their great indignation, all were interviewed by the Board of Trade, to create a repository of their individual **depositions**, before they were even allowed to see their families, let alone catch the train home to Southampton. Around half were kept at the docks overnight. In total, the Board of Trade accumulated statements from over two hundred crew members, although fewer than fifty were called to London to give evidence.

Those depositions disappeared at some point during World War II, a loss to historians that also means we don't know to what extent the inquiry hand-picked its witnesses. Some crew members certainly felt that they weren't invited to testify in person because their stories were **inconvenient**. Greaser Walter Hurst, for example, wrote to Walter Lord in 1955 that, "I went to London on The Inquiry but was not called. I am sure it was because I spoke of The Boats Leaving half Empty."

On Monday 6 May, as the inquiry team toured the *Olympic* in Southampton, the *Celtic* arrived in Liverpool carrying the first batch of crew members who had testified in Washington. She was followed four days later by the *Californian*. Although her return attracted little public attention, the local "Receiver of Wreck" took statements from the *Californian*'s captain, officers and crew. As a result, several were summoned to London to testify. Finally, the following day, the *Adriatic* arrived in Liverpool with **Ismay** and the *Titanic*'s surviving officers.

Thanks to having access to the entire crew, the UK inquiry gleaned a much fuller picture of what went on below decks during the sinking than had been possible in Washington. Among the crew members who appeared in London during its first week was fireman **Frederick Barrett**, who thereby achieved the unique distinction of testifying to the British inquiry *before* the American one (see p.153).

The inquiry spent two days investigating the role of the *Californian*; for a full discussion of the issues raised, see p.204 onwards. Additional evidence having come to light since **Captain Lord** appeared in Washington, he was subjected to much more intensive cross-examination. The Attorney General in particular gave Lord a hard time, at one stage becoming so exasperated by his self-righteous prevarications that he warned him, "do really try and do yourself justice!" While Captain Lord clearly made a very bad impression, he was not on trial, so he was not recalled for further questioning after the testimony given by his junior officers appeared to contradict his own.

Lightoller in London

The *Titanic*'s senior surviving officer, **Charles Lightoller**, wrote an extensive account of the British and American inquiries in his autobiography, published 23 years later. Pouring scorn on Senator Smith's investigation, he said it was "such a contrast to the dignity and decorum of the Court held by Lord Mersey".

Despite his supposed respect for the proceedings in London, however, Second Officer Lightoller boasted that he had lied to the British inquiry: "It was very necessary to keep one's hand on the **whitewash brush** … Sharp questions that needed careful answers if one was to avoid a pitfall … leading to a pinning down of blame on to someone's luckless shoulders". His motivation was very clear: "I had no desire that blame should be attributed either to the Board of Trade or the White Star Line, though in all conscience it was a difficult task".

Under cross-examination by the Solicitor General, Lightoller's replies sounded **rehearsed** and polished. He stated point blank that he had no idea why the *Titanic* had collided with the iceberg, and that he had not discussed it with Captain Smith or anyone else during the hours that followed.

In his book, Lightoller admitted that, "one had known, full well, and for many years, the ever-present possibility of just such a disaster". He presented the collision to the inquiry, however, as a **freak occurrence** that could never have been predicted: "Of course we know now the extraordinary combination of circumstances that existed at that time which you would not meet again in a hundred years; that they should all have existed just on that particular night shows of course that everything was against us … In the first place there was no moon … Then there was no wind, not the slightest breath of air. And most particular of all in my estimation is the fact, a most extraordinary circumstance, that there was not any swell. Had there been the slightest degree of swell I have no doubt that berg would have been seen in plenty of time to clear it."

Parts of Lightoller's autobiography showed palpable fury, as for example when he condemned the behaviour of the *Californian*. Describing the UK inquiry, however, he made the whole thing sound strangely like a game, which "I think in the end the Board of Trade and the White Star Line won." He prided himself that once the battle of wits was over, he and his opponents "parted very good friends". His one regret was that his employers at the White Star Line had failed to appreciate his efforts: "what an endless strain it had all been, falling on one man's luckless shoulders … fortunately they were broad. Still, just that word of thanks which was lacking … would have been very much appreciated."

All of which begs the question, what exactly was Lightoller hiding? In his book, he admitted that he'd managed to obscure two specific charges at the inquiry: the "utter inadequacy of the lifesaving equipment" aboard the

Titanic, and the fact that she was carrying too few seamen to launch and manage her lifeboats. From his tone, however, you can't help suspecting that he knew much more than he was prepared to say. In 2010, his granddaughter Louise Patten revealed what she claimed were the **secrets** Second Officer Lightoller had confided only to his wife (see p.184).

The strange case of the missing passengers

Only two passengers were invited to give evidence to the British inquiry – **Sir Cosmo** and **Lady Duff Gordon**. Many stories had been circulating about their escape from the sinking ship aboard Boat 1, the so-called "Money Boat" (see p.200), and so the couple were given the opportunity to clear their names, and allowed legal representation. Their appearance attracted a great number of society spectators, including the wife of the prime minister.

Not one passenger from the *Titanic*'s **lower decks**, however, appeared as a witness – even though the inquiry was supposedly hoping to establish whether the third-class passengers had been held back from reaching the lifeboats. There were of course obvious practical impediments. Most of the steerage passengers were dead, while the rest had been deposited as penniless and bereaved immigrants on the other side of the Atlantic.

In any case, Lord Mersey had no interest in hearing what the passengers might have to say. Quizzed on 11 June by Mr Harbison, the counsel for the third-class passengers, as to when such passengers might be called, Mersey responded that "Survivors are not necessarily of the least value".

As the inquiry drew to a close, and it was clear that no ordinary passengers would be asked to appear, the Attorney General explained: "We found it useless to call passengers who could only state what had been already stated by the officers and crew." In Washington, Senator Smith had agonized as to whether he could take the officers at their word; if Sir Rufus had such doubts, he overcame them.

The verdict in London

The **final report** of the British Wreck Commissioner's Inquiry was delivered two months after its American equivalent, on 30 July. Strictly speaking, it consisted of a single sentence: "The Court, having carefully inquired into the circumstances of the above mentioned shipping casualty, finds … that the loss of the said ship was due to collision with an iceberg, brought about by the excessive speed at which the ship was being navigated."

The fruits of the inquiry's investigations were expanded in an "annex", which included full specifications of the *Titanic* along with a detailed account of the voyage and collision. Section 7 answered twenty-six itemized questions about the disaster, many of them with similar brevity: "4. (a) Was the *Titanic* sufficiently and efficiently officered and manned? Yes"; "17. Was proper discipline maintained on board after the casualty occurred? Yes".

The British and American inquiries are generally described as having reached the **same conclusions**. That was certainly the feeling at the time. The *New York Tribune* for example reported the UK verdict with the headline, "Experts say 'ditto' to laymen", while in Britain the *Engineering News* stated that, "contrary to the general expectation, the two reports are essentially the same in effect".

There was at least one major **difference**, however, and it had been predicted from the very start. Senator Smith described the "laxity of regulation and hasty inspection" by the Board of Trade as the main cause of the tragedy; the Board of Trade itself however concluded that it had done nothing wrong. In that respect, it's easy to agree with Officer Lightoller's depiction of the British inquiry as a "whitewash".

That doesn't invalidate all its other conclusions, however. Defenders of **Captain Lord** of the *Californian* like to suggest that he made a convenient scapegoat for the Board of Trade, to distract from its own failings. What's

THE LEGACY OF THE *TITANIC*

As a direct result of the *Titanic* disaster and the recommendations of the US and British inquiries, extensive **new laws** were introduced to regulate shipping. The American government was the first to act. The Smith Bill, as proposed by Senator Smith at the end of his inquiry, was implemented, and the navy sent cruisers to patrol the North Atlantic looking for ice.

Between November 1913 and January 1914, the first-ever **International Conference for the Safety of Life at Sea** met in London, with Lord Mersey as its president. Besides setting new standards in many aspects of shipbuilding and navigation, delegates agreed the following regulations:

• All ships must carry sufficient **lifeboats** to carry every passenger aboard.

• All ships must have **round-the-clock wireless** service of an agreed level of power, with two operators and an auxiliary power source in case of emergencies.

• Any ship travelling at night in an area where ice has been reported must **slow down** or steer clear.

• An international **distress signal** – a Roman candle or an aerial rocket – must only be fired to signal distress.

• The creation of an internationally funded **Ice Patrol**, to be run by the US Navy as an expansion of its existing patrols. This provision created what soon became the US Coast Guard.

more striking is that both the British and American inquiries examined the evidence and came to substantially the same verdict. Asking itself, "What vessels had the opportunity of rendering assistance to the *Titanic* and, if any, how was it that assistance did not reach the *Titanic* before the SS *Carpathia* arrived?", the court in London decided: "The *Californian*. She could have reached the *Titanic* if she had made the attempt when she saw the first rocket. She made no attempt."

Lord Mersey also concurred that the **steerage passengers** had been free to reach the lifeboats. His explanation for why so few failed to do so, however, was somewhat different to Senator Smith's. He suggested they'd been too reluctant to leave their loved ones and possessions below decks, and afraid to trust their lives to the lifeboats. He did not accept that **J. Bruce Ismay** had had "some moral duty" to go down with the ship, and felt his conduct in boarding a lifeboat had been blameless. "Had he not jumped in he would merely have added one more life, namely, his own, to the number of those lost." The **Duff Gordons**, however, he damned with fainter praise (see p.204).

In reaching its verdict on **Captain Smith**, the British court opted for an intricate piece of sophistry. It acknowledged that the *Titanic*'s excessive speed at the time of the collision was a "very grievous mistake" by her captain. He had not however been negligent, because: "he was doing only that which other skilled men would have done in the same position". Smith could not be blamed, in other words, because the world had not yet learned what happens when a ship smashes into an iceberg. "What was a mistake in the case of the *Titanic* would without doubt be negligence in any similar case in the future."

Chapter 8
The *Titanic* rediscovered

As soon as the *Titanic* sank, the popular imagination was seized by the idea that the wreckage might be **located** and even **recovered**. Hundreds of well-meaning Americans wrote to the US inquiry suggesting how to raise her from the ocean floor, and rescue any survivors still trapped in underwater air pockets. Senator Smith felt obliged to respond by ruling out any such possibility – and was therefore ridiculed by the world's press.

Some of the wealthiest bereaved families, including those of John Jacob Astor IV and Benjamin Guggenheim, commissioned a specialist company to investigate the feasibility of a **salvage** operation. They were swiftly told that the necessary technology did not exist. In 1914, a Denver inventor published a scheme to haul the *Titanic* back to the surface using **electromagnets** attached by a submarine, but failed to attract investors.

Over the decades that followed, the sheer **impossibility** of raising the *Titanic* took on proverbial status. Simultaneously, the myth grew that the wreck held some great treasure in gold or jewels, doomed to lie out of reach forever. On a more prosaic level, scientists believed that the **Grand Banks Earthquake** of 1929, a major underwater tremor 250 miles south of Newfoundland, might well have buried or destroyed whatever remained of the *Titanic*. In 1953, an **expedition** actually got as far as venturing out into the North Atlantic. The Southampton-based salvage ship *Help* detonated explosives in the hope of tracing the *Titanic* through echo patterns, without success.

Expeditions and innovations

The first crucial moment in the process that culminated in the *Titanic*'s rediscovery came in **1966**. A US B-52 bomber on a practice mission crashed while refuelling in mid-air over southern Spain. Three of its cargo of live **H-bombs** fell on dry land, but the fourth ended up at the bottom of the Mediterranean. Desperate to retrieve it, the **US Navy** called in the aid of the experimental three-man submarine *Alvin*, which had recently been developed by the **Woods Hole Oceanographic Institution** (WHOI) in Massachusetts. *Alvin* duly found the bomb, 2550 feet down, after a systematic hunt. Although an initial attempt at recovery ended when the lethal cargo was dropped a further five hundred feet deeper, *Alvin* re-located it, and the bomb was brought to the surface.

Based on Cape Cod since 1930, **WHOI** was an autonomous organization whose mapping of underwater geology helped to prove that the continents had once formed part of a single land mass. Its members funded their research by hiring out their expertise and technology, most obviously to the **US Navy**. Lent a newly glamorous image as a kind of reflection of the space programme, underwater exploration was booming during the 1960s; WHOI liked to think of itself as a "wet NASA".

Alvin's proven abilities as an underwater search vehicle led to a fresh round of improvements. In 1973, the substitution of **titanium** for steel in her hull doubled her maximum operational depth from 6500 to 13,000 feet. Named on account of the metal **Project Titanus**, the programme also, purely by coincidence, made *Alvin* just strong enough to reach the *Titanic*.

In 1975, French diver **Jacques Cousteau**, whose televised exploits attracted worldwide attention, found the wreck of the ***Britannic***, the *Titanic*'s sister ship, lying four hundred feet below the surface off the coast of Greece. Originally intended to be named the *Gigantic*, the ship was launched in Belfast in 1914, and sunk by a German mine in November 1916.

Rivals enter the race

During the mid-1970s, an underwater geologist at Woods Hole, **Dr Robert Ballard**, realized that the quest for the *Titanic* was the perfect lure to attract **investors**. The sums involved were so large, however, that negotiations with potential sponsors such as Disney or the BBC repeatedly broke down. Other schemes smacked too much of profiteering; thus one company wanted to sell the *Titanic* off chunk by chunk, as paperweights. Ballard did get as far as sailing to the approximate site of the sinking in 1977, aboard the ***Alcoa Seaprobe***. Although this was a drilling ship, the plan was to use its technology not to drill but to lower a camera-equipped "pod" to the ocean floor. After a few days, however, the drill pipe snapped, and the expedition was abandoned.

The greatest rival of the Woods Hole scientists was the similar **Scripps Institute of Oceanography**, in La Jolla, California. In 1980, together with the Lamont-Doherty Geological Observatory of Columbia University, they teamed up with Texas oilman and entrepreneur **Jack Grimm**. A veteran of previous searches for Noah's Ark, the Loch Ness Monster and the Abominable Snowman, Grimm dispatched a new expedition on the geophysical research ship *H.J.W. Fay*.

Directed by **Dr Fred Spiess** from Scripps, the *Fay* surveyed roughly four hundred square miles of ocean floor. After focusing initially on the location of the *Titanic*'s **distress signal**, it then extended the search further east. There its attention came to centre on a long underwater "valley", oriented northeast to southwest, which it dubbed **Titanic Canyon**. When bad weather and malfunctioning equipment forced it to concede defeat, the team concluded that it had failed to spot the *Titanic* herself because the wreckage was obscured or shadowed by some large geologic feature. They drew up a list of fourteen possible sites for future investigation.

Grimm was so confident that a follow-up expedition would succeed that he was himself aboard the *Gyre* when it returned to the North Atlantic in 1981. Instead, they missed the *Titanic* once again, albeit this time only narrowly. The twin mistake was to concentrate overmuch on Titanic Canyon, where all fourteen of the putative hiding spots were ruled out, and to place too much faith on the *Titanic*'s distress location.

During the voyage home, the crew of the *Gyre* slowly worked their way through the colour video footage acquired by their deep-sea submersible. Amid great excitement, they came across a murky sequence that appeared to show one of the *Titanic*'s mighty **propellers**. Even though his scientists refused to make a positive identification, Grimm went ahead and informed the world's press. Hardly anyone was convinced, and two more years went by before Grimm raised funds for a brief return to the "propeller" site, which once again proved fruitless.

Ballard tries again

As the three Grimm expeditions unfolded, **Robert Ballard** had been watching from the sidelines, convinced that his moment had passed. Their ultimate failure, however, gave Ballard the opportunity to put together a new expedition. It was clear that for any future mission to succeed, he needed to be able to draw on any or all of several distinct devices. These included a **sonar scanner** that could be towed underwater to search for anomalous objects, a **magnetometer** to detect which such objects were made of metal, and a **submersible** capable of providing a visual record of specific targets.

And then of course there was the question of **where to look**. Ballard was convinced that the location transmitted in the *Titanic*'s distress calls,

The ghostly remains of the Titanic's *prow, photographed in 1995.*

as calculated by Fourth Officer **Joseph Boxhall** (see p.130), must be wrong. The most telling evidence for that conclusion was the speed with which the *Carpathia* had reached the survivors in the lifeboats. Ballard was convinced that the ship could not have travelled as far as Captain Rostron originally thought. Working on the same basis, Grimm's expeditions had assumed that Boxhall's given location was too far west, and that the *Titanic* lay within ten miles to the east. As for the **source** of the error, it most likely consisted of a combination of Boxhall overestimating the *Titanic*'s speed, failing to make accurate allowance for the complicated shifts in the ship's local time, and underestimating the effects of any currents.

Dr Ballard finally managed to secure sponsorship from the US Navy for an expedition in the summer of **1985**. The scientific pretext was to test two new pieces of equipment: *Argo*, a towed, remote-controlled deep-sea video vehicle, and its smaller companion *Jason*, which Ballard described as a "swimming robot on a long cable-leash". Once the navy had put up the money for three weeks, Ballard persuaded the French National Institute for Oceanography, **IFREMER**, to fund a separate four-week operation.

The two distinct phases of the joint American–French programme had to be squeezed into the brief window between mid-July and mid-September, the only time when weather conditions where the *Titanic* sank allow for

The starboard propeller of the Titanic, *slowly rusting away on the seabed.*

underwater search operations. In the first, American and French scientists aboard the French ship *Le Suroit* planned to use a sonar scanner to map out the entire area. In the second, the same team, now on the American *Knorr*, would send *Argo* and *Jason* to investigate whatever *Le Suroit* might find.

The sonar scanner was designed to search the ocean floor in a process similar to **mowing the lawn**. Having made a slow, straight pass over a long strip measuring around a thousand yards wide, it would turn around and return along a parallel and slightly overlapping strip, then repeat the process, ad nauseam. Actually managing to carry out such a meticulous operation on churning seas was a very different matter. Ballard likened it to **towing a kite** on a two-and-a-half-mile string. The scanner had to be weighed down to stop it trailing behind, and somehow kept an even distance from the ocean floor, not least to avoid potentially disastrous collisions. Each time the waves on the surface dropped or lifted the ship ten feet, they had the same effect on the scanner far below.

Le Suroit eventually returned to port having mapped roughly seventy percent of the target area without any luck. (It later transpired that it had come tantalizingly close to the actual site, only just missing it thanks to adverse currents.) With time now running short, Ballard decided to adopt a different approach for the second stage of the expedition, aboard the *Knorr*. Although *Argo* was perfectly capable of continuing with the sonar scanning, he would use its TV cameras to make a **visual search** instead.

THE STATE OF THE WRECK

Until the *Titanic* was found, no one knew whether the ship remained in **recognizable** condition. Despite having broken into two main segments, with further remains scattered across the seabed, the wreckage turned out to be remarkably complete, as well as still standing upright. While the stern portion had been crushed by the pressure, the bow seemed almost pristine, and the first pictures of the *Titanic*'s intact prow swiftly became iconic.

In the decades since then, the *Titanic* has **deteriorated**. Each successive expedition has tended to accuse its predecessors of **harming** the vessel in some way, whether by pulling her apart in the quest for hard-to-reach artefacts, or bashing her to pieces by landing submersibles on exposed areas. As an **archaeological site**, the wreck is ruined; no one has made a comprehensive survey of what lay where, and many items seem to have simply been picked up and squirrelled away as and when they were found.

The most serious, and unavoidable, damage to the *Titanic* is however entirely **natural**. Robert Ballard was the first to notice, and name, the **rusticles** – icicle-like tendrils of rust – that appear to dribble from the *Titanic*'s hull. These are created by **rust-eating bacteria** that thrive in the absence of oxygen, which are progressively dissolving the steel of the ship. Several species are to blame, including one first identified there, dubbed *Halomonas titanicae*.

Even at the rate of decay that has seen steel plates that originally stood one inch thick dwindle to barely a quarter of that, the *Titanic* would have perhaps thirty years to live. In fact, long before that, the hulk is likely to become too flimsy to support its own weight.

Ballard's experience with other deep-sea wrecks had shown that any sinking object **breaks up** as it falls. Each fragment is then caught by any prevailing current. While the heaviest objects drop straight down, the rest end up strewn across the ocean floor. The resultant **debris field** is much like a comet, stretching from a dense core along an ever-fainter tail. At a depth of two and a half miles, the *Titanic*'s debris field could be anticipated as being anything from half a mile to a mile long. While the sonar scanner remained the best tool for locating the *Titanic* itself, a visual search might succeed in spotting the debris field.

Success

In the early hours of **1 September 1985**, the ocean was as calm as the night that the *Titanic* went down. Viewing conditions were perfect. *Argo* had spent eight days underwater, and ruled out various potential targets, including all of Titanic Canyon and, as was thought, Grimm's supposed propeller site – although in fact Grimm had deliberately released the wrong coordinates. And then, just before 1am, the night shift monitoring live footage from *Argo* finally **spotted something**.

While clearly **man-made**, the first pieces to be seen were too small to be identified. Then a large circular object came into view. The leader of the French contingent, Jean-Louis Michel, produced a copy of the 1911 *Shipbuilder* article detailing the *Olympic* and *Titanic*. He swiftly confirmed that they were looking at a **boiler** from the *Titanic*.

Ballard was roused from his bunk, and he quickly ordered that *Argo* be raised to an altitude of a hundred feet above the sea floor – which proved to be only just enough for it to avoid slamming into the actual wreck. Although they knew they'd found the *Titanic*, the team had no idea what state it was in – whether for example the wreck was still in one major piece, or whether the funnels or rigging remained intact or erect.

It was now possible to locate the main body of the wreckage using the *Knorr*'s own basic sonar scanning system. The next morning, *Argo* was sent across the top for the first time. In six quick minutes, she established that the wreckage was upright, with the funnels missing, and offered a quick glimpse of the **Boat Deck**. Only on her third pass did the watching scientists realize that the **stern** of the *Titanic* was **missing**.

With the weather deteriorating fast, it became unsafe to deploy *Argo* any further. Ballard therefore lowered *Angus*, which was basically a heavy sled equipped with still cameras. In that pre-digital age, *Angus* simply shot thousands of random photos, which had to be developed later, back on the *Knorr*. It took several months before those images were analysed sufficiently to reveal that the *Titanic*'s stern – or rather, most of it – stood as a second enormous piece of wreckage around two thousand feet south of the bow.

Ballard immediately told Woods Hole of his discovery, so the international **media** was soon full of the news. In a strange and still unexplained twist, the London *Observer* had actually gone to press announcing the finding of the *Titanic* at the precise moment that she was actually found – in other words, before the story could possibly have been authentic.

Releasing the news

The *Knorr* returned to Woods Hole on 9 September 1985, to be greeted by news teams from all over the world. Ballard, who had given countless radio interviews during the voyage home, contented himself with a brief statement:

"The *Titanic* lies in 13000 feet of water on a gently sloping alpine-like countryside overlooking a small canyon below. Its bow faces north and the ship sits upright on the bottom. There is no light at this great depth and little life can be found. It is a quiet and peaceful and fitting place for the remains of this greatest of sea tragedies to rest. May it forever remain that way and may God bless these found souls."

Sadly, relations between WHOI and IFREMER fell apart the moment the *Knorr* reached dry land. The French members of the expedition had been assured that video footage of the wreck would be released **simultaneously** in France and the US. Instead, Woods Hole succumbed to pressure from the major American networks, and allowed them to use the material straight away. As a result, the world gained an impression the French have never been able to correct, that the *Titanic* had been re-discovered by an entirely American team.

Safeguarding the site

Robert Ballard's much-publicized view that the *Titanic* should remain **undisturbed** on the seabed, and that nothing should be removed from the site, struck a chord with many people. Several survivors spoke of the wreck as being an underwater **grave**, where the victims of the disaster should be allowed to rest in peace. Although all trace of **bodies** had disappeared long before the *Titanic* was found, matching pairs of **shoes**, side by side on the seabed, made it clear where many had lain.

As the *Titanic* sank in **international waters**, however, no individual government could enact legislation to protect it. Just ten days after the wreck was rediscovered, the **RMS Titanic Memorial Act** was introduced in the US Congress in a bid to preserve the site's integrity. Although it became law in 1986, all it actually did was to express the desire "to encourage international efforts to designate the shipwreck of *RMS Titanic* as an international maritime memorial and to provide for reasonable research, exploration, and, if appropriate, salvage activities". Attempts to enlist the support of the governments of France, Britain and Canada met with little response, and no such compact has ever been agreed.

Going back to *Titanic*

Numerous expeditions have **revisited** the *Titanic* since she was re-located, amid much the same spirit of rivalry and acrimony that characterized the race to find the wreck. All have filmed extensively at the site; chronicles of several specific trips are available on **DVD**, as reviewed in Chapter 10.

Ballard himself returned to the *Titanic* in 1986, again without collecting artefacts. The next year, however, the French scientists from IFREMER handled the operational side of an expedition that was financed by **Titanic**

Ventures Ltd. As well as raising 1800 objects from the wreck and the surrounding debris field, which were taken to France for conservation, they also managed to film the ship's name on the bow, which was to erode away within the next ten years (the footage can be seen on rmstitanic.net).

In 1991, the Canadian movie company **IMAX** chartered a Russian research ship, the *Akademik Keldysh*, along with the manned submersibles *Mir I* and *Mir II*, to explore the wreck. The voyage resulted in the giant-screen film *Titanica*, although without damaging or recovering artefacts.

The next year, a consortium spearheaded by **Jack Grimm**, Marex-Titanic, claimed that it now held the rights to the *Titanic* site, having somehow got hold of a couple of items illegally raised by the Russian expedition. After lengthy legal battles, Titanic Ventures – by now renamed **RMS Titanic, Inc** – was awarded exclusive salvage rights to the wreck by a court in Virginia in 1994. While they are entitled to put retrieved artefacts on public display, they can't sell any, and if it's possible to identify an item's original owner, it must be handed over to their rightful heirs.

To maintain its official status as "salvor in possession", RMS Titanic, Inc, is obliged to make regular returns to the ship. Their 2010 expedition marked the eighth in total. The single most impressive artefact recovered was the 22-ton **Big Piece**, an enormous chunk of the outer wall of two starboard cabins on C Deck. Measuring 13 feet by 22 feet, it was spotted in 1996 and finally reached the surface in 1998; it's currently on display in the Luxor hotel in Las Vegas.

Although only RMS Titanic, Inc, is entitled to retrieve items from the *Titanic*, further legal proceedings have established that other expeditions can film at the site. The best known visitor has been **James Cameron**, who first chartered the *Akademik Keldysh* and its two submersibles while filming *Titanic* in 1995, and has returned twice since then. It's even possible to go yourself, aboard one of those same *Mir* submersibles, with **Deep Ocean Exhibitions** (deepoceanexpeditions.com). The fare currently stands at $60,000.

Chapter 9
Questions, controversies and conspiracies

Since the moment the *Titanic* vanished into the icy Atlantic, speculation has swirled around the many **mysteries** of the disaster. This chapter sets out to explore all the great questions and conundrums, from what the iceberg actually did to the *Titanic* to why the nearby *Californian* never came to her aid. As well as exploring sensational allegations of shootings and bribery while the lifeboats were being loaded, it considers some of the most enduring **myths** and sheds light on the murkiest **conspiracy theories.**

The entire story will never be told, but taking a long hard look at a century's worth of evidence makes it possible to come a little closer to understanding what really happened, far out on the unforgiving ocean, either side of midnight on Sunday, 14 April 1912.

1. What damage did the iceberg do?

The one fact that everyone knows about the *Titanic* – that she collided with an iceberg – might seem enough to explain why she sank, but it conceals an essential paradox. Had she crashed straight into the iceberg, she would probably have survived. Instead, she struck it such a glancing blow that most of her passengers and crew didn't even notice; and yet that was enough to destroy her. So what **damage** did the iceberg actually do?

The *Titanic*'s division into sixteen **watertight compartments**, detailed on p.30, was designed to protect her from any conceivable accident. The idea was that if the hull was holed, water would not spread to flood the entire ship, but simply rise to fill a single compartment. Even if two compartments were flooded, and probably as many as four, the ship would still remain afloat. Her precise fate would depend on which specific compartments might fill, as the effect of such a great weight of water on the overall balance of the ship would vary according to where it entered the hull.

As a result, her designers thought, no collision could sink her. If the *Titanic* ran head-on into something, her foremost compartments would be crushed, but no water would reach the rest of the ship. If something else, presumably another ship, ran into her at an angle, the worst that could happen would be for the point of impact to be at a bulkhead, which might open up two adjoining compartments. The idea that a scrape, let alone a slice, might cause more severe injury doesn't appear to have been considered.

Assessing the impact

For the benefit of the British inquiry, **Edward Wilding**, a naval architect with Harland & Wolff who helped design the *Titanic*, drew up an accurate assessment of where and at what rate the water entered the ship. He was aided by testimony from Fireman Frederick Barrett, who was in Boiler Room 6 at the time of the collision, and other survivors who had observed the water levels at different times in different areas. Their evidence revealed that all the first six watertight compartments – which from the bow were the forepeak and three cargo holds, then Boiler Room 6 and Boiler Room 5 – had been pierced, while Boiler Room 4 had sustained lighter damage. Calculating that sixteen thousand tons of water had entered the ship in the first forty minutes after the collision, he concluded that the total holed area amounted to around **twelve square feet**.

Wilding described the hole as being on average three-quarters of an inch wide, and said that if it was 200 feet long that would account for the volume of water. He neither said nor thought that the *Titanic* had been sliced open along a **300-foot gash**, although that's how the story entered

A fanciful illustration from **The Sphere** *in 1912, depicting the* **Titanic** *hitting the iceberg; no one knows what the underwater portion of the berg actually looked like.*

popular consciousness. Instead, he suggested that there were several separate **puncture wounds**. One, in cargo hold 1, was thought to be a large hole through which the iceberg had penetrated more than three feet into the ship. Others were smaller tears and gashes, while the last of all, in Boiler Room 4, was not in the side of the hull, but somewhere in the double bottom, and thus caused water to rise from beneath the firemen's feet. Each wound, Wilding felt, might have been created by a different spur of ice, ending when each snapped off in turn.

There was much discussion at the inquiry as to whether the *Titanic* might have survived if her forward bulkheads had risen higher in the ship, as far as C Deck. The conclusion was no – too many compartments had been holed for that to make a difference. According to Wilding, the crucial factor was the damage to Boiler Room 4, even though that particular wound was relatively minor in itself.

How the ship sank

In every *Titanic* movie, there's a classic scene in which designer Thomas Andrews explains to Captain Smith that the ship is **doomed** because as the water rises in each watertight compartment, it will drag the bow deeper, and allow water to overflow into the next compartment. That is indeed why Andrews could be sure the *Titanic* was going to sink, but her hull was so badly torn that it's not what actually happened.

No **eyewitness accounts** suggest that the sinking was caused by water rising to the upper decks, flowing along them, and then cascading down into previously dry sections of the ship. Instead, several compartments filled at once, at differing rates; open portholes and hatches enabled the sea to spill in; and further weaknesses in the system, perhaps exacerbated as the ship listed to each side in turn, allowed water to burst through horizontally at unexpected places and times.

Most historians accept Wilding's calculation of the extent and pattern of the damage. Debate focuses instead on whether the iceberg really did puncture the hull with a series of holes, or whether instead it **rammed** it hard enough to buckle its steel plates, causing rivets to pop out and "unzipping" the seams.

Robert Ballard hoped that his discovery of the wreck in 1985 would enable him to settle the issue once and for all. In fact, the *Titanic*'s bow turned out to have ploughed too deep into the ocean-floor mud for anything forward of her second cargo hold to be visible. Further aft, Ballard saw no sign of a long gash, or of individual wounds, just places where heavy knocks to the hull had caused the plates to separate at the seams. Sonar imaging of the wreck, on the other hand, carried out by subsequent expeditions, appeared to show narrow slits in the relevant areas, but it's hard to be sure which damage resulted from the *Titanic*'s collision with the iceberg, and which from her impact against the sea bottom.

As for how a block of ice could do serious harm to solid steel, the key lies in the sheer **mass** of the iceberg. For it to be tall enough for pieces to break off and fall onto the forward well deck, it must at a conservative estimate have risen fifty feet above sea level. Given the rule of thumb that eight ninths of an iceberg's bulk lies below the surface, it would have stretched hundreds of feet down underwater. Not that its sides were vertical; instead the *Titanic* must have scraped against a massive, irregularly shaped slope of ice, banging into one protrusion after another. Some may have been jagged enough to pierce or slice the hull; at other points, the colossal pressure was simply enough to cave in the steel panels, and open the seams.

2. Was the *Titanic* made with substandard steel?

The idea that **low-quality steel** was used to make the hull of the *Titanic* gained currency thanks to tests conducted by Canadian government scientists in 1991. Examining a small "Frisbee-shaped" piece of hull that was illegally retrieved that year by the expedition that filmed the IMAX movie *Titanica*, they concluded that the steel became **brittle** as its temperature approached freezing point. This discovery was widely publicized as being a significant, or even crucial, factor in the *Titanic*'s demise. The hull might have become so weak in those icy waters that it simply shattered on impact with the iceberg.

Subsequently, however, extensive **metallurgical tests** on other samples by Jennifer Hooper McCarty and Tim Foecke, detailed in their book *What Really Sank the Titanic* (see p.239), have revealed a different story. The original Frisbee sample was not representative of the ship as a whole, while it (and some but not all of other pieces collected later) was only shown to be brittle in response to a specific form of blow that was very unlike the long grinding impact actually experienced by the *Titanic*. Although the *Titanic*'s steel contained too much sulphur and too little manganese to meet modern standards, it was entirely acceptable for 1912, and the same would have been true for any ship of the era.

McCarty and Foecke then turned their attention to the *Titanic*'s **rivets**. Two kinds of rivet were used to hold the hull together; **steel** ones wherever the hydraulic riveting machines could reach, and **iron** ones in the less accessible areas towards both the bow and the stern, where they were driven into place manually (see p.17). Testing revealed the iron rivets to be composed of exceptionally low-quality iron, which the researchers said Harland & Wolff had been forced to buy to cope with their huge demand.

McCarty and Foecke believe that wide variations between the strength of the rivets left some parts of the hull much **weaker** than others, and that when the *Titanic* hit the iceberg the weakest rivets yielded, allowing her to rip open along the most vulnerable seams. They point to the fact that the tearing started near the bow, and appears to have stopped at the point where the iron rivets ended and the steel ones began. Their argument is basically a question of degree; they acknowledge that some rivets would have burst however strong they were, and some seams would have opened, but suggest that without her abnormally weak rivets the *Titanic* might have been wounded that little bit less, enough to keep her afloat long enough for rescue to arrive.

3. Was the *Titanic* on fire?

When the *Titanic* arrived in Southampton on Thursday 4 April, the coal in bunker number 10, on the starboard side of Boiler Room 6, was **on fire**. It was still burning when the ship sailed on her maiden voyage, and only finally extinguished on Saturday 13 April, when a team of around ten firemen finished removing all the coal from the bunker. We know all this because the fire was reported to the White Star Line in Southampton, and because some of the firemen who put it out – including their leader, **Frederick Barrett** – survived to testify at the subsequent inquiries.

It would be misleading to think of the fire as a dangerous blaze; it was much more of a persistent **smoulder**. Such fires were frequently caused by spontaneous combustion, and alarmed no one. When the Board of Trade officer who inspected the *Titanic* on the morning she left Southampton was asked if he should have been told about the fire, he replied: "Hardly, it is not an uncommon thing to have these small fires in the bunkers."

The fire acquired added significance after the disaster because it had taken place very close to the spot where the *Titanic* received her most conspicuous injury from the iceberg. Barrett and his colleague Charles Hendrickson described the fire as having heated the bulkhead between boiler rooms 5 and 6 at that point enough to make it "ding", or become slightly concave. Barrett also described water as having burst through horizontally between the two boiler rooms during the disaster.

It has therefore been suggested that the bulkhead gave way as the ship filled with water because of damage from the fire, and in doing so it caused one too many watertight compartments to be flooded for the *Titanic* to remain afloat. That would make the fire the crucial factor that caused the *Titanic* to sink. However, experts – from designer Edward Wilding at the time to modern metallurgists – have argued that the fire could not have damaged the bulkhead to that extent. It is probably true that the bulkhead did collapse, but it was not due to the fire, and in any case the collision with the iceberg had caused quite enough harm to sink the ship without that making a difference.

4. Was the *Titanic* going too fast, due to pressure from J. Bruce Ismay?

The *Titanic* was clearly going too fast when she hit the iceberg. Any speed that meant she couldn't avoid an iceberg in her path was by definition too fast. As the British inquiry put it, in its one-sentence summary of the disaster, the collision was "brought about by the **excessive speed** at which the ship was being navigated".

Not only was the *Titanic's* speed excessive, but faced with the most dangerous conditions of the voyage, and armed with explicit warnings of ice ahead, she was going faster than she had ever previously travelled. Witnesses disagree on the precise figure, but it was at least 21 knots, and more likely 22 knots, which translates to just over 25 miles per hour.

After the disaster, it swiftly emerged that such speeds were standard on the North Atlantic crossing. No captain would dream of slowing down – even in the vicinity of ice at night – until his ship actually encountered an obstacle, at which point he

White Star Line chairman J. Bruce Ismay.

would take evasive action. Hence the verdict of the British inquiry on Captain Smith, that in the light of "practice and of past experience" he had not been negligent, but that anyone who failed to learn from his mistake in future would indeed be negligent.

A more damning allegation has circulated ever since that Smith was guilty of something worse than overconfidence – that the *Titanic* was driven to disaster in a bid to set a new speed record. Several of the surviving passengers, and much of the world's press, further claimed that Smith was not the real culprit. Instead, they charged that **J. Bruce Ismay**, who was both chairman of the White Star Line and president of the corporation that owned her, had pushed Smith to ignore his own better judgement.

A record-breaking run

The *Titanic* was not physically capable of capturing the legendary **Blue Riband**, awarded to the ship that made the fastest crossing of the Atlantic. The record was then held by the *Mauretania*, for a 1909 voyage at an average speed of just over 26 knots. Like her sister Cunard liners, the *Mauretania* was built for speed; the *Titanic* and *Olympic*, on which the priority was style and luxury, could never hope to match such a pace.

A different record, however, did lie within the *Titanic's* grasp – beating the time set by the *Olympic* on her own maiden voyage. The *Titanic* was officially scheduled to arrive in New York on Wednesday morning, just as the *Olympic* had done almost a year earlier. Were she to arrive on Tuesday evening instead, it would be a publicity coup for the White Star Line.

Captain Smith liked to pretend that such matters meant little to him or his employers. At the end of the *Olympic*'s maiden voyage, he had told *The New York Times* that: "there will be no attempt to bring her in on Tuesday. She was built for a Wednesday ship." In fact, on her second trip, the *Olympic* arrived in New York on a Tuesday night.

Rumours and records

J. Bruce Ismay always accompanied Captain Smith on the maiden voyages of new White Star liners. On the *Titanic*, as ever, he travelled as a first-class passenger, in one of the finest suites on the ship, although naturally he didn't pay for his ticket. In a statement after the sinking, he insisted that: "During the voyage I was a **passenger** and exercised no greater rights or privileges than any other passenger. I was not consulted by the commander about the ship, her speed, course, navigation, or her conduct at sea". Passengers who had sailed with him on previous voyages spoke up in his defence. However, in the same statement Ismay continued: "I was never on the bridge until after the accident". In other words, he obviously did feel that he had the right to intervene in a time of crisis.

However careful Ismay may have been to observe proprieties, he was no ordinary passenger. He had after all come up with the very concept of the *Titanic*, and been involved in every detail of her design, including the decision to carry twenty rather than forty-eight lifeboats. He was also well aware of the dangers of ice at sea, having himself chaired the 1898 conference in London that established shipping routes across the North Atlantic to minimize the risk of encountering ice.

That said, Smith had been captaining White Star liners for over twenty years, and the *Titanic* was his seventeenth command. He knew what was expected of him, and the occasional reminder from Ismay that he'd like the *Titanic* to have a triumphant maiden voyage would surely not have influenced him to go against his own instincts as a seaman.

Ismay made himself a conspicuous figure among the first-class passengers, and relished appearing to be at the centre of things. Passenger Elisabeth Lines recalled overhearing a conversation between Ismay and Captain Smith in the First Class Reception Room at lunchtime on Saturday, in which Ismay repeatedly stated: "We will beat the *Olympic* and get in to New York on Tuesday".

On the morning of the disaster, the *Titanic* seemed certain to make a record-breaking trip. **Lawrence Beesley** described his fellow passengers as having followed the ship's progress day by day, and been confident that she would arrive on Tuesday. **Colonel Gracie** said that the captain himself had "prophesied that, with continued fair weather, we should make an early arrival record". The most telling argument of all comes from the actual distances already covered, which prove that at the time of the collision, the *Titanic* was on target to surpass the *Olympic*'s crossing time, and reach New York on Tuesday.

As Sunday wore on, however, the lust for speed took on a more sinister aspect, when the *Titanic*'s wireless room received an avalanche of warnings of **ice ahead**. The most notorious evidence of Ismay's possible role in the disaster centres on the message received from the *Baltic* at 1.42pm. For some unknown reason, after reading it, Captain Smith passed the Marconigram – the actual piece of paper – on to Ismay when he happened to meet him on A Deck. Ismay kept it in his pocket for several hours, until the captain, who presumably had retained the basic information in his head if nowhere else, asked for it back at 7.15pm.

Ismay meanwhile showed the message, which described "icebergs and large quantities of field ice", to several passengers. Excited rumours of icebergs ahead began to circulate. One passenger, Mahala Douglas, later recalled a shipboard associate, **Emily Ryerson**, saying that late on Sunday afternoon: "I went to Mr Ismay and said: 'Oh, Mr Ismay, I have heard that the wireless has reported a large number of icebergs in the path of our ship. Are you not going to order her to slow down?" He replied to me: 'On the contrary, Mrs Ryerson, we are going to go along faster than we have been going'. And we did go faster."

That the story is hearsay doesn't necessarily mean that it's untrue, but it's telling that when Senator Smith of the US inquiry – no friend of Ismay – interviewed Mrs Ryerson, she called it an "exaggeration", and refused to swear to it. By that time, nonetheless, it was in the public domain, where it has remained in some form ever since.

Captain Smith's only known action in response to the ice warnings came at around 5pm that evening. The *Titanic* was following what was known as the "southern route", which consisted of a long southwesterly arc from southern Ireland to a spot known as **The Corner**, at 42°N 47°W. At that point ships would normally adjust their course and head more directly westwards to New York. According to her surviving officers, the *Titanic* reached the Corner at 5pm, but continued to follow the same arc for another three quarters of an hour before turning west. It's thought that Smith delayed the turn in the hope of taking his ship south of the ice field. Neither then nor later, however, did he slow down her engines; the *Titanic* continued to speed toward her fate.

Heroes and villains

The crucial reason why Ismay has so often been made out to be a **villain** of the *Titanic* disaster, and Smith a **hero**, is surely the fact that Ismay survived and Smith did not. If Smith was at fault, he paid the penalty, and he did so nobly. Ismay, on the other hand, escaped the consequences of his actions, and escaped them in a highly unedifying manner into the bargain.

The abiding image of J. Bruce Ismay is depicted in James Cameron's *Titanic* movie: having generally got in everyone's way as the ship was sinking, this nasty, shifty-looking character sneaks into a lifeboat at the last minute, to the silent contempt he'll endure for the rest of his life. Whatever the literal truth may have been, Ismay's presence on the *Carpathia* the next day was hugely resented by his fellow survivors, and their anger was widely reflected in the press coverage once they reached land. In the US, he was lampooned as **J. Brute Ismay**. The stance of the *New York American* was typical: "Mr Ismay cares for nobody, but himself... He crawls through unspeakable disgrace to his own safety". Ismay received a more sympathetic welcome back home in Britain. The British inquiry accepted Ismay's story that he'd simply jumped into Boat C as it was being lowered with no one else around, and stated in its report that: "Had he not jumped in he would merely have added one more life, namely, his own, to the number of those lost".

> "... for capitalism and for our existing social system his [Ismay's] escape – with five and fifty third-class children waiting below to drown – was the abandonment of every noble pretension."
>
> H.G. Wells, writing in the *Daily Mail* (1912)

Even if Ismay played no part in the actual sinking, as the man responsible for the *Titanic*'s shortage of lifeboats he bore a definite burden of **guilt**. Officer Lightoller told the US inquiry that aboard the *Carpathia*, Ismay "was obsessed with the idea, and kept repeating, that he ought to have gone down with the ship". That self-reproach seems to have stayed with him for the remaining 25 years of his life. He did not quite withdraw from the world, as is often suggested, and he continued a career in business after retiring from the White Star Line and IMM, but he never again sought the public eye.

5. Did Quartermaster Hichens turn the wheel the wrong way?

It has often been speculated that the *Titanic* failed to avoid the iceberg because of some **navigational mistake** on the bridge. The latest author to advance such a theory, **Louise Patten**, has remarkable credentials – she's the granddaughter

TILLER ORDERS AND RUDDER ORDERS

A great deal of confusion surrounds the order given by First Officer Murdoch when the iceberg was spotted. Why did he order **"Hard a-starboard"**, when he wanted the *Titanic* to turn to **port**?

As you might expect, to turn the ship to port, the helmsman turned the wheel to port. That in turn moved the **rudder** to port. The order "Hard a-starboard" dated back to the era of sailing ships, when to move the rudder to port you had to put the **tiller** – a long lever, attached to the rudder and pivoting around a post – to **starboard**. Such **Tiller Orders** remained standard even on those sailing ships that used steering wheels to control the tiller.

As steam took over from sail, from the late nineteenth century onwards, the use of Tiller Orders was progressively supplanted by **Rudder Orders**, which referred to the movement of the rudder and the ship itself. Under Rudder Orders, anyone ordered "Hard a-starboard" would turn the wheel to starboard, and the ship would turn to starboard. The changeover was only completed in Britain and America during the 1930s.

Note that under both sets of orders, it was always the case that turning the wheel to port would turn the ship to port; it was simply the order used to describe the action that changed.

of the *Titanic*'s senior surviving officer, Second Officer **Charles Lightoller**. She claims that her grandfather told his wife, Sylvia Lightoller, the true story of the disaster, and that after his death in 1952, her grandmother in turn passed the family secret on to her.

According to Patten, Quartermaster **Robert Hichens**, who was at the wheel of the *Titanic* when the iceberg was spotted, responded to First Officer **William Murdoch**'s order of **"Hard a-starboard"**, by turning the wheel to starboard, when he should have turned it to port. Hichens was crossing the North Atlantic for the first time. In his panic, he momentarily forgot that the *Titanic* was using **Tiller Orders**, which required him to turn the wheel to port (see box above). His previous experience, on the India run and in the Baltic, had been with Rudder Orders, under which turning the wheel to starboard would have been correct.

In Patten's version of the night's events, Officer Murdoch was the first to spot the iceberg, from the bridge. It was then 11.36pm, and the iceberg was just under two miles away. He gave Hichens the order "Hard a-starboard", and Hichens turned the ship the wrong way. It's worth remembering that the wheelhouse was entirely enclosed, and Hichens could not see out; he could not have turned the wheel "instinctively" to avoid the iceberg. Murdoch immediately noticed his error, and corrected it. At that point, Lookout Fleet

The stanchion that held the wheel of the Titanic, *still standing proud underwater.*

sighted the iceberg straight ahead, but it was now too close to avoid, and the collision happened exactly as it's usually described.

After the collision, Patten continues, Murdoch ordered the engines to stop. Ten minutes later, however, **J. Bruce Ismay** arrived on the bridge. Despite being told by Captain Smith that the *Titanic* was seriously damaged, Ismay, in his eagerness to complete the voyage on schedule, insisted that the engines were restarted. The ship was ordered "slow ahead" for ten minutes, then stopped, and then ordered "slow astern" for five minutes. This motion supposedly worsened the damage to the *Titanic*'s hull, by forcing water in at high pressure. Only after a final shut-down was the order given to prepare the lifeboats.

Officer Lightoller supposedly learned these details when the *Titanic*'s surviving officers gathered after the collision. None of his senior colleagues – Murdoch, Captain Smith, and Chief Officer Wilde – survived. During the subsequent investigations, the truth was hushed up so the White Star Line could claim on their insurance. That would not have been possible if White Star had been found guilty of negligence.

Guilty secret or old wives' tale?

Patten's description of the many conversations that she, as an ill teenager, had with her grandmother on the subject of the *Titanic* gives her story a certain plausibility. The theory also helps to explain several **anomalies** in the known facts about the sinking, and focuses rather neatly on its most enigmatic **characters**.

Officer Lightoller's references in his autobiography to how necessary it was at the British inquiry "to keep one's hand on the **whitewash brush**", and that he'd had to deal with "sharp questions that needed clever answers", leave a strong impression that he knew secrets that he'd managed to conceal. J. Bruce Ismay was very clearly burdened with **guilt** after the disaster; Captain Rostron, for example, described him as being "mentally very ill" when he was aboard the *Carpathia*.

Guilt might also explain Officer Murdoch's rumoured suicide, though whether he killed himself remains pure speculation (see p.197). And as for Hichens himself, his subsequent behaviour on Boat 6 was so appalling (see p.125) that it suggests he was seriously traumatized. He remained troubled for the rest of his life, and served five years in jail for attempted murder during the 1930s.

On the other hand, it does seem unlikely that Hichens would make such a basic mistake, especially since with that much warning there was no reason to panic anyway. In some ways the more intriguing aspect of Lightoller's "secret" is the charge that it was Ismay who demanded that the *Titanic* resume its forward progress. Several witnesses spoke of the ship moving after the collision, but the issue was not adequately explored at the inquiries. Even on that score, however, modern experts say that it would probably not have further damaged the hull.

As an interesting footnote, when **Walter Lord** was writing *A Night to Remember* in 1955, Sylvia Lightoller became aware of the project, and wrote to him that "Naturally my husband discussed the disaster freely with me so I know all the details". Rather amazingly, Lord replied that, "Lightoller's record was so brilliant and his testimony so clear and vivid that I think I have everything I need." It sounds very much as though Officer Lightoller's widow was prepared to reveal the secret at that point. Had Lord accepted her offer, the story might now be regarded as the definitive explanation of the tragedy, instead of just the latest alternative theory. (For a review of *Good as Gold*, the novel in which Louise Patten sets out her story, see p.242.)

6. Were the third-class passengers impeded from reaching the lifeboats?

One of the great mysteries about the sinking of the *Titanic* is that although more than two thousand people were on board, and the ship took well over two hours to sink, witnesses described the Boat Deck as being **empty** when certain lifeboats were being loaded. At several specific moments, the crew called for women and children to step forward, but there were none to be seen, and the boats departed half full.

So where was everybody? And most specifically, given the huge discrepancies in the survival rates for different classes of passengers, where were the **third-class passengers**? Controversy has raged ever since over the suspicion that they were in some way prevented from reaching the lifeboats.

There's no arguing with the statistics. Of the female first-class passengers, 97 percent survived, as opposed to 46 percent of the women in third class. All except one of the children travelling first and second class survived, compared to only 32 of the 89 children in third class. And only 16 percent of third-class male passengers survived, which was just under half the rate for men in first class.

As the report of the UK inquiry put it, stories circulated after the tragedy "that the third-class passengers had been unfairly treated; that their access to the Boat Deck had been **impeded**, and that when at last they reached that deck the first- and second-class passengers were given precedence in getting places in the boats." The inquiry itself delivered a no-nonsense verdict – "There appears to have been **no truth** in these suggestions". However, only when the question is phrased in its most extreme form – "Was a systematic, ship-wide policy enforced to keep all third-class passengers below decks in order to give other passengers priority in boarding the lifeboats?" – is it possible to answer it with a definite "no". Qualify that assertion in any way, and the doubts immediately creep in.

Gates and barriers

To avoid the potential spread of disease, the owners of the *Titanic* were legally obliged, throughout the voyage, to deny the third-class or **steerage** passengers access to the upper decks. In some parts of the ship, **locked gates** were used to achieve that goal; elsewhere, a sailor would be stationed at a moveable barrier. All that it would have taken to "impede" the third-class passengers was for the normal restrictions to remain in place.

Most obviously, restrictions clearly were placed on the male third-class passengers. On the upper decks, when the call went out for "**women and children first**", the "gentlemen" were free to escort their wives and families up to the Boat Deck, and then stand nobly aside. From the third-class areas, however, only the women and children were initially allowed to leave. Their menfolk, driven out of their cabins by rising water, and ignorant of the situation on the higher decks, were forced to remain below. Similarly, while the crew throughout the *Titanic* set out to avoid panic by downplaying the danger, in steerage that had the additional effect of encouraging women to stay with their husbands.

Sifting through the many contradictory accounts, it's impossible to establish exactly which gates and stairways were locked at the time of the collision, and which may have been subsequently locked or unlocked. Neither is anyone entirely sure what the gates actually looked like. Movies tend to depict them as floor-to-ceiling lattices, but they may have been simply waist-high gates which usually made effective deterrents, but in an emergency could be easily climbed.

The situation was further complicated by the closing of some but not all of the **watertight doors** that were supposed to make the ship unsinkable. Bear in mind that only the doors down in the engine rooms were electrically operated. Those in the passenger areas, usually kept open to allow ease of movement, had to be closed by hand in the event of an emergency.

Even if all the doors and barriers were open, the ship itself was designed to make it hard for steerage passengers to reach the upper decks. During the voyage, the third-class passengers would have learned how to get around the warren of passageways down below, but acquired little sense of what lay above.

Steward Hart's story

The most detailed testimony as to what happened below decks was given by Third-Class Steward **John Hart**. Awakened in the communal quarters he shared on F Deck, he was instructed by the head steward to: "Get your people roused up and get lifebelts placed upon them". Responsible for a cluster of cabins close to the stern on E Deck, he woke his passengers, and put life belts on those willing to wear them. He was told to reassure them that the damage was not serious; asked why at the inquiry, he replied, "to keep them quiet; it is quite obvious."

After a short wait, his next order came through at about 12.20am: "Pass your women up on the Boat Deck". He led a group of around thirty women and children up the main third-class staircase to the **aft well deck**, then along most of C Deck – passing various barriers which he said would normally have been closed but were not at that time – all the way to the Grand Staircase. From there, they climbed three more decks, up to the Boat Deck. Most of his party then boarded **Boat 8**, though several immediately bolted back indoors again, to get out of the cold.

Hart then went back down to get another group of twenty-five. This time, he told the British inquiry, "I had some little trouble in getting back owing to the males wanting to get to the Boat Deck". Quite what that trouble was, or how those men were thwarted in their desire, he didn't specify. His second batch did get through, however. This time, he put them on **Boat 15**, and also climbed in himself, on the orders of Officer Murdoch. Hart also testified that all his fellow third-class stewards were doing the same thing, while yet more stewards were lining the route to show everyone the way.

Prayer and pandemonium

At the time of the collision, most passengers were in their cabins. In steerage, that meant they were close to either end of the ship, with the single men near the bow and the couples and families at the stern. The obvious immediate reaction was to head outside to see what was happening. Steerage passengers thus gravitated to the open deck areas with which they were already familiar – the forward well deck on **D Deck**, and the aft well deck on **C Deck**. All would have originally boarded the ship via one or other of those decks, and returned to it for recreation during the voyage. Few if any, however, would have climbed any higher in the main superstructure, or been aware of possible routes. Instead, many of those on C Deck retreated into the warmth of the adjoining general and smoking rooms. Witnesses later spoke of communal singing and prayer.

The single men at the bow, especially on **G Deck** where water was soon sloshing underfoot, were the swiftest to realize that something was seriously wrong. When the call for the women and children went out, however, they seem to have been ignored. The stewards knew the women were at the stern, so that's where they established a human chain to gather them together and guide them up.

Not only was the forward well deck several feet lower than its counterpart at the stern, but all this while, the *Titanic* was going down by the head. As the sinking progressed, the men became increasingly desperate. Some of the few who did escape described climbing a ladder towards the higher decks, whereupon a sailor appeared and locked a gate at the top that had previously been unlocked. The men broke through anyway.

As described on p.28, the only practicable lower-deck route between the forward and aft portions of the ship was **Scotland Road**, the long narrow corridor on **E Deck**. Soon after the collision, it became filled with crowds of third-class passengers, struggling with their heavy baggage. As emigrants, they were travelling with all their worldly possessions, and were loath to leave anything behind. As the waters rose and time ran out, however, they abandoned their belongings where they stood. The corridors started to fill with floating detritus, making movement yet more difficult.

This was the most obvious route for anyone seeking to escape from the bow to follow. At around 1am, a sudden influx of sodden and bedraggled men came streaming aft on E Deck, and joined the family groups waiting at the bottom of the aft staircase. Desperation turned to something uglier.

According to Steward Hart, there was actually a quicker route to the upper decks; he noticed that an emergency door on Scotland Road was open, which led onto a smaller staircase. Hart saw no one using it, but third-class passenger **Berk Pickard** testified at the US inquiry that he passed through it, and continued straight up to the Boat Deck where he boarded a lifeboat.

It's sobering to think what the third-class passengers on the aft well deck could see. They would have watched the rockets go off, and some at least of the lifeboats being lowered, though not near enough at hand for any of them to actually jump in. They would also have seen the lifeboats in the water, and realized that those boats would soon be at the same level as the deck. They would have seen the "Mystery Ship" on the horizon. They could not on the other hand see how few lifeboats were left to be launched.

The only hope of escape lay in reaching the **Boat Deck**. A 26-year-old Norwegian fisherman, **Olaus Abelseth**, told the US inquiry that the gate leading from the aft well deck into the *Titanic*'s superstructure was closed: "I do not know whether it was locked, but it was shut so that they could not go that way". He therefore joined a stream of men who were climbing the **cargo cranes**, and inching along their long horizontal arms to drop on the far side of the railings of B Deck.

While it's not clear from Abelseth's testimony whether the barrier was physical or human, it seems unarguable that at the very least, at certain times and in certain places, some passengers were forcibly restrained to the lower decks. **Paul Maugé**, the secretary in the à la carte restaurant, gave a more explicit account of how the ship's stewards refused to allow his fellow restaurant workers to leave their accommodation on E Deck. Only he and the chef, who were in civilian clothes, were permitted to pass; the remaining sixty were kept down, and died.

Eventually, anyone on the lower decks who was not actually locked in or trapped simply had to leave, as the *Titanic* became flooded with icy seawater. At that point, verbal constraints, ropes stretched across gangways, even locked gates must have lost their power. Of the various witnesses who described the moment when the steerage passengers finally did break free, several characterized them as an **angry mob**. Colonel Archibald Gracie was more restrained: "there arose before us from the decks below, a mass of humanity several lines deep, covering the Boat Deck, facing us, and completely blocking our passage towards the stern".

Walter Lord, in *A Night to Remember*, concluded that there was no overall policy to hold back third-class passengers. Considering that there's little evidence of consistent policies about anything whatsoever on that chaotic night, it seems reasonable to agree. That's a very different thing, however, to saying that such restraint didn't happen at all. Moreover, the fact remains that there was a direct correlation between each individual's **location** on the ship, and his or her chances of survival. The third-class passengers, along with the engineers, firemen and stokers, were the most likely to die. Given that their location on the ship also intimately reflected their social status and personal wealth, that hardly seems a coincidence.

7. Did the band play on?

One of the few facts that everybody "knows" about the *Titanic* is that the **band** went down with the ship, playing "**Nearer My God to Thee**" even as she sank beneath the waves. The story holds a substantial kernel of truth, mixed in with a great deal of myth.

To put it briefly, although the *Titanic* didn't have a "band" as such, an ad hoc group of musicians did indeed play on the deck as the lifeboats were loading. None survived, but it's not known what exactly they played when, or at what point they finally stopped.

The great problem, of course, is there were so few witnesses to the *Titanic*'s final moments. Most of the survivors escaped on lifeboats well before the actual sinking. For many of them, seeing and hearing the musicians provided their last abiding memory of the ship. However, they were in no position to know what happened later on.

The musicians

A total of eight **musicians** were hired to play aboard the *Titanic*. They performed in two separate combinations, both devoted almost entirely to the amusement of the first-class passengers in the public spaces on A Deck. The man later eulogized as the *Titanic*'s **bandleader**, violinist **Wallace Hartley** from Lancashire, in fact led a **quintet**, made up of two violins, one cello, one double bass and a piano, which usually played in the First Class Lounge. A distinct **trio** of violin, cello and piano, which included a Frenchman and a Belgian, was based in the Reception Room adjacent to the à la carte restaurant.

Much like the wireless operators, the musicians on the great transatlantic liners formed a small coterie of inveterate voyagers with little allegiance to any one ship. Until early 1912, they had at least signed on as members of the crew for each specific voyage. Now, however, agents in Liverpool, C.W. and F.N. Black, had negotiated deals to provide all the steamship lines with musicians. Individual performers had thus been forced to accept pay decreases, from the previously typical £7 per month down to just £4 per month.

Being a musician was a young man's game. At thirty-three, Hartley was the oldest of the eight; the youngest, French cellist Roger Bricoux, was just twenty. Though officially travelling as second-class passengers, they all shared quarters down on E Deck, with their instruments in an adjoining room. With the possible exception of the final hours, the two groups never performed together.

The final concert

It seems likely that not all eight musicians were in the group that assembled in their uniforms in the First Class Lounge, half an hour after the collision with the iceberg. Not long afterwards, now wearing life belts, they moved up to the

The story that the band played "Nearer My God to Thee" as the ship went down is perpetuated by this Titanic *memorial postcard.*

top of the Grand Staircase on the **Boat Deck** – where, as in the lounge, they would have had use of a piano. Once the lowering of the lifeboats began, they moved out on deck, taking up a position outside the gymnasium.

What role, if any, was played by the two pianists once the band was outside is not known. Similarly, there's been much pedantic speculation among *Titanic* historians as to how anyone could perform on either a cello or a double bass on the sloping deck of a sinking ship. That said, Lawrence Beesley specifically described seeing a cellist "run down the now deserted starboard deck, his cello trailing behind him, the spike dragging along the floor". This may well have been the French-speaking Roger Bricoux, described by second-class passenger Bertha Lehmann as having helped her into her lifejacket. The fact that he had his valuable instrument with him, of course, doesn't prove that he'd been actually playing it.

According to French survivor Pierre Maréchal, the band had been **ordered** to start playing, as part of the general attempt to prevent panic. A musician who had played with Hartley aboard the *Celtic* later recalled that "he often said music was a bigger weapon for stopping disorder than anything on earth", and stopping disorder was clearly the aim. Some have argued, however, that the music lulled passengers into a false sense of security, by contributing to the dreamlike unreality of the proceedings, and held them back from boarding the half-filled lifeboats. **Colonel Archibald Gracie**, on the other hand, who incorporated the experiences of many fellow survivors into his book about the disaster, was in no doubt: "the band began to play, and continued while the boats were being lowered. We considered this a wise provision tending to allay excitement."

As for what **music** they were actually playing, Gracie added, "I did not recognize any of the tunes, but I know they were cheerful and were not hymns." Other witnesses described a mixture of popular styles – ragtime, jazz and waltzes – that included the biggest hit of 1911, Irving Berlin's "Alexander's Ragtime Band". Second Officer Charles Lightoller, supervising the loading of the lifeboats, later wrote: "I could hear the band playing cheery sort of music. I don't like jazz music as a rule, but I was glad to hear it that night. I think it helped us all." The legend that the band played "**Nearer My God to Thee**" as the ship went down is based on very flimsy evidence – a single newspaper interview with Vera Dick. Although she left on Boat 3 at 1am, she claimed to have heard the tune wafting across the waters at the crucial moment – a time of course when the *Titanic* was breaking apart, and the air would have been filled with screams. There's an additional problem with the "Nearer My God" legend, in that the hymn at the time was sung to two different settings in Britain, and a third in the

> "If, as has been reported, 'Nearer My God to Thee' was one of the selections, I would assuredly have noticed it and regarded it as a tactless warning of immediate death to us all ... all whom I have questioned or corresponded with ... testified emphatically to the contrary."
>
> Colonel Archibald Gracie, *The Truth About the Titanic* (1913)

US, so British and American passengers would not have recognized it from the music alone.

One alternative explanation is that even if the band weren't playing, those assembled on deck may have been **singing** hymns. As Steward Alfred Pugh, safely ensconced in a lifeboat at the time, wrote to Walter Lord over forty years later, "I had not heard the Band Playing, but in the distance I could hear people singing 'For Those In Peril On The Sea'".

Gracie was among the few survivors who remained on the *Titanic* until the very end. He said that the band **stopped** playing around the time the last lifeboat departed, half an hour before the ship actually sank. First-class passenger Algernon Barkworth, who scrambled aboard collapsible boat B as the ship went down, told much the same story "when I first came on deck the band were playing a waltz. The next time I passed where the band had been stationed, the members had thrown down their instruments, and were not to be seen."

Wireless operator **Harold Bride**, on the other hand, who emerged from the Marconi room just as the *Titanic* was about to go down, recalled: "From aft came the tunes of the band. It was a rag-time tune. Then there was 'Autumn'". For many years, Bride was assumed to be referring to an obscure hymn, but sterling research by musicologists has shown it to be much more likely that it was a then-popular **waltz**, "Songe d'Automne". As for the conflict in the timing, he was presumably remembering what he'd heard on a previous venture out from the wireless cabin, half an hour earlier.

8. Were shots fired as the *Titanic* went down?

By the time the *Titanic* survivors reached New York, three days after the disaster, speculation was rife as to whether **gunfire** had been necessary to keep order on the sinking ship. Lurid stories were already circulating that desperate passengers, attempting to storm their way onto the lifeboats, had been gunned down, and that a senior officer, possibly even Captain Smith, had shot himself in the head as the ship went down.

Such tales stood in stark contrast, of course, to the notion that the *Titanic's* final moments had been characterized by heroism and bravery, and that her male passengers in particular had accepted their fate with quiet dignity. So do they remain unproven and under-examined because the truth might be uncomfortable – or simply because they weren't true?

The most basic facts are easy to establish: yes, the *Titanic* carried revolvers for the use of the crew, and yes, they were distributed to her officers by Chief Officer Wilde shortly after the collision. And yes, at least one of those revolvers was fired. Asked at the US inquiry, "Did you hear

Second Officer Charles Lightoller (left) arrives in Liverpool, 11 May, 1912.

any pistol shots?," **Fifth Officer Harold Lowe** replied, "I heard them, and **I fired them**".

Beyond that, however, the waters are murkier. Different witnesses appear to speak of shots being fired at three or more locations, with varying consequences. Lowe himself claimed to have fired three times as **Boat 14** was being lowered on the port side, fearful that what he described as "Latin people … glaring, more or less like wild beasts" might attempt to leap onto the already overloaded lifeboat and cause its ropes to snap. Lowe was adamant that he hadn't hit anyone: each shot was aimed not at a person, but fired parallel to the side of the *Titanic*, in the gap between lifeboat and ship, and intended solely as a warning. That said, any such "warning" could only be of his preparedness to shoot to kill, and one witness recalled his shouting: "If any man jumps into the boat I will shoot him like a dog".

Very similar stories are told of **Second Officer Lightoller**, this time about the loading of **Boat 4**. Some say he too fired between the lifeboat and the

Titanic, or up into the air. In Lightoller's own memoirs, he simply refers to "vigorously flourishing my revolver", and claims it wasn't loaded.

First Officer Murdoch, however, is at the centre of the bloodiest allegations. As he failed to survive the sinking, he could not be questioned at the inquiries, and the issue was never officially investigated. Three separate witnesses spoke of him shooting either one or two men, possibly stewards, either as they attempted to climb into **Boat C**, or as they were already in the boat and refused to leave. In the latter version, the bodies were simply tipped into the sea. The incident appears, slightly distorted, in James Cameron's *Titanic*, with Jack's best friend Tommy Ryan as one victim, while a recent book by Leila Salloum Elias, who collected testimony from the Syrian survivors, was able to name specific men claimed by their relatives to have been shot by an officer.

As well as the relatively clear-cut issue of men being shot for attempting to usurp seats in the lifeboats, other less specific stories describe shots being fired amid a general **panic**, especially when there was a sudden rush of third-class passengers onto the upper decks. Journalist Logan Marshall's generally discredited 1912 book, *The Sinking of the Titanic*, described "half a dozen healthy, husky immigrants … Shouting curses" who were shot down as they stormed the first lifeboat. Even more shockingly, the book spoke of Captain Smith dispatching armed men to the boiler rooms to ensure that the stokers and engineers stayed at their posts; by the time it was published, however, it was already an accepted part of *Titanic* lore that the crew below deck had been every bit as heroic as the officers above.

Suggestions of suicide

The most controversial question concerning shootings on the *Titanic* is whether an officer committed **suicide**. While conflicting stories surround the death of **Captain Smith**, as described on p.112, they consistently draw a fine distinction between the heroic act of a captain going down with his ship, and an actual suicide. By that token, swimming away from rescue into the icy Atlantic counts as self-sacrifice rather than suicide.

Instead the charge is most frequently levelled at **First Officer Murdoch**. The most detailed story appears in a letter written four days later by survivor **George Rheims** to his wife, whose account of the shootings described above continues: "Since there was nothing left to do, the officer told us, 'Gentlemen, each man for himself, goodbye.' He gave us a military salute and shot himself. That was a man!" At least two more witnesses claimed to have seen the incident, and others to have heard the shots and/or seen Murdoch's body. Surviving officers on the other hand, especially Lightoller, refused to countenance the idea.

This same story has also at times been attached to **Chief Officer Wilde**. Both are known to have been in the same area during the ship's last moments, and confusion appears to have been rife among the passengers between the first officer and the chief officer, what with their similar titles and the fact that Murdoch had briefly been the *Titanic*'s chief officer.

The exact **motive** for any such suicide remains a puzzle, however. The officers may have been in the best position to judge that they were certain to die, and to have had the clearest sense of the form their deaths would take. Even if passenger Rheims appeared to approve wholeheartedly of Murdoch's supposed act, however, the *Titanic* had not yet sunk at the moment in question, so his duties were arguably not yet over, and in any case four of his fellow officers did somehow manage to survive.

It has been suggested that because Murdoch was in charge in the hours before the collision, and according to some rumours he had failed to slow down even after previous encounters with icebergs, he saw himself as primarily responsible for the disaster, and took his life in despair. His descendants protested angrily after James Cameron's *Titanic* showed him not only shooting himself but also accepting a bribe to allow a first-class passenger onto a lifeboat.

Although the truth will never be known, the consensus among historians is that an officer may well have committed suicide; we just can't be sure it was Murdoch.

9. Was the *Titanic* really called unsinkable?

Whether or not the *Titanic* was **unsinkable** was settled on 15 April 1912. Two further issues have been debated to this day, however. Did her makers **claim** that she was unsinkable? And did the world at large – and above all, her passengers – **believe** her to be unsinkable?

For *Titanic* researchers, discovering a newspaper or magazine article from before the disaster that called the ship "unsinkable" would be akin to finding the Holy Grail. Despite a century of searching, however, only the faintest of pre-tragedy references to her supposed unsinkability have been discovered.

The prime evidence comes from a White Star Line **brochure** from 1911, covering both the *Olympic* and the *Titanic*. Describing the system of watertight compartments, it explained how in the event of an accident the captain could close the watertight doors, thereby "practically making the vessel unsinkable".

A special issue of *The Shipbuilder* later that year, again devoted to both ships, repeated the text from that brochure almost word for word. Here the crucial phrase became "**practically unsinkable**", though far from singling out the *Titanic*, the author referred to the system as "usual in White Star Lines".

The Shipbuilder being a specialist trade publication, it's unlikely that the general public would have been aware of the claim, and it wasn't picked up by the mainstream press.

Out of the great mass of promotional material issued by the White Star Line, only one other item makes a comparable claim. A little-known 1910 leaflet rather modestly asserted that, "as far as it is possible to do so, these two wonderful vessels" – the *Olympic* and the *Titanic* – "are designed to be unsinkable".

On the very day the *Titanic* sank, on the other hand, the word "unsinkable" seemed to rise to the surface. The man largely responsible was **Philip Franklin**, vice president of the White Star Line. When the first rumours reached New York on the morning of Monday 15 April, he responded: "We place absolute confidence in the *Titanic*. We believe that the boat is unsinkable". After the news was confirmed, later the same day, he told *The New York Times*: "I thought her unsinkable, and I based [my] opinion on the best expert advice. I do not understand it."

The arrogance of imagining any ship to be unsinkable tied in perfectly with the notion of the *Titanic* being destroyed by hubris. Early reports of the disaster were liberally peppered with the word "unsinkable". Journalists seeking facts and figures may well have drawn on the account in *The Shipbuilder*, and come across it there as well.

Survivors of the sinking swiftly started to use the term. Less than a month later, **J. Bruce Ismay** testified at the British inquiry that: "I think the position was taken up that the ship was looked upon as practically unsinkable; she was looked upon as being a lifeboat in herself". Archibald Gracie, who was on the deck of the *Titanic* as its fate became horribly apparent, described the male passengers as seeking to "reassure the ladies" by repeating "the much advertised fiction of 'the unsinkable ship'".

Richard Howells devoted a fascinating chapter of his 1999 book *The Myth of the Titanic* to examining the issue in great detail. He concluded that the idea that she was considered unsinkable was "an essentially retrospective invention". His most powerful argument took the form of a "control experiment". The *Olympic* was all but identical to the *Titanic*, built in the same shipyard at the same time and to the same safety standards, and sailed on her maiden voyage less than a year earlier, on the same route and even with the same captain. At no time however was she hailed as being unsinkable; only the *Titanic* became known as the "unsinkable ship", precisely because she did in fact sink.

No one would dispute that the *Titanic*'s passengers, and for that matter her captain and crew, thought they were aboard an exceptionally safe ship. Few appreciated that, as described on p.30, she was in fact considerably less safe than such predecessors as the *Great Eastern*. While that overconfidence may not have caused the collision itself – racing at breakneck speeds towards dangerous ice fields was pretty much standard practice at the time – it did ultimately cost lives, because it was surely the main reason why so few passengers came forward to board the earliest lifeboats. Only once the *Titanic* sank, perhaps, did people realize quite how invulnerable they had imagined themselves to be, a blind faith best articulated by the term "unsinkable".

10. Did the Duff Gordons bribe their way to safety?

In the aftermath of the disaster, the story of **Boat 1**, which became known as the **Money Boat**, was engulfed in suspicion, speculation and innuendo. Lurid gossip suggested that even though the lifeboat was almost empty, **Sir Cosmo Duff Gordon** had **bribed** its crewmen to row away from the sinking *Titanic*, rather than return to pick up survivors. He might even have bribed his way off the ship in the first place.

Sir Cosmo and his wife Lucy – the celebrated fashion designer **Lucile** – denied all such allegations. The British inquiry, which investigated them in detail, absolved the couple of bribery without quite wiping the slate clean. Sir Cosmo's character remained besmirched for the rest of his life.

The Money Boat

As described on p.94, **Boat 1** held just twelve people when it was lowered from the *Titanic*. While all those on board agreed on the general circumstances of its **launch**, their stories varied in crucial respects. Officer Murdoch did not survive the sinking, and thus could not explain why he'd ordered the boat to be lowered less than half full. **Lookout George Symons**, however, was clearly mystified: "I could not tell why he gave the order. I could not criticise an Officer. He gave the order to lower away, and I had to obey orders."

As for how the **Duff Gordons** came to be aboard, Lady Duff Gordon described an implausibly civilized exchange with Murdoch: "my husband went forward and said, 'Might we get into this boat?', and the officer said in a very polite way indeed, 'Oh certainly, do; I will be very pleased'". Lucile, who was also accompanied by her maid, Laura Francatelli, had no intention of leaving the *Titanic* without her husband. She had already refused to go aboard three previous lifeboats without Sir Cosmo.

One of the two American first-class passengers who brought the boat's complement up to a dozen, **Charles E. Stengel**, told the US inquiry that he and his (male) companion jumped in, with permission, as it was being lowered. In other words, Murdoch had actually ordered it to be lowered with just ten people aboard, and the Duff Gordon party as the only passengers. Stengel also said that he and Sir Cosmo were responsible for choosing the direction in which the boat was rowed – away from the *Titanic*, and towards the lights of the so-called Mystery Ship.

Boat 1 was stationary in the water, either two hundred yards (according to the sailors and firemen) or half a mile (as Sir Cosmo would have it) from the *Titanic* when she finally went down. Not long afterwards, Lady Duff Gordon consoled her maid for the loss of her possessions, saying, "**there goes your beautiful nightdress**". A fireman retorted: "Never mind about your nightdress madam, as long as you have got your life". Sir Cosmo and the crew members alike recalled that a general conversation then ensued, about how the crew had lost everything. In Sir Cosmo's version, one fireman said: "we have lost all our kit and the company

> **"Even in that terrible moment I was filled with wonder at the American wives who were leaving their husbands without a word of protest or regret, scarcely a farewell. They have brought the cult of chivalry to such a pitch in the States that it comes as second nature to men to sacrifice themselves and to women to let them to do it. But I had no such ideas about my husband."**
>
> Lady Duff Gordon, *Discretions and Indiscretions* (1932)

won't give us any more, and what is more our pay stops from tonight. All they will do is to send us back to London." He replied: "You fellows need not worry about that; **I will give you a fiver each** to start a new kit."

When they were all aboard the *Carpathia* the next morning, Sir Cosmo delivered on the promise, writing each man a cheque for £5. They all posed for a photograph together on the deck of the *Carpathia*, and signed a life belt for Lady Duff Gordon to keep as a souvenir.

Investigation and exoneration

Once the *Carpathia* reached New York, rumours began to spread that the Duff Gordons had refused to allow the crewmen to row back to help the desperate swimmers. By that reckoning, the £5 was either a payment not to go back, a **reward** for not doing so, or a **bribe** to keep their mouths shut. There were hints too that Sir Cosmo had also paid Murdoch for his seat on the boat, and for launching it as soon as he was aboard.

The crucial question was, when exactly did the conversation mentioned above take place, and what precisely was being agreed? Lady Duff Gordon always insisted that Sir Cosmo had simply made a generous gesture to men who were in financial trouble, and that the real mystery was why other *Titanic* survivors had not done so as well.

MADAME LUCILE

Lady Lucy Duff Gordon was a pioneer of the fashion industry. One of the first internationally successful designers, known to the world as **Madame Lucile**, she's credited with inventing the "mannequin parade", precursor of today's catwalk shows. At the time she boarded the *Titanic*, she employed around two thousand people, and was earning a six-figure income.

Lucy Sutherland was born in London in 1863, to Canadian parents. After her father died two months later, she was brought up in Canada and Jersey, before returning to London as a young woman. When her first marriage ended in divorce, she set up Maison Lucile, a shop selling custom-designed clothing for women, with the help of her sister, the novelist **Elinor Glyn**.

The business prospered, especially after she remarried in 1900. Her new husband was a Scottish baronet, **Sir Cosmo Duff**

Lady Lucy Duff Gordon, fashion designer.

Gordon. Memorably characterized by Beryl Bainbridge, in *Every Man for Himself* (see p.242), as "a pink porpoise of a man", his connections gave her an entrée at court. Queen Mary herself became a client. Meanwhile, Sir Cosmo, who was independently wealthy, with no need to work, pursued manly activities such as **fencing**, at which he won an Olympic silver medal.

Despite the notoriety she acquired from her role in the *Titanic* disaster – or perhaps, as she defiantly insisted, because of it – Lady Duff Gordon continued to thrive thereafter. Her activities became increasingly centred in the US. She dressed the Ziegfeld Follies girls on Broadway, and became a fixture in Hollywood, where her screenwriter sister popularized the notion of "It" during the 1920s, working with the "**It Girl**" Clara Bow.

Eventually, however, the fashion world moved away from Lady Duff Gordon's voluminous and extravagant designs. She died in relative obscurity in London in 1935, four years to the day after her husband.

At the **US inquiry**, Lookout Symons said that Boat 1 had held between fourteen and twenty people, and that it had indeed gone back to search for survivors in the water, but been unable to find any.

By the time the **British inquiry** investigated the issue, however, no one was pretending that the boat had held more than twelve, or that they'd made the slightest effort to go back. The evasive testimony of everyone on board left the strong impression that when the *Titanic* went down, and the cries of the suffering filled the air, they rowed away from the sound, partly perhaps because the rowing itself obscured the dreadful screams. Lady Duff Gordon said she was too seasick to know what was going on, and Sir Cosmo that he was too concerned about his wife to notice. Fireman **Charles Hendrickson**, on the other hand, said that he had wanted to go back, but that the Duff Gordons had begged the crew not to do so.

Who had overall responsibility for the decision was highly contentious. Although Lookout Symons had been placed in command by Officer Murdoch, in that deferential era the innate authority of a British aristocrat carried a lot of weight.

Symons returned home from America a few days after Hendrickson's testimony, and appeared before the inquiry during the following week. He insisted that, "I never heard anybody of any description, passengers or crew, say anything as regards going back". He went on to say that in fact he had heard nobody say **anything at all**, for the entire five hours they were in the boat. Referring repeatedly to himself as the "**master of the situation**", he claimed that "I used my own discretion", fearing that the boat would be swamped by desperate swimmers.

Under cross-examination from the British Attorney General, however, Symons admitted that during the preceding weekend he'd been visited at home by an anonymous "gentleman" who was acting on behalf of the Duff Gordons. This gentleman had talked him through his forthcoming evidence, and invited him to agree with a number of statements that included the phrases "master of the situation" and "used my discretion".

The Attorney General summed up Symons' testimony in damning terms: "If I understand correctly what you say, your story to my Lord is; the vessel had gone down; there were the people in the water shrieking for help; you were in the boat with plenty of room; nobody ever mentioned going back; nobody ever said a word about it; you just simply lay on your oars. Is that the story you want my Lord to believe?" Symons replied: "Yes, that is the story"

Sir Cosmo was then subjected to his own gruelling **cross-examination**. The various members of the inquiry returned again and again to the issue of whether Boat 1 could or should have picked up survivors. Sir Cosmo blustered and flailed, with such answers as: "It is difficult to say what occurred to me. Again, I was minding my wife, and we were rather in an abnormal condition, you know. There were many things to think about, but of course it quite well occurred to one that people in the water could be saved by a boat, yes." At one point, he expostulated: "We had had **rather a serious evening**, you know."

Asked, "Was not this rather an exceptional time, 20 minutes after the *Titanic* sank, to make suggestions in the boat about giving away £5 notes?", Sir Cosmo replied, "No, I think not. I think it was a most natural time." Another lawyer pursued the issue: "Why do you suggest that it was more natural to think of offering men £5 to replace their kit than to think of those screaming people who were drowning?" "I do not suggest anything of the sort", responded Sir Cosmo.

In its final report, the inquiry concluded that: "The very gross charge against Sir Cosmo Duff Gordon that, having got into No.1 boat he bribed the men in it to row away from the drowning people is **unfounded** … The members of the crew in that boat might have made some attempt to save the people in the water, and such an attempt would probably have been successful; but I do not believe that the men were deterred from making the attempt by any act of Sir Cosmo Duff Gordon's. At the same time I think that if he had encouraged to the men to return to the position where the *Titanic* had foundered they would probably have made an effort to do so and could have saved some lives."

Although exonerated of the worst accusations, Sir Cosmo was **disgraced** by his public humiliation. His appearance before the inquiry had attracted an extraordinary array of society figures and minor royalty, and, according to Lady Duff Gordon, "he never lived down the shame". He died in London in 1931.

11. Why did the *Californian* not come to the rescue?

The most controversial aspect of the *Titanic* disaster is the role played by the Leyland liner ***Californian***. Was she the so-called **Mystery Ship** that was visible from the decks of the sinking ship? Did her captain and crew ignore the *Titanic*'s distress signals? Could the *Californian* have steamed to the site and rescued some or all of the *Titanic*'s passengers and crew?

While historians have advanced numerous theories to explain exactly what happened that terrible night, they remain broadly divided into two opposing camps. Most insist that the *Californian* was in the wrong; those who disagree, and defend her captain, **Stanley Lord**, against charges of negligence, are widely known as **Lordites**.

Both the 1912 inquiries into the disaster concluded that the *Californian* was at fault. The report of the **US inquiry** stated that the *Californian*'s officers and crew had seen the *Titanic*'s distress signals and "failed to respond to them in accordance with the dictates of humanity, international usage, and the requirements of law". "Such conduct", it continued, "whether arising from indifference or gross carelessness, is most reprehensible". The **British inquiry** decided that the *Californian* had been "not more than eight to ten miles" from the *Titanic*, and that, "When she first saw the rockets the *Californian* could have pushed through the ice to the open water without any serious risk and so have come to the assistance of the *Titanic*".

Several entire books have been devoted to the mystery of the *Californian*. While there's no room here to detail every intricacy of the argument, everything hinges on the **distance** between the two ships. Was it as little as five miles, in which case they would have been perfectly visible to each other, or as much as twenty-five miles, which would absolve the *Californian* of all blame?

Eyewitnesses aboard the *Californian* and the *Titanic* gave conflicting testimony. Some of the inconsistencies, especially from those who were facing death aboard the *Titanic*, can be put down to human error. It's clear that some at least of those aboard the *Californian*, on the other hand, must have been lying. At both inquiries several crew members, including Captain Lord, floundered under questioning, flatly contradicting each other, while in addition Lord made hugely misleading statements to the American press.

There is also some less subjective evidence. Each ship gave its **position** in wireless messages before as well as during the disaster, while the *Californian* was seen the next morning by several other ships, most notably the *Carpathia*. And when Robert Ballard found the wreck of the *Titanic* in 1985, he finally solved the riddle as to where precisely she sank.

A most peculiar night

As far as possible, the account that follows is an attempt to set out the basic narrative of what took place aboard the *Californian* during what Captain Lord later described as "a most peculiar night". It avoids any disputed issues, and omits the details of conversations if the participants later gave different accounts.

The *Californian* sailed from Liverpool, bound for Boston, on Friday 5 April. A 477-foot, 6223-ton cargo steamer, she belonged to the Leyland Line, which in turn belonged to the International Mercantile Marine; she therefore had the same owners as the *Titanic*. Although she had space for 47 passengers, she was carrying none on this voyage. Her captain, **Stanley Lord**, came from Lancashire, and was aged 34.

As night approached on Sunday 14 April, the *Titanic*, speeding west at almost double the *Californian*'s twelve knots, was about to overtake the *Californian* en route to North America. The *Californian*, however, was the

A PATTERN OF LIGHTS

There's no disputing that watchers on the *Californian* and the *Titanic* alike could see another ship at the time of the disaster; the debate is whether each was seeing the other, or a different unknown vessel. Spotting a distant ship on that deathly still, moonless night, required an observer to pick out a pattern of **lights** on the horizon, a challenging task against the backdrop of brilliant stars.

The *Titanic*, with her sheer bulk and her rows of bright windows and portholes, must have been more conspicuous than the low-lying *Californian*. If we accept that the two ships saw each other, that helps to explain why the *Californian* spotted her unidentified ship significantly earlier than the *Titanic* saw hers.

As well as **white** masthead lights, each ship – as remains standard – displayed a **green** light on its starboard side, and a **red** light on its port side. In principle, the northernmost of two ships sailing west, which we know in this instance to have been the *Californian*, would when looking south at the other see its green light; the more southerly of the pair, looking north, would see the red light of the other.

Eyewitness testimony from both ships has been scrutinized at great length in the attempt to establish who saw which colour light, when. The task is hugely complicated by the fact that each ship stopped sailing westward – the *Californian* when she was halted by the ice, and the *Titanic* after she hit the iceberg – and then swung around to some unknown extent, quite possibly exposing a different colour light to the other.

Furthermore, the *Titanic* was in motion in all sorts of other ways. As she attempted to steer round the iceberg, for example, she might well have switched from offering the *Californian* a view of her brightly lit side, and exposed instead her smaller and darker stern. In the hours that followed, as her stern went down, the angle of her lights changed from the horizontal; row after row of portholes were extinguished as she sank deeper in the water; and ultimately her lights disappeared altogether.

There's also a further disincentive against undertaking the almost impossible task of untangling the morass of evidence about the lights. For anyone who comes to the conclusion that several *Californian* crew members did not tell the full truth to the inquiries, it becomes rather pointless to trust their testimony as to which lights they saw.

first to reach the ice that stretched across their path, just after 10.20pm, and swiftly became surrounded by loose field ice. Captain Lord, who had never previously encountered ice, decided to stop for the night, and went below to the chart room. At 11pm, he asked his wireless operator, **Cyril Evans**, to warn nearby ships. Evans got through to Jack Phillips in the *Titanic*'s wireless room, but his signal was so loud that Phillips angrily cut him off before he could give him the message, or, crucially, the *Californian*'s position. Soon afterwards, Evans shut his wireless system down, and went to bed.

Standing on the bridge at 11.10pm, Third Officer **Charles Groves** "made out a steamer coming up a little abaft our starboard beam", and estimated it was "10 to 12 miles away". Within fifteen minutes, Groves went below to tell Captain Lord that a passenger steamer was approaching. Lord told him to contact the ship with the Morse lamp; Groves was attempting to do so at 11.40pm, when the steamer's lights suddenly went out. At that point, Lord briefly reappeared on the bridge, and Groves pointed the ship out to him.

Groves also indicated the ship to Second Officer **Herbert Stone**, when Stone took over the watch shortly after midnight. Groves then went below, and called in at the wireless room, where he woke Evans and had a short conversation. He put on the wireless headphones to see if he could hear a signal, but didn't realize the system needed to be wound up before it could work; hearing nothing, he took the headphones off. This was about the time the *Titanic* was sending out her first distress signal.

Meanwhile, an apprentice, **James Gibson**, had joined Stone on the bridge. He too saw a passenger ship in the distance, which appeared to be signalling in Morse. Gibson attempted to signal back, but soon concluded he was mistaken, and that all he had seen was a flickering masthead light. Gibson then went below, leaving Stone alone on the bridge.

At around 12.45am, Stone suddenly saw a "white flash in the sky immediately above this other steamer". After four more such flashes, at 1.10pm, he called Lord, who was now in his cabin, via the speaking tube, and told him he'd seen **five white rockets**. Just after that, Gibson came back up to the bridge, and Stone told him about the five rockets. While Gibson tried once more to contact the ship via Morse, they both saw three more rockets go off. At 1.20am, Stone told Gibson that he could see the ship steaming away towards the southwest. Later he exclaimed, "Look at her now … **she looks very queer out of the water**; her lights look queer". Gibson remarked: "she looks rather to have a big side out of the water".

Not until 2am did Stone decide to disturb Lord again, sending Gibson down to tell the captain that the ship had fired eight rockets and was disappearing in the southwest. Captain Lord's only response was to ask what colour the rockets were. Twenty minutes later, Stone called Lord via the speaking tube to say the ship had vanished from view. Lord again asked about the colour of the rockets.

At around 3.40am, Gibson saw another bright white light, on the southwestern horizon. He called Stone to his side, and together they saw two

The **Californian,** *a photograph taken in 1912, possibly from the* **Carpathia.**

more. This time, they didn't inform Lord, but when Chief Officer **George Stewart** took over the watch at 4am they told him the full story of the night. Stewart thereupon spotted a stationary ship, which Stone had somehow failed to notice; Stone told him that she wasn't the same ship that he'd originally seen. Half an hour later, Stewart woke Captain Lord, who came on deck to see the new ship for himself. At that point, finally, Lord gave the order for the wireless operator to be woken. As soon as Evans turned on his equipment, he learned that the *Titanic* had sunk during the night. The *Californian* turned on her engines and pushed her way slowly towards the rescue site. She arrived just as the *Carpathia* was picking up the last of the survivors.

Interpreting the evidence

By far the most obvious **interpretation** of the above sequence of events is that the observers aboard the *Californian* watched the *Titanic* turn as she approached the iceberg; stop after she hit it; send up rockets as she sank; and finally disappear at a strange angle beneath the waves. They then saw the *Carpathia* fire rockets in turn as she arrived on the scene.

There are genuine **problems** with that version, however. Even when the issue was first investigated, it was difficult to reconcile the position reported

ROCKETS, SOCKETS AND COMPANY SIGNALS

As the lifeboats were leaving the *Titanic*, Fourth Officer **Joseph Boxhall** attempted to summon help by firing **rockets**. In his testimony at the two inquiries, Boxhall described the rockets as "socket distress signals", which were "exploded by a firing lanyard". They flew into the air like a ball with a luminous tail, and then burst into bright white stars.

In 1912, there was no agreed convention for how to use rockets to signal **distress** at sea. One option was to send up a rocket that exploded like a firework with a spray of stars; it was not obliged to reach any specific height or make any noise. Alternatively, you could use a cannon-like gun to shoot a "detonating rocket", which made a loud noise. These latter were supposed to be fired at one-minute intervals, and to be white.

Ships that belonged to the same steamship line, however, were also allowed to use detonating rockets as **company signals**, for such purposes as exchanging greetings at night. Apologists for the *Californian* therefore argue that Boxhall got it wrong; what the *Titanic* was firing were not strictly speaking rockets, and thus he should have fired them at precise one-minute intervals. Because he did not do so, the argument runs, anyone seeing his signals was justified in not taking them seriously.

However, company signals were not random, but tightly regulated. Each company was only allowed to use a very specific form of signals, and all were distributed in a published list. Very few used white rockets; almost all were coloured. What's more, they were required to take a form that couldn't possibly be confused with a distress signal. Conversely, were they to be used in anything other than the prescribed fashion, they were to be interpreted as distress signals. Even Captain Lord acknowledged as much, before he realized that his own conduct was under suspicion: "you never mistake a distress rocket".

Leslie Reade, author of *The Ship That Stood Still*, worked his way through all the agreed signals of the time and demonstrated that no ship that was entitled to use white signals could have been nearby. He concluded that: "In 1912 company signals were so rarely used on the high seas that it was highly unreasonable for any master to think that a reported rocket (or rockets) would have been a company signal".

Second Officer Herbert Stone was watching from the deck of the *Californian* as the rockets were fired. Under intense questioning at the British inquiry, he acknowledged that he'd commented: "A ship is not going to fire rockets at sea for nothing".

by the *Californian* when she stopped for the night – at which time there would have been no conceivable reason to lie – with the SOS position given by Officer Boxhall on the sinking *Titanic*. When the wreck of the *Titanic* was found in 1985 a further thirteen miles southwest, it rendered the calculations used by the two inquiries redundant.

It's also impossible to resolve the inconsistencies between the witnesses. Some, though not all, of those aboard the *Titanic* (including Boxhall himself) were convinced that the Mystery Ship they saw was **moving**, and that it eventually steamed away out of sight. The *Californian*, on the other hand, definitely remained in one spot for the whole night.

And while the **timings** given above, for specific observations from the *Californian*, seem to dovetail very neatly with known events aboard the *Titanic* as she sank, it has to be acknowledged that time itself is a hugely complicated issue. We're used these days to adjusting our watches by several hours after a transatlantic flight. In 1912, ships crossing the Atlantic would make repeated incremental adjustments to their clocks, so that ship's time would match the appropriate local time when they reached their destinations. Thus the *Titanic* was due to move her clocks back 23 minutes at midnight; it's thought that some clocks did change, but some did not, meaning that different witnesses were working to different clocks. As for the *Californian*, some authors say she was seventeen minutes ahead of the *Titanic*, others that she was twelve minutes behind.

At its simplest, the **Lordite case** is that the *Californian* and the *Titanic* were too far apart to see each other, but both could see another, smaller ship directly in between them. This **third ship**, not the *Californian*, was the Mystery Ship seen from the *Titanic*. As seen from the *Californian*, the *Titanic*'s rockets appeared to explode directly above the third ship. Understandably puzzled to see a ship that was clearly not in distress firing rockets, and then steam away, the crew of the *Californian* can be excused for doing nothing to investigate.

A further ramification of that theory suggests that there may have been **four ships** in a line, with the *Californian* and the *Titanic* as bookends. Some Lordites have also suggested that at least one ship other than the *Titanic* was firing rockets that night, though that seems extremely unlikely given that no one aboard the *Titanic* saw any such rockets.

All of which begs the question as to what those other ships were. No plausible candidate has ever been identified. There was much excitement in 1962 when the BBC reported that the Norwegian ship **Samson** had been poaching seals nearby, and that her crew had supposedly thought the *Titanic*'s rockets were a signal that she had been spotted, and fled. It has since been proved, however, that the *Samson* could not have been in the area.

Testimony from the *Californian*

Between learning of the disaster on Monday morning, and their arrival in Boston on Friday night, the captain and officers of the *Californian* had five days to examine their consciences. At that point, they had little reason to imagine that their conduct was going to be the focus of any significant investigation, but they must nonetheless have picked over the events of the night.

For anyone who now seeks to defend their reputation, it's a very tough task to portray their subsequent behaviour in a positive light. The first evidence of what smacks of a **cover-up** is that the ship's log contained no mention whatsoever of the rockets and/or unknown ships seen that night, while the "scrap log" – the rough minute-by-minute notes from which a ship's log is compiled – disappeared altogether.

The possible involvement of the *Californian* in the tragedy first came to public attention due to a mistake. Roy W. Howard, news manager for the United Press, who happened to be aboard the *Olympic* at the time of the tragedy, sent an erroneous wireless message that the *Californian* had picked up some of the bodies. Crowds were therefore waiting to greet her in Boston, where Captain Lord granted a number of newspaper interviews. He told *The Boston Post* that his ship "had sighted **no rockets or other signals** of distress", and *The Boston Journal* that "nothing of the kind was seen by [Officer Stewart] or any of the men who were on watch with him". To *The New York Herald*, he stated that, "with the engines stopped, the wireless was, of course, not working". That was not true: the wireless could operate as usual when the engines were stopped.

The appearances of Lord and various crew members at the British and American inquiries was largely prompted by newspaper reports that two *Californian* crewmen, assistant donkeyman **Ernest Gill** and carpenter **W.F. McGregor**, had described the ship as having seen the *Titanic*'s distress rockets and failed to respond. The British inquiry in particular homed in on the crucial questions. What did Stone and Gibson think was happening when they saw the rockets going off? Why did Lord not come up to see for himself? Why was he so sure the rockets were not distress signals? And above all, why did he not wake the wireless operator to find out what was going on? In response, they met with a quite extraordinary array of evasions and prevarications.

Reading the transcripts, the sheer recalcitrance of Stone, with his monosyllabic answers, and Lord, who at one point was admonished by the Attorney General: "Do really try and do yourself justice!", is stunning. Both squirmed to avoid admitting that it had ever occurred to them to take the firing of white rockets as a distress signal, although in the end Lord grudgingly conceded, "it might have been". Lord's basic defence boiled down to the fact that he'd been **asleep** all night. Not only could he not explain why he'd kept

THE ROUGH GUIDE TO THE TITANIC

asking about the colour of the rockets, he claimed that he'd been speaking in his sleep and couldn't remember the conversations. When he was asked why he hadn't woken the wireless operator when the rockets were going off, he was frankly incredulous, expostulating: "When? At 1 o'clock in the morning?" Above all else, he always insisted that he was sure the ship he'd seen from the bridge of his stopped ship was not the *Titanic*.

The afterlife of Captain Lord

Following his public condemnation by the two inquiries, Captain Lord was asked to resign from the Leyland Line. He was not however **prosecuted**, on the grounds that he'd testified to the British inquiry freely, without being warned that he might incriminate himself. Instead, he secured another command, as captain of the *Anglo-Saxon*, and remained at sea until 1928.

Lord was still alive when his namesake Walter Lord published *A Night to Remember* in 1955. Both that and the subsequent film were highly critical of his behaviour. In 1958, therefore, he presented himself at the offices of the Mercantile Marine Services Association, and announced: "I am Lord of the *Californian*, and I have come to clear my name". Lord himself died in 1962, but Leslie Harrison, the General Secretary of the union, became a passionate advocate of his cause, and twice petitioned the Board of Trade on his behalf, to no avail.

Following the rediscovery of the *Titanic*, the British government agreed in 1992 to a **new investigation** of the *Californian* question. Two Department of Transport inspectors reconsidered the evidence, and came to different conclusions. One decided the *Titanic* and the *Californian* had been between five and ten miles apart; the other that the distance had been more like eighteen miles, and that while the *Californian* had indeed seen the distress signals, Lord himself had done nothing wrong, and the blame lay instead with Officer Stone for failing to report what had happened.

As for the *Californian*'s officers, Charles Groves wrote to Walter Lord in 1955 that, "I have never had the slightest doubt whatsoever that the ship which I saw on the evening in April 1912 whilst we were stopped in the ice was the *Titanic*." He also stated that Herbert Stone "knew without a shadow of doubt that there was trouble aboard the vessel from which the distress signals had been fired", but was too intimidated by his authoritarian captain to disturb him. Walter Lord also contacted Stone's son, who told him that in later years his father had made it clear that he'd always been sure that what he had seen were distress signals.

The verdict on the *Californian*

It's almost impossible to escape the conclusion that the *Californian* saw the *Titanic*'s distress signals. The only alternative explanation would be that some other ship, seen by nobody other than the *Californian*, fired eight rockets at very much the same time as those fired by the *Titanic*, and then left the scene.

It's slightly more possible that the *Californian* saw the rockets but not the *Titanic* herself. Much more likely, however, is that with the abnormally high visibility of that remarkable night, observers aboard the *Californian* saw what they thought was a small ship perhaps five or six miles away, but was in fact an enormous ship a dozen miles away. That distance would explain why the rockets were not audible, and why attempts at Morse signalling failed.

It does not explain, however, the *Californian's* failure to respond to the distress signals. It seems reasonable to speculate that Captain Lord was so reluctant to restart his ship in the dead of night and push her through the ice – a perilous situation of which he had no previous experience – that he somehow convinced himself that whatever ship might be signalling was not in immediate danger.

The question as to whether the *Californian* was near enough to the *Titanic* to save any lives is irrelevant to the **moral issue**. Having seen the rockets go off – irrespective of how far away the *Titanic* may have been, or even whether they came from the *Titanic* at all – the *Californian* was duty bound to respond.

What might have happened if the *Californian* had gone to the rescue is too hypothetical to resolve. If the *Californian* was the Mystery Ship, however, it's surely relevant that she was first seen from the *Titanic* two hours before the ship finally sank, and that Captain Smith was convinced she was close enough to come to his aid.

The ultimate solution depends not only on the exact distance between the two ships, but also at what moment we imagine the *Californian* springing into action. If Stone had indeed chanced to hear the *Titanic's* wireless messages, or if Gibson had rushed to wake his captain as soon as he saw the first rocket go up, then perhaps the *Californian* might have arrived in time. Any later than that, and she would probably have been too late to do more than pick up the survivors from the lifeboats.

12. Was the *Titanic* swapped for the *Olympic* and sunk as an insurance scam?

Other than a certain perverse entertainment value, the one **conspiracy theory** that everyone seems to know about the *Titanic* – that she was somehow **swapped** with the *Olympic* just before her maiden voyage, and that the ship that sank was actually the *Olympic* – has no merit whatsoever. The brainchild of one man, **Robin Gardiner**, it draws ingeniously on various coincidences and anomalies, but rests on no credible evidence.

Sisters under construction: the Olympic (in front) and the Titanic at Harland & Wolff shipyards, Belfast, 1910.

The theory runs that the *Olympic* sustained such severe damage in her September 1911 collision with HMS *Hawke* that she was no longer fit for use. Because the naval inquiry into that incident ruled unfairly against the White Star Line, they were unable to claim on their insurance. Facing financial ruin, therefore, they took the damaged *Olympic* back to Belfast, and swapped her with the almost-completed *Titanic*. When the world thought it saw the *Olympic* return to service six weeks later, it was actually seeing the hastily finished *Titanic* masquerading in her place.

Supposedly, White Star planned to patch the *Olympic* up just enough to send her back to sea, as the *Titanic*, and then deliberately sink her in such a way that they'd be able to claim the insurance after all. On the night of 14 April 1912, everything was going smoothly, as the "*Titanic*" approached its designated point of rendezvous with two ships that were waiting to pick up her passengers and crew.

Just as Captain Smith was looking for a **convenient iceberg** to smash into, however, he ran accidentally into one of those ships, lurking in pitch darkness. That ship was so surprised that it fled, having first set off eight white rockets and thereby baffled its companion, the *Californian*, which was standing by, waiting for the prearranged signal of coloured rockets from the

Titanic. Meanwhile, Captain Smith was so shocked that he briefly **forgot** the plan altogether, and steamed away south. Only then did he discover that his ship had been seriously damaged in the collision, and it sank beyond reach of rescue. Neither of the waiting ships, incidentally, was the *Titanic's* "Mystery Ship"; that was yet another vessel which happened to be in the wrong place at the wrong time. In conclusion, Gardiner states: "the *Titanic* was damaged in a **freak accident** while her officers were trying to stage a fake one".

A very sinkable theory

There are so many **flaws** in that preposterous theory that it's hard to know where to begin. To name but a few: why, if the whole thing was an insurance fraud, did the White Star Line not fully insure the *Titanic*? Even Gardiner acknowledges that the ship was only insured to around two thirds of her value. How could they in any case have been so sure that they'd never claim the insurance for the damaged *Olympic*, when the case in fact dragged on through the courts until November 1914? For that matter, there's no evidence that the *Olympic* was damaged nearly as severely as he suggests. What on earth made the White Star Line think that they'd be able to find an iceberg at the appointed time and place? And how could they possibly think that deliberately sinking a ship with over two thousand people on board was the way to salvage their finances and maintain their reputation?

> "All they needed to do was sail the damaged ship out into the middle of the North Atlantic, somewhere nice and deep, and a staged collision with an iceberg would do the rest."
>
> Robin Gardiner, *Titanic – The Ship That Never Sank* (1998)

Gardiner also completely glosses over such **practical** issues as how the swap was physically effected, let alone how such a major operation, involving the workforce of Harland & Wolff and the White Star Line, could have been carried out in such total secrecy that even after the disaster not a whisper of the truth emerged. On the *Titanic* itself, he claims that only the senior officers – Smith, Wilde and Murdoch, all of whom, rather conveniently, died – knew about the plan.

In their excellent book, *Olympic and Titanic: The Truth Behind the Conspiracy*, authors **Steve Hall** and **Bruce Beveridge** meticulously **compare** every detail of the two ships, and demolish the case that the two could have been swapped. Whether you choose to believe them, or Gardiner's prime informant, a mysterious *Titanic* crewman called **Paddy the Pig** – who can't be found on the ship's roster, was still at sea, off Australia, 56 years after the disaster, and died shortly after telling his story to a fellow sailor in the late 1960s – is entirely up to you.

13. Was the sinking of the *Titanic* predicted before it ever happened?

Even as the *Titanic* was sinking, some people were already claiming to have **foreseen** the disaster. Survivor Archibald Gracie described standing at the rail of the doomed ship as the distress rockets were being fired: "It was at this point that Miss Evans related to me the story that years ago in London she had been told by a fortune-teller to '**beware of water**'."

Fiction or fact?

The best known of the various **fictional** accounts that presaged the tragedy is **Morgan Robertson**'s 1898 novella *Futility, or the Wreck of the Titan*. Read the whole thing and you'll spot plenty of differences, but it can't be denied that Robertson's **Titan** is "the largest craft afloat", built to almost exactly the same specifications as the future *Titanic*, and carrying tow thousand passengers and insufficient life boats. Despite being "practically unsinkable" thanks to its watertight compartments, it sinks in the North Atlantic after crashing into an **iceberg** on a cold April night. Robertson further boosted his credentials as a prophet with his 1914 story "Beyond The Spectrum", in which a war between America and Japan begins with a sneak Japanese attack on Hawaii, and ends with the devastating use of an ultra-powerful American "searchlight".

An edition of the American *Popular Magazine* published shortly before the *Titanic* sailed contained a story by **Mayn Clew Garnett** entitled "The White Ghost of Disaster". This tells how the huge liner *Admiral*, en route between Liverpool and New York, sinks after failing to spot an iceberg. Once again, the casualties are especially heavy due to the inadequate provision of lifeboats.

Two separate stories by journalist **W.T. Stead** carry the additional eerie resonance that Stead himself sailed to his death aboard the *Titanic*. The first appeared in March 1886 in the *Pall Mall Gazette*, of which Stead was the editor. He prefaced "How the Mail Steamer Went Down in Mid Atlantic" with the warning that: "This is exactly what might take place and **what will take place** if the liners are sent to sea short of boats". Following a collision with another vessel, the narrator finds that the steamer has only enough lifeboats to save fewer than half her passengers. Even those are launched with "half their proper complement", as desperate officers fire their pistols to hold back "a maddened host of cowardly men and hysterical women". Finding himself in

THE CURSE OF THE *TITANIC* MUMMY

Over dinner aboard the *Titanic* on the evening of 12 April, the celebrated journalist **W.T. Stead** regaled his fellow diners with the story of an **Egyptian mummy**, a priestess of Amen-Ra, which had been dug up a few years earlier by four Englishmen. Whosoever should repeat aloud the inscription on the mummy's case, he said, would activate a terrible curse… and then went on to do just that. By the time Stead finished spinning his saga, cataloguing the various misfortunes and untimely deaths that the mummy had brought to its successive owners, the clock had passed midnight.

Only one man seated at that table, first-class passenger **Frederic Seward**, lived to tell the tale. His account became ever further embroidered as it passed from teller to teller, until it became widely believed that Stead himself had not only bought the mummy, but he had smuggled it aboard the *Titanic*, and that the disaster itself was the latest and deadliest manifestation of its curse. In due course, some even said the mummy had somehow made its way onto a lifeboat, and then on to the *Lusitania* for the return trip to England.

It may be that Stead really did tell his companions that the mummy now lay beneath their feet. He had **invented** the whole story, after all. Over the years, Stead and his friend Douglas Murray had first concocted, and then combined, two separate fictions, one about a cursed mummy excavated in Egypt and brought to England, and another inspired by the lifelike portrait they'd seen on an Egyptian coffin lid in the British Museum. Imagining it to represent a soul in anguish, they had asked the museum for permission to hold a séance over the coffin, but been refused. They had been recounting the story ever since, embellishing it with whatever new details sprang to mind.

Stead would surely have relished the fact that the legend is still going strong a century later. As for the coffin, it too survives; it never left the British Museum.

the water amid a "blackened, wriggling sheet of drowning creatures", he does however manage to struggle on to a lifeboat.

In December 1892, the Christmas edition of *The Review of Reviews* – again edited by Stead – held his tale "From the Old World to the New". This centres around a fictional voyage on a real-life ship, the White Star Line's *Majestic*, captained as she then truly was by none other than Captain Smith of *Titanic* fame. An Irish woman aboard, gifted with second sight, persuades Smith to divert the *Majestic* and rescue a group of survivors stranded on an iceberg after their own ship has sunk. Once more the details of the sinking, with desperate swimmers disappearing one by one beneath the icy waters, sound awfully familiar.

An ominous voyage

Several accounts of the actual voyage of the *Titanic* reveal the worries and **premonitions** of those aboard. Second-class passenger Robertha Watt later recalled her "mother and some ladies having tea", when one decided to "read the tea cups … in one cup she said 'I can't see anything, it's like there was just a blank wall and nothing beyond'". Another survivor, Edith Russell, posted a letter when the *Titanic* called at Queenstown saying, "I cannot get over my feeling of depression and premonition of trouble". In another letter from Queenstown, bedroom steward George Beedum bemoaned more poignantly than prophetically that, "the last 3 days I've felt rotten, & what with no dusters or anything to work with **I wish the bally ship at the bottom of the sea**". He did not survive.

A number of incidents also served to fuel passengers' fears. The most notorious came when a **blackened face**, seen by some as a death's head, suddenly emerged from the *Titanic*'s fourth funnel off Queenstown. The funnel was actually a dummy, not connected to the boilers but serving as a ventilation shaft, and the face simply belonged to a stoker who had climbed up inside, either as a joke or simply to enjoy the view. And then there's the story of Nellie Hocking, who told her fellow passengers that from her cabin she'd heard a **cock crowing** at nightfall, something that in her native Cornwall was considered a dreadful omen. Strangely enough, perhaps she did; there were indeed live roosters aboard, caged not far below.

Finally, if anyone can truly claim to have had a premonition of the *Titanic*'s fate, it would be those who bought tickets for the crossing but then **cancelled** their trip. At least 55 did, including legendary financier J. Pierpont Morgan, Henry Clay Frick and Mr and Mrs George W. Vanderbilt, whose unfortunate servant however remained aboard with their luggage. Most such cancellations were for mundane reasons, of course – Morgan would habitually book several liners at once, then cancel those he didn't need – but Mr and Mrs E.W. Bill, from Philadelphia, chose to change their plans after Mrs Bill dreamed that the *Titanic* was wrecked.

Part 4

RESOURCES

Chapter 10
The *Titanic* in the media

The *Titanic* story has been explored, dissected, celebrated and mythologized in movies, books and popular culture for a full century. Whether you want to voyage deeper into the history and secrets of the great ship, or marvel at her onscreen splendour, this chapter will point you towards the true highlights of the *Titanic*'s media afterlife.

Feature films

The very first **movie** about the *Titanic* started shooting in New Jersey within a week of the disaster. *Saved from the Titanic* starred 22-year-old survivor **Dorothy Gibson**, who had escaped on the first lifeboat (see p.91). Already an established star with the Éclair company, Gibson also wrote the script, in which she re-enacted her ordeal while wearing the same silk skirt and polo coat as on the night of the sinking, and then found love with a sailor. Released in May 1912, the film was an international hit, but only a few tantalizing stills now survive.

Cinemas of the era also showed **newsreels** that supposedly depicted the tragedy. Footage of Captain Smith on the *Olympic*, for example, was displayed as though filmed aboard the *Titanic* ten minutes before she sailed, and juxtaposed with images of icebergs. Since then, filmmakers have repeatedly returned to the story. The section that follows describes the most important *Titanic* films to have appeared in the course of a century.

IN NACHT UND EIS (IN NIGHT AND ICE) Germany 1912, 34 min
Director Mime Misu **Cast** Mime Misu, Waldemar Hacker, Otto Rippert

Commissioned within a fortnight of the disaster, the silent German movie *In Nacht und Eis* was released in August 1912. By that time, according to researcher Michael Wedel, cobbled-together footage of icebergs and the *Titanic* had become so familiar that the trade papers were reporting that "they don't attract audiences any more".

Much of the film was shot aboard the *Auguste Victoria*, a 677-foot, 24,600-ton vessel belonging to the Hamburg-Amerika line, and consists of lengthy scenes of ordinary shipboard life, such as playing games on deck and dressing for dinner. No characters are named, though recognizable figures include Isidor Straus, John Jacob Astor IV and the bearded Captain Smith, played by the film's Romanian director, **Mime Misu**. There's no sign of the steerage passengers at all, though we do see the firemen hard at work in the hellish boiler rooms. Frequent shots of the band are accompanied by captions explaining what they're playing; it's thought live musicians in each cinema would play the corresponding tunes, most obviously in the climactic "Nearer My God to Thee".

In the actual collision, a twenty-foot model of the *Titanic* is rammed into a block of ice, whereupon passengers in the Café Parisien tumble to the floor. Rather than panicking crowds and a rush for the lifeboats, the horror is conveyed by the consternation of the captain, and shots of wireless operator Jack Phillips remaining at his post as the water rises around him. The caption "The ship is sinking deeper and deeper" is shown repeatedly, and the film ends as the swimming captain disappears beneath the waves. The original release is said to have featured one more final shot, of a giant death's head rising up behind the iceberg.

In Nacht und Eis was long assumed to have been lost, until a German collector found a copy in 1998. It can now be seen on YouTube.

ATLANTIC England 1929, 90 min
Director Ewald André Dupont **Cast** Franklin Dyall, Madeleine Carroll, John Stuart, Monty Banks

Atlantic was the **first talkie** to tell the *Titanic* story. It was made in England, but German director Ewald Dupont filmed different actors on the same sets to produce parallel English and German versions. (The German version was the first-ever all-German talking picture.)

The **play** on which *Atlantic* was based, *The Berg* by Ernest Raymond, took place in the lounge of an unnamed liner that sinks after hitting an iceberg. Rather than a chronicle of actual events aboard the *Titanic*, it was a philosophical two-hander in which an atheist author and a priest faced death in their separate ways. While the **film** retained the late-1920s setting (and costumes) of the theatrical production, the ship is immediately recognizable as the *Titanic*, even though pressure from the White Star Line forced its producers to call it the *Atlantic* instead, and the characters are at least nominally fictitious.

Almost all the dialogue in the movie is still spoken in the very static environs of the lounge, where the "dangerous" author John Rool both occupies centre stage and serves as the moral centre. Unlike the play, he's now surrounded by a more extensive cast of passengers and crew, among whom the priest is a peripheral figure. As Rool is confined to a wheelchair, the other actors approach him to speak their lines in turn and then withdraw. Both that and the uniformly ponderous enunciation must have helped with recording the sound, but the funereal pace of the interior scenes is in stark contrast with the dramatically intercut shots of pandemonium out on deck (filmed on a genuine liner anchored on the Thames).

Even so, and despite the paring of the play's religious themes to a minimum, the film offers a powerful depiction of how the realization of their own impending death spreads slowly from man to man. Most are quietly stoical about their fate; there's little sign of heroism, and Rool comments to an officer that "you've destroyed the proud faith I had in the calm of sailors when faced by an emergency". The officer rather resignedly responds that: "I shall obey orders I suppose", while the gentlemen in the bar proclaim, "let's get drunk". Meanwhile, just outside, frantic women are lowered into wildly swaying lifeboats amid a cacophony of alarm bells, exploding rockets and shrieking.

Some moments in *Atlantic* now seem jarring, such as the band playing "Oh Dear! What Can the Matter Be?" out on deck, or two black men being gunned down as they fight their way onto a lifeboat. Several familiar tropes also make an appearance, including the philandering husband who finds redemption by saving his wife and daughter, and the massed crowd on deck singing "Nearer My God to Thee". The understated ending is a triumph; as the throng in the lounge finish reciting the Lord's Prayer, the screen simply goes blank. The filmmakers did shoot scenes of the ship going down, but, it being just seventeen years since the real thing, decided not to use them.

The entire film can be watched on YouTube, and is also available on DVD as *Titanic: Disaster in the Atlantic*.

TITANIC Germany 1943, 85 min
Directors Herbert Selpin and Werner Klingler **Cast** Hans Nielsen, Sybille Schmitz, E. F. Fürbringer, Karl Schönböck, Otto Wernicke

Made in Nazi Germany at the height of World War II, and personally commissioned by **Joseph Goebbels**, the 1943 **Titanic** movie was an overt piece of propaganda that attributed the disaster to English greed and disregard for life. As the onscreen text at the end put it, the sinking is "an eternal condemnation of England's quest for profit".

The story therefore centres on the struggle between "Sir Bruce Ismay" and John Jacob Astor – here depicted as an Englishman – for control of the White Star Line, which is in deep financial trouble due to the cost of building "the first unsinkable ship in the world". Ismay announces that the *Titanic* will capture the Blue Riband for the fastest-ever Atlantic crossing, and promises Captain Smith $1000 for every hour by which he beats the scheduled arrival time in New York.

The usual cast of fictitious passengers, from decadent English gentry to young lovers in steerage, are for once complemented by an invented crew member, the young German officer **Petersen**. Very much the conscience of the film, Petersen repeatedly tells Ismay that the *Titanic* is going too fast, with too few lifeboats, into an ice zone; he calls it "a ship run not by sailors but by stock speculators". When the inevitable happens, both Ismay and Astor try and fail to buy their way onto a lifeboat, only for Petersen to secure Ismay's safe escape so that he can later be held accountable for his actions. Petersen himself is also rescued, after he finds a little girl weeping in her cabin, swims out to a lifeboat carrying her, and is helped aboard. The two men have a final confrontation at the subsequent Board of Inquiry, only for Ismay to be exonerated, and all blame placed on Captain Smith.

While all the emphasis on share prices rather detracts from the human drama, there's still time to include such episodes as a girl rejecting the hopes of her parents to follow the man she loves, a debauched dance in the third-class dining room and even, as in James Cameron's film, a jewel thief being rescued from the ship's jail by the judicious use of an axe. What's more unusual is the brief scene of the crew of the *Californian*, watching and discussing the *Titanic*'s rockets, and failing to respond on the basis that they're white flares rather than appropriate distress signals.

Much of the action takes place in the *Titanic*'s implausibly vast ballroom. Shortly after the collision, the steerage passengers come up en masse to find out what's happened, and appear to be struck dumb by its opulence, before dutifully returning below. Until the sinking, there's little sense of being aboard a real ship; the whole thing is so stable that there's even a billiards table. Later scenes however were filmed aboard the ***Cap Arcona***, a liner that had been requisitioned by the German Navy. After director **Herbert Selpin** complained about the behaviour of the real-life German officers, his co-writer Walter Zerlett-Olfenius denounced him to the Gestapo. Within twenty-four hours Selpin had been interrogated by Goebbels himself, and found **hanged** in his cells; the project was completed by Werner Klingler.

The *Cap Arcona* also met a grisly fate; it was sunk by British fighter planes the day before the war ended. An estimated five thousand concentration camp inmates, who were being shipped to an unknown destination, lost their lives.

After the cinema in Germany that was due to host its premiere was bombed, the film was first shown in Paris at the end of 1943. Goebbels soon withdrew it from circulation, supposedly because its depictions of panic and disaster were inappropriate for German audiences experiencing nightly bombing raids. Historian Jared Poley has however argued that the real problem, at a time when internal opposition to the Nazi regime was growing, may have been the film's focus on a morally upright hero who stands up against his corrupt leaders.

TITANIC USA 1953, 98 min
Director Jean Negulesco **Cast** Barbara Stanwyck, Clifton Webb, Robert Wagner, Thelma Ritter, Audrey Dalton, Richard Basehart

Despite sticking to its initial promise to be scrupulous with the navigational aspects of the disaster, the 1953 Hollywood rendition of the *Titanic* story shows little interest in period detail or authenticity. Instead it focuses on two parallel stories – an estranged couple, Mr and Mrs Sturges (played by Clifton Webb and Barbara Stanwyck), tussling over their adolescent children, and the shipboard romance of their daughter Annette (Audrey Dalton) with student Giff Rogers (Robert Wagner).

There's little lingering over the *Titanic* itself, seen steaming in to Cherbourg at the start with no mention of England, or any suspense as to whether she's going to hit the iceberg – in fact the very first shot of all, before the credits, shows the berg cleaving from the side of a glacier. Even the collision itself, and the response of the crew, are presented with minimal excitement. Captain Smith is a hero, and not in any sense to blame, while the loading of the lifeboats is an orderly and very decent operation. Fifteen hundred doomed people line up on deck and sing "Nearer My God to Thee" as the ship goes down.

The whole thing serves as a backdrop for Stanwyck and Webb to play out their mutual antagonism, while proto-teenager Robert Wagner woos Audrey Dalton with his glee-club singing and the latest ragtime dances. The dialogue is sparky enough for the screenplay to have won an Oscar. When disaster strikes, Mr and Mrs Sturges find reconciliation in the face of death. In the emotional climax, Mr Sturges, previously an ageing roué, finds redemption in his love for his son. Having rescued the women of the family, the two go down together. It's almost peripheral that both the young lovers survive; we never even see their happy reunion.

A NIGHT TO REMEMBER England 1958, 118 min
Director Roy Ward Baker **Cast** Kenneth More, Honor Blackman, Michael Goodliffe, David McCallum, Robert Allen, Ronald Ayres

While writing his bestselling book, *A Night to Remember*, in 1955, Walter Lord told the daughter of Captain Smith that: "I just want to recreate the night the *Titanic* went down so that anybody can picture exactly what it was like." The **film** of the book, made three years later, took that process a stage further. More of a docudrama than a conventional narrative, and filmed in black and white, it has very little dialogue, and devotes scant attention to individual characters other than its stern-jawed hero, Second Officer Charles Lightoller (Kenneth More).

Like the book, the film consists instead of multiple vignettes and glimpses, which allow the audience to build up a cumulative portrait of the action from every imaginable vantage point. These start before the *Titanic* has even sailed, with shots of passengers of all classes setting off from their homes, from aristocrats leaving their stately piles to Irish immigrants bidding their grieving families farewell. Everything moves swiftly towards the fatal collision with the iceberg, which arrives half an hour in. Thereafter the *Titanic* sinks, if not quite in real time, then at least in 75 drawn-out, suspense-filled minutes.

Several **survivors** of the disaster acted as consultants, including Fourth Officer Joseph Boxhall and author Lawrence Beesley, and the action is peppered with incidents drawn from memoirs and eyewitness testimony. Even so, it's very much an authored view, reflecting Lord's own opinions. Unspecified foreigners make trouble as the lifeboats are loaded, panic erupts, and an officer restores order by firing four shots. Steerage passengers gather at a locked grating below decks, and eventually break through with an axe, only to arrive on the Boat Deck once the last lifeboat has left. The band carry on playing "Nearer My God to Thee" even after they're told their duty is done.

More controversial issues are also addressed. We're repeatedly shown the crew of the *Californian*, in plain sight of the *Titanic* and yet with inexplicable obtuseness watching her distress signals without responding. Towards the end Captain Smith addresses the distant ship with the words "God help you", as though it's the *Californian* that's the real victim of the tragedy. Meanwhile, J. Bruce Ismay insists, "I'm just an ordinary passenger on this ship", and interferes with the loading of the lifeboats before sneaking onto one himself. He's never named, however, being referred to only as "the chairman".

Despite the quest for authenticity, some scenes were invented. The very first, for example, shows the *Titanic* being launched with a bottle of champagne, even though the film's producer, **William MacQuitty**, had actually attended the launch and there was no such baptism. Certain characters too are composites, representing particular groups of passengers. There's even a rather cursory Irish–Scandinavian romance featuring a couple of emigrants;

Second Officer Lightoller, played by Kenneth More, fires a gun into the air during A Night to Remember.

both seem to survive, though we never see them reunited. The ending instead focuses on Lightoller's existential angst, as he guides his collapsible lifeboat towards rescue: "I don't think I'll ever feel sure again, about anything".

Even with the mundane surroundings of Ruislip Lido standing in for the open Atlantic, and Cricklewood Pumping Station serving as the *Titanic*'s engine rooms, *A Night to Remember* was at the time the most expensive film ever made in Britain. It had at one stage been arranged to shoot the climactic scenes aboard a Shaw Savill liner docked at Tilbury; that was cancelled when the company chairman turned out to be Ismay's real-life son-in-law.

The film is now packaged together on DVD with a fascinating "making of" documentary, featuring a memorable scene of a giant Gulliver-like figure wading through a mass of clockwork lifeboats.

TITANIC USA 1997, 194 min

Director James Cameron **Cast** Leonardo DiCaprio, Kate Winslet, Billy Zane, Gloria Stuart, Frances Fisher, Bill Paxton, Kathy Bates, Danny Nucci, Bernard Hill, Victor Garber

Before it was released, director James Cameron made no bones about his intentions in making **Titanic**: "The film is primarily a kind of 'you are there' experience, involving the sinking of the *Titanic* in the presence of a very powerful love story". Pundits predicted the movie would itself prove to be a memorable disaster; instead it swiftly became the most financially successful film in a century of cinema, won eleven Oscars, and has been converted into 3D format to mark the great ship's centenary.

As the "you" who Cameron wanted to place aboard his *Titanic* were young movie-goers, he created a scrupulous reconstruction of the doomed liner, peopled it with a full cast of real-life characters that included her actual crew and most famous passengers, and then unleashed a pair of glowing and magnificently anachronistic modern teenagers to rampage through it. These two berg-crossed lovers – **Leonardo DiCaprio** as Jack Dawson and **Kate Winslet** as Rose DeWitt Bukater – cast their radiance into *Titanic*'s murkiest corners and breathe fresh air into the liner's stifling Edwardian world.

For anyone enthralled by the true-life drama of the *Titanic*, the movie is irresistible. When Cameron chooses to aim for strict historical accuracy, his vision and resources make almost anything possible. Thus the story is book-ended by two stunning and utterly convincing no-expense-spared showpieces, in each of which the colossal *Titanic* herself shares the screen with hundreds of swarming human individuals. The first is our initial sweeping view of the mighty liner in all her majesty, taking her passengers aboard as she prepares to sail from Southampton on her maiden voyage; the second, at the other end of the film, is our final view of the wounded ship in her death throes, shaking herself free of her human encumbrances as she plunges beneath the waves.

Cameron's trump card in all this is the footage he shot aboard the **wreck** itself. Repeatedly segued into the action at crucial moments, it effectively asserts his ownership of the truth about the *Titanic*, and thus allows him to stray from that truth as and when he feels like it. The narrative framing device, in which the 101-year-old "**Old Rose**" is brought back to the site of the disaster, achieves much the same purpose; the story begins when Rose, and the audience with her, are asked: "Are you ready to go back to *Titanic*?" We know that we're about to learn what really happened.

Designed to serve as "an emotional lightning rod for the audience", Jack and Rose roam throughout the ship, and manage to be present at countless crucial incidents during the voyage. They play out their romance, raging against the rigid class structure that keeps them apart, and pledge undying love at the very moment that the iceberg looms into view. All this time, of course, they've been oblivious to the grim statistic on which their story is predicated: a first-class female passenger aboard the *Titanic* had a 97 percent chance of survival, whereas a third-class male passenger had an 85 percent likelihood of an icy death.

Befitting Cameron's desire to "tell our story within an absolutely rigorous, historically accurate framework", the movie takes a stance on many iconic

Young lovers Jack (Leonardo DiCaprio) and Rose (Kate Winslet) flee Rose's vengeful fiancé Cal through the sinking ship, in James Cameron's Titanic.

controversies. Thus we see White Star Line chairman **J. Bruce Ismay** encouraging Captain Smith (Bernard Hill, who played Lookout Frederick Fleet in *A Night to Remember*) to run the *Titanic* too fast in the attempt to reach New York early. The ship's designer **Thomas Andrews**, on the other hand, is a benign twinkling Irishman, who explicitly states that "I was overruled" when the canny Rose notices that the vessel is carrying too few lifeboats. The third-class passengers are indeed kept locked below decks while the lifeboats are being loaded (Cameron joked, "we're holding just short of Marxist dogma"); and First Officer Murdoch **shoots** and kills a couple of passengers as the lifeboats are loading, including Jack's friend Tommy Ryan, before shooting himself. It does steer clear of some issues, however; there's no mention of the ***Californian***, let alone whether she was the notorious "Mystery Ship" seen during the sinking. Here, instead, the *Titanic* goes down in an endless expanse of empty black sea.

Historians tend to decry Cameron's more fanciful inventions, like the ludicrous chase scene, in which Jack and Rose are pursued through the flooding lower decks by her pistol-toting fiancé Cal (Billy Zane). Such objections, however, ignore the film's overall success in humanizing the tragedy to an extent a strictly documentary approach could never achieve. Far from being diminished by its fictional elements, the meticulous depiction of the sinking itself, during which the *Titanic* breaks in two, in line with the latest research, benefits because we see its impact on specific characters. For

A REAL-LIFE JACK AND ROSE

The doomed lovers in James Cameron's *Titanic*, Rose DeWitt Bukater and Jack Dawson, are entirely fictitious. Perhaps the closest romantic parallels among those on board are with 37-year-old **Henry Morley** and 19-year-old **Katy Phillips**. Morley was already married when he started an affair with Miss Phillips, who worked in one of the three sweetshops he owned in the Worcester area, and they decided to run away together to America. Under the name of "Mr and Mrs Marshall", they shared a second-class cabin on the *Titanic*, and Miss Phillips proudly displayed her new sapphire necklace to other passengers.

The couple were forcibly separated as the lifeboats were loading, and only Phillips survived. Soon after she returned home, however, she discovered that she had conceived a child on board. That child, **Ellen Walker**, lived on into the twenty-first century. She sold the necklace to a collector in the 1980s, and died aged 92 in 2005. Her final years were marred by a bitter dispute as to whether she could truly be considered the youngest *Titanic* survivor, which culminated in her expulsion from the British Titanic Society. She left her estate to the Royal National Lifeboat Institution, and asked to be buried at sea.

Finally, movie fans left flowers and even film tickets on the grave dedicated to "J. Dawson", one of the 121 *Titanic* victims buried in the Fairview Lawn Cemetery in Halifax, Nova Scotia. The body it holds, however, is that of a 23-year-old Irish trimmer, Joseph Dawson, who has no connection with the character in the film.

anyone left wanting yet more historical detail, the DVD release of the film includes material that was omitted from the three-hour final cut, including scenes on the *Californian*.

Actual filming took place aboard the *Akademik Keldysh*, the Russian ship used by Cameron's expedition to the site; on an underwater replica of the interior of the wreck; and on a vast ocean-front set erected in Baja California, Mexico. They only reconstructed the starboard half of the *Titanic*; any shots that show her port side, such as her departure from Southampton, were filmed in mirror image and then flipped.

Documentaries

Dozens of documentaries have explored the *Titanic* story over the years, and many more have been produced to mark the centenary of the sinking. In addition, since the wreck was located in 1985, most of the expeditions that have returned to the site have been chronicled in their own films, while all have produced more undersea footage. With no survivors now remaining to be interviewed, and the ship itself steadily deteriorating, new documentaries tend to be dependent on re-hashing familiar material. While there's always scope to cast fresh light on the tragedy, therefore, the films listed below are unlikely to be surpassed.

SECRETS OF THE TITANIC 1987, 51 min

This National Geographic production centres on Dr Robert Ballard's return to the wreck site in 1986, the year after he found it. This was the first expedition to send a manned submarine down to the wreck, and thus shows the ship in the best condition in which it was ever filmed. In its most compelling underwater footage, the remote-controlled mini-sub *Jason* enters the wreck through the vast hole left by the vanished Grand Staircase, and finds a chandelier still hanging in place far below.

TITANICA 1993, 65 min

The first IMAX film of the wreck, captured by the 1991 expedition, and complemented by a decent run-through of the historical background and the night of the disaster. While the image quality is exceptional, the camera always flies over the ship rather than entering it.

TITANIC – THE COMPLETE STORY 1994/1998, 300 min

This three-disc History Channel set provides an all-but definitive overview of the tragedy. The first programme, *Death of a Dream*, is especially good on the building of the *Titanic*, while the last, *Beyond Titanic*, offers an entertaining romp though the ship's onscreen afterlife.

ANATOMY OF A DISASTER 1997, 104 min

A detailed study of how and why the *Titanic* sank, based largely on the 1996 IFREMER expedition that located, and unsuccessfully attempted to retrieve, the so-called "Big Piece" (see p.174). Made by the Discovery Channel, the film is also available as part of a generally repetitive six-disc set.

GHOSTS OF THE ABYSS 2003, 58 min

For anyone tantalized by the glimpses of the wreck in James Cameron's *Titanic* – in which many of the internal shots were in any case filmed on a replica – this spectacular documentary, originally filmed in 3D IMAX format, is an essential purchase. Drawing on the director's subsequent dives,

A **Mir** *submersible is launched from the Russian research ship* **Akademik Keldysh.**

and beautifully photographed, it's by far the best of the underwater docs. Cameron's highly manoeuvrable ROV "bots" (remote-controlled mini-subs), *Jake* and *Elwood*, managed to penetrate several specific cabins, including those occupied by Molly Brown and J. Bruce Ismay, as well as the wireless room. As for the "ghosts", Cameron uses the same eerie technique as in his blockbuster movie, albeit with different actors, of fading fictionalized reconstructions into the wreck itself.

The *Titanic* in music

Although **popular music** at the time the *Titanic* went down was usually sold in the form of printed sheet music rather than on record, **songs** about the tragedy rapidly entered the culture, and are preserved on recordings made a few years later. Artists have returned to the subject ever since, making it hard to restrict the following listings to a simple, chronological, **Top Ten**. Sadly, it proved impossible to include – or even listen to – Celine Dion's tearjerker, "My Heart Will Go On", which was originally written as an instrumental for James Cameron's *Titanic*.

1 *BE BRITISH* Robert Carr, 1912

Arguably the first ever charity record, "Be British" was produced in England within weeks of the disaster to raise money for the Titanic Relief Fund. Having celebrated the fact that "our men knew how to die", and Captain Smith's supposed exhortation to "Be British", **Robert Carr** encourages his listeners to "Be British" themselves, and "show that you are willing, with a penny or a shilling, for those they left behind".

2 *THE TITANIC* Ernest Stoneman, 1924

Although this is the first known recording of that staple of a thousand scout camps, the song that tells how "It was sad when that great ship went down", an early version of the lyrics is said to have been circulating as sheet music within a week of the disaster. **Ernest Stoneman**, a bluegrass musician from Virginia who accompanied himself on autoharp and harmonica, is said to have sold over a million copies. William and Versey Smith cut a much wilder blues version three years later, and there have been countless other renditions since then.

3 *THE SINKING OF THE TITANIC* Richard "Rabbit" Brown, 1927

Himself a singing boatman in his native New Orleans, **Rabbit Brown** was a songster who was best known for performing blues, but here delivers a self-composed ballad. Following a meticulous blow-by-blow account of the disaster, including the successive wireless messages from Captain Smith to the *Carpathia*, he rounds things off with a verse or two of "Nearer My God to Thee".

4 *LAST SCENE OF THE TITANIC* Frank Hutchison, 1927

Often regarded as the first white bluesman, **Frank Hutchison** was a coal miner from West Virginia who cut powerful versions of many classic folk tunes between 1926 and 1929. "Last Scene of the Titanic" seems to reflect his own take on the disaster, however, in that it's a fabulous hoedown that recreates only the first half of the voyage. Down on the lower decks, "everybody's fiddling and dancing and having a big time"; up on the bridge Captain Smith is checking his compass and heading for a world record. He sees an iceberg a mile ahead, but is sure his unsinkable ship will plough right through it. And there, uniquely, the song ends, before the collision ever happens.

5 *GOD MOVES ON THE WATER* Blind Willie Johnson, 1929

A gruff-voiced itinerant preacher who conjured extraordinarily eerie sounds playing slide guitar, **Blind Willie Johnson** made several bestselling gospel records at the end of the 1920s. He didn't write his own songs, and one of his vocal trademarks was to sing only the first half of a line, then complete the phrase on guitar, knowing that his audiences would be familiar with the words. He never sings the entire phrase "God moves on the water" here, which suggests it was a well-known song, even if his was the first recording. While the lyrics state that "many gunshots were fired" and mention E.J. Smith by name, they don't say that God sank the *Titanic* as a judgement; the suggestion is more that "over water" is simply one of the mysterious ways in which He moves.

6 *DOWN WITH THE OLD CANOE* Dixon Brothers, 1938

The most explicit musical statement of the view that God sank the *Titanic* to "cut down all her pride", performed as a bluegrass duet by the two **Dixon Brothers** from South Carolina. Though they start by saying that "It was 25 years ago", they may have adapted the song from an earlier version. After explaining that "this great ship was built by man, that is why she could not stand", they make the disaster an explicit warning to their listeners: "Your *Titanic* sails today", and "if you go on in your sins", you too will go "down with that old canoe".

7 *THE TITANIC* Leadbelly, 1948

In his preamble to this recording, veteran bluesman **Huddie "Leadbelly" Ledbetter** recalls that "The Titanic" was the first song he learned to play on the twelve-string guitar, back in 1912 when he used to accompany Blind Lemon Jefferson on the road in Texas. Some critics have argued that he composed it himself, much later, though you can certainly hear strong echoes of Virginia Liston's 1926 "Titanic Blues" in its refrain of "Fare thee, *Titanic*, fare thee well". In any case, Leadbelly's gift for a tune, and knack with paring lyrics down to the bare essentials, make this the catchiest *Titanic* song of them all. Historically it's most noteworthy for its reference to heavyweight champion Jack Johnson, allegedly refused passage on the ship: "Jack Johnson wanted to get on board, captain he says, 'I ain't hauling no coal'".

8 *THE LEGEND OF THE U.S.S. TITANIC* Jamie Brockett, 1969

New England folkie **Jamie Brockett**'s archetypal 1960s extravaganza is a thirteen-minute "talking blues" along the lines of Arlo Guthrie's "Alice's Restaurant". It's loosely built around Leadbelly's "The Titanic", with a substantial walk-on part for Jack Johnson, but Brockett introduces an entirely new character, a first mate with a penchant for smoking hemp rope. Naturally he turns Captain Smith on to his poison of choice, with disastrous consequences...

THE LEGEND OF JACK JOHNSON

The legend that boxer **Jack Johnson**, the first black world heavyweight champion, had been **denied passage** on the *Titanic* because of the colour of his skin spread rapidly among African–Americans in the wake of the disaster. Several songs and folk poems attributed the sinking to divine retribution for this racial slur.

In the literal sense that Johnson was in Chicago on the relevant April night, it's definitely not true. He had been in England in 1911, and returned to New York that December as a first-class passenger aboard the White Star Line's *Celtic*.

Whether Johnson had ever been turned away from a transatlantic liner is a more contentious issue. He was a hugely controversial figure at the time, and was subjected to racist harassment that culminated in two arrests for supposed immorality later that same year. However, no evidence of any such incident with a ship has yet been found.

9 *THE SINKING OF THE TITANIC* Gavin Bryars, 1975

Composed in 1969, and first recorded for Brian Eno's appropriately named Obscure label in 1975, British composer **Gavin Bryars'** 24-minute epic imagines the *Titanic*'s band as continuing to play even after the ship is underwater. Inspired by wireless operator Harold Bride's description of the actual music played as being the hymn "Autumn" – although sadly historians now believe it was a popular waltz of a similar name – it incorporates various settings of the hymn, as well as fragments of interviews with survivors, random dialogue and Morse signals. At the start, the dying ship is perpendicular to the ocean, while the band stands on the open, now-horizontal doors of the gymnasium. As *Titanic* and musicians alike slide beneath the water, the music acquires ever more haunting reverberations.

10 *TITANIC* General Echo, 1979

In which Jamaican reggae DJ **General Echo**, who was shot by police the next year and is more usually associated with "slackness", or sexually explicit material, makes great play of his grandmother's failure to board the *Titanic*. "It is a lucky thing me granny get sick, or else she would have sink in the *Titanic*". Fortunately the doctor orders her to stay home in bed, and so she misses the rest of the story – the captain sighting the iceberg, the people singing "Nearer My God to Thee", the whole sorry saga.

THE ROUGH GUIDE TO THE **TITANIC**

Books

Literally hundreds of **books** have been written about the *Titanic*. The following list includes those that proved most useful in the writing of this Rough Guide. For anyone setting out to build their own *Titanic* library, the best places to start are Walter Lord's classic *A Night to Remember*, and the eyewitness accounts of Lawrence Beesley and Colonel Archibald Gracie.

It's also possible to buy full transcripts of the official British and American inquiries in book form, though as described on p.244 the entire text of both is available online.

Eyewitness accounts and primary sources

Lawrence Beesley *The Loss of the S.S. Titanic* (1912)

The single best first-hand account of the disaster, written by a 34-year-old widowed English schoolmaster who was travelling second class to visit his brother in Canada. Evident throughout his easy, flowing narrative, Beesley's observational skills make him the most reliable witness as to what the passengers did, saw and felt on the night of the disaster. Aged eighty, he was a consultant on the filming of *A Night to Remember* in 1958, and attempted to hide among the extras so he could finally go down with the ship.

Dave Bryceson *The Titanic Disaster as Reported in the British National Press* (1997)

An invaluable anthology of entire reprinted newspaper articles from the days and months that followed the tragedy. Most are from the *Daily Sketch*, with a handful from *The Times* as well.

Colonel Archibald Gracie *The Truth About the Titanic* (1913)

The bluff American counterpart to the more measured Beesley, first-class passenger Colonel Gracie is the biggest character in his rip-roaring memoir of his dramatic escape from the sinking ship. He also complemented his own experiences with extensive interviews with fellow passengers, to produce a very creditable account of the overall sequence of events. Gracie was travelling on the *Titanic* to relax after writing *The Truth About Chickamauga*, an account of the Civil War battle in which his father fought for the Confederacy. Sadly, worn out by his gruelling ordeal, he died in December 1912, shortly before his *Titanic* book was published.

Violet Jessop *Titanic Survivor* (1997)

By the time the memoirs of stewardess Violet Jessop, who survived the sinking of not only the *Titanic* but also her sister ship the *Britannic* in 1916, were published in 1997, she'd been dead for 26 years. The slim manuscript she wrote in 1934 was annotated and expanded by author John Maxtone-Graham. While nothing like as detailed as other eyewitness accounts, with just a few pages on the *Titanic*, it's a welcome glimpse of the world of the Victualling Crew.

Charles Lightoller *Titanic and Other Ships* (1935)

The *Titanic*'s senior surviving officer devoted only six of the forty-five chapters in his autobiography to his time on the ship. Essential reading for any *Titanic* enthusiast, they offer a fascinating perspective on the view from the Boat Deck, and include what at the time were new revelations. Besides assorted other yarns from a life at sea, the book is also intriguing for what Lightoller doesn't say – what exactly did he hold back from the two inquiries?

Tim Maltin *Titanic, First Accounts* (2012)

The best anthology of eyewitness accounts and contemporary reports, including substantial extracts from both Archibald Gracie and Lawrence Beesley, as well as crucial testimony from the inquiries, and lesser-known newspaper interviews.

General histories

Nick Barratt *Lost Voices from the Titanic* (2009)

Setting out to provide "the definitive oral history", this paperback compiles extensive quotations from a wide range of sources, many of them seldom found elsewhere, to tell the story of the ship from construction to sinking.

John P. Eaton and Charles A. Haas *Titanic: A Journey Through Time* (1999)

Large, extensively illustrated hardback that takes a chronological approach to the disaster, shifting from day by day to minute by minute as the drama reaches its peak. The authors also give detailed coverage of the 1998 expedition to the wreck, in which they took part.

Robin Gardiner and Dan van der Vat *The Riddle of the Titanic* (1995)

So long as you ignore the ridiculous *Titanic–Olympic* swap segments (as discussed on p.213), which only form a small proportion of the text and were disowned even by co-author van der Vat, this international bestseller is an entertaining read. Digging around in lesser-known sources, it added a refreshing note of scepticism to the familiar narrative. Also published as *The Titanic Conspiracy*.

Walter Lord *A Night to Remember* (1955)

Still the must-read introduction to the *Titanic* story, Lord's international bestseller was the first book to be written about the ship for forty-two years, and rekindled popular interest. A short but very gripping read, it focuses unerringly on the nub of the story, evoking the supreme tension of the *Titanic*'s final hours. Lord's interviews and correspondence with eyewitnesses remain invaluable.

Don Lynch *Titanic: An Illustrated History* (1992)

The best fully illustrated account of the *Titanic* and its fate. Its large format allows familiar photos to be reproduced at unusual size, but the real selling point is the sumptuous large colour paintings, diagrams and cutaways by artist Ken Marschall.

Geoffrey Marcus *Maiden Voyage* (1969)

Written at a time when there was still new eyewitness testimony to find, with a wider focus and depth of research than Walter Lord, this remains among the very strongest overall accounts of the tragedy. Marcus's coverage of the British inquiry is especially useful.

Filson Young *Titanic* (1912)

Although he completed this account of the *Titanic*'s short life just 23 days after she sank, and included many of the already ubiquitous myths about the tragedy, Ulster-born journalist Filson Young wrote so beautifully that this slim volume should not be missed. He also had the advantage of having visited the Harland & Wolff shipyards while the *Olympic* and *Titanic* were being built.

Aspects of the story

Dr Robert D. Ballard *The Discovery of the Titanic* (1987)

The compelling story of the race to find the wreck, written by the leader of the winning team. As well as giving clear descriptions of the technology and procedures involved, and both the monotony and the tensions of the hunt, Ballard provides plenty of discussion about the *Titanic* herself, with an intriguing exploration of the implications of the location and state of the wreckage.

Robin Gardiner *Titanic – The Ship That Never Sank* (1998)

In which Robin Gardiner sets out his notorious theory that the damaged *Olympic* sank in the *Titanic*'s place, as part of a huge conspiracy that also involved Captain Lord of the *Californian*. Even though Gardiner has clearly familiarized himself with a vast range of information about both ships, he fails to provide the slightest credible evidence of his absurd fantasy. See p.213 for more details.

Steve Hall and Bruce Beveridge *Olympic and Titanic: the Truth Behind the Conspiracy* (2004)

The definitive riposte to the theory that the *Olympic* was secretly swapped with the *Titanic* and then deliberately sunk (see p.213). Hall and Beveridge work through every aspect of the physical evidence, from the collision between the *Olympic* and the *Hawke* to a detailed comparison with the *Titanic*. It's a shame it had to be written, but it's a worthy addition to any *Titanic* library.

Jennifer Hooper McCarty and Tim Foecke *What Really Sank the Titanic* (2008)

After years investigating samples brought up from the *Titanic*, two metallurgists show that the steel was not "brittle", but suggest the rivets may well have been weak (see p.179). It's fascinating even for non-scientists, thanks to the authors' obvious passion for the ship, while their objectivity makes a welcome change from the polemic of so many other books.

David F. Hutchings and Richard de Kerbrech *RMS Titanic Owner's Workshop Manual* (2011)

While it's not quite what you might imagine from the title, lacking new blueprints and diagrams, this slim hardback nonetheless does a good job of detailing the design, construction and internal workings of the great ship. It also features copious contemporary photographs from the Harland & Wolff shipyards.

Donald Hyslop, Alistair Forsyth and Sheila Jemima *Titanic Voices* (1994)

Produced by Southampton County Council, and drawing heavily on interviews by its Oral History Unit, this copiously illustrated large-format hardback vividly portrays the impact of the disaster on Southampton itself. For anyone wanting to understand the experiences of ordinary crew members and passengers as well as their families, there's no better source.

Walter Lord *The Night Lives On* (1986)

After the *Titanic* was rediscovered in 1985, the doyen of *Titanic* studies revisited the topic, using recent research to illuminate several of the most intriguing aspects of the "night" he helped to make immortal.

Tim Maltin and Eloise Astin *101 Things You Thought You Knew About The Titanic… But Didn't!* (2010)

More of a handy reference work than a book to read beginning to end, this very readable compendium addresses a century's worth of myths and controversies about the sinking.

Senan Molony *Titanic and the Mystery Ship* (2006)

In the most persuasive and comprehensive exposition of the "Lordite" case, Molony argues that Captain Lord was unfairly scapegoated by the two inquiries, and that his ship, the *Californian*, was not the "Mystery Ship" seen from the sinking *Titanic*.

Leslie Reade *The Ship That Stood Still* (1993)

The definitive volume on the *Californian*, her role in the disaster and the enigmatic Captain Lord. Although Reade completed his manuscript in 1975, Lord's defender Leslie Harrison (see p.212) managed to block publication, and the book only appeared four years after Reade's death in 1989. While the issue may never be settled beyond all doubt, this hefty volume stands as a massive indictment of Captain Lord, supported by extensive research and explained with intricate diagrams.

Wyn Craig Wade *The Titanic: End of a Dream* (1979)

This unique and compelling book treats the disaster from an entirely American standpoint, focusing especially on its immediate aftermath. Wade single-handedly restores the reputation of the Senate inquiry's chairman, Senator William Alden Smith, long besmirched by British commentators, with a detailed biography and a day-to-day account of his energetic and probing investigation.

Gavin Weightman *Signor Marconi's Magic Box* (2003)

Only twenty pages of this excellent history of Guglielmo Marconi and the development of wireless are devoted specifically to the *Titanic*, but the entire book is invaluable in explaining the operation and significance of Marconi's invention.

Culture and media

Tim Bergfelder and Sarah Street (eds) *The Titanic in Myth and Memory* (2004)

Originally delivered at a *Titanic* conference at Southampton University in 2000, the various papers collected here range across several disciplines, but are especially useful for anyone interested in how the disaster has been represented in literature and film.

Steven Biel *Down with the Old Canoe* (1996)

A ground-breaking and very enjoyable romp through the cultural history of the *Titanic* disaster, exploring the many ways in which the story reached and remained a part of American popular culture. Biel deserves huge credit for finding and interpreting all sorts of little-known texts, songs and artefacts. A revised edition has been prepared to mark the centenary of the sinking, while many of Biel's prime discoveries are reproduced at length in his companion anthology, *Titanica* (1998).

Richard Howells *The Myth of the Titanic* (1999)

The rather more academic but still imaginative and absorbing British equivalent of Biel's *Down with the Old Canoe*, focussing on British popular culture and similarly updated to commemorate the centenary. Howells takes a forensic look at several of the most abiding myths of the tragedy, and teases out what they say about our own times as well as the Edwardian era.

David M. Lubin *Titanic* (1999)

In this British Film Institute monograph on James Cameron's *Titanic*, a film historian rejects the charge that what was at the time the most successful movie ever made was merely lightweight fluff, and considers whether its audience appeal was rooted in its treatment of class, gender and other issues.

Ed W. Marsh *James Cameron's Titanic* (1997)

Glossy, large-format, official account of the making of the blockbuster movie. While filled with behind-the-scenes technical details, it's most interesting for Cameron's own introduction, explaining his fascination with the story and recounting his dives to the wreck itself.

The *Titanic* in fiction

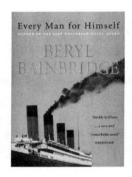

Beryl Bainbridge *Every Man for Himself* (1996)

The best fictionalized rendition of the *Titanic* saga won the Whitbread Prize and was shortlisted for the Booker Prize. Deftly using the ship to represent the Edwardian world in miniature, Bainbridge peoples it with a mixture of real and invented characters, and tells a short but powerful story of star-crossed young love.

Louise Patten *Good as Gold* (2010)

The sinking of the *Titanic* is a peripheral subplot in this readable romp of a novel, in which Patten rather eccentrically chose to reveal what she claims is the secret explanation of the disaster that her grandfather, Second Officer Charles Lightoller, told only to his wife. She also describes how Quartermaster Robert Hichens turned the wheel the wrong way in a short non-fiction "Afterword"; the story is discussed on p.184 of this Rough Guide.

Titanic websites

The **websites** listed below are those that proved especially useful in the research and writing of this book. Sites designed to promote a particular book or author have not been included, and neither have those belonging to the museums and exhibitions listed on p.246 onwards.

Encyclopedia Titanica encyclopedia-titanica.org

This huge and highly recommended site is by far the most comprehensive online source of *Titanic* information. As well as full lists of passengers and crew, with whatever biographical details are known and links to relevant press cuttings, it holds an archive of authoritative articles and an enormous message board, in which leading experts and neophytes alike contribute to discussions on every

FICTIONAL VICTIMS OF THE *TITANIC*

The most famous **fictional victim** of the *Titanic* disaster is probably **Jack Dawson**, the character played by Leonardo DiCaprio in James Cameron's *Titanic*. There have been many others, however:

Fantômas, *La fin de Fantômas.* The dastardly, psychopathic Fantômas figured as the anti-hero in no fewer than 32 crime novels published by French authors Marcel Allain and Pierre Souvestre between 1911 and 1913. Although the exhausted pair then killed off their creation by placing him aboard the *Titanic*, Allain later brought him back to life, to star in thirteen more books. He continues to feature in movies and graphic novels.

Edward Marryot and **Edith Marryot**, *Cavalcade.* The honeymooning young Marryots in Noël Coward's 1931 play, and 1933 movie, established one of the great tropes of *Titanic* fiction; the audience only discovers the couple are aboard the doomed ship when, after excitedly discussing their future together, they move away from the rail to reveal a *Titanic* life belt.

Lady Marjorie Bellamy, *Upstairs Downstairs.* Having been the central figure in the first two series of the 1970s' TV drama, Lady Marjorie is lost aboard the *Titanic*. Her ladies' maid survives, however, along with her jewellery box.

Charles Fitzgerald, **Kate Winfield** and **Bert Winfield**, *No Greater Love.* After Edwina Winfield, the feisty heroine of Danielle Steel's 1991 novel, later a TV movie, loses her fiancé and both parents as they voyage home to America, she battles to hold the family publishing empire together.

James Crawley and **Patrick Crawley**, *Downton Abbey.* The deaths of this father and son pair, the next two heirs to Lord Grantham of Downton Abbey, served as the springboard to the 2010 TV series.

conceivable topic. If you're looking for any specific nugget of information about the *Titanic*, this is the place to start, and even if you don't find it, you're bound to stumble across something else equally fascinating.

Titanic-Titanic titanic-titanic.com

While not as comprehensive as Enyclopedia Titanica, this general *Titanic* site is strong in certain areas, and what it lacks in text it tends to make up for in well-researched images. As well as all the latest news, it features a good section on *Titanic*-related sites, useful links for buying books, DVDs and memorabilia, an archive of articles, and a busy forum.

Titanic Inquiry Project titanicinquiry.org

A wonderful resource for any *Titanic* researcher: the full transcripts of both the British and American 1912 inquiries into the disaster. Testimony is organized witness by witness as well as day by day, making it easy to compare between the two inquiries, and you'll also find the final reports. You can even download the whole thing. The one drawback is that it can be hard to search for specific statements or topics.

Discovery Channel: Titanic Explorer tinyurl.com/6cm3e4a

The Discovery Channel website holds various short clips of the wreck, but its most useful feature is this massive, zoomable set of plans of the *Titanic*, which sadly cannot easily be saved or printed.

BBC Archive: Survivors of the Titanic bbc.co.uk/archive/titanic

A dozen fascinating historic recordings from the BBC archives, including twenty-minute accounts of the disaster from both Second Officer Lightoller (recorded in 1936) and Fourth Officer Boxhall (1962), and filmed reminiscences from several other survivors.

RMS Titanic rmstitanic.net

The official website of the "salvors in possession" of the *Titanic* details their current exhibitions of artefacts, and holds an interactive section on their most recent expedition to the wreck, with plenty of good footage.

Mark Chirnside's Reception Room markchirnside.co.uk

Mark Chirnside has written several authoritative works on the *Titanic* and her sister ships. Among interesting articles on his website, his dissertation succinctly refutes the allegation that the *Titanic* and the *Olympic* were swapped.

Bill Wormstedt's Titanic wormstedt.com

Titanic enthusiast Bill Wormstedt's personal site contains several interesting articles and features. The highlight is the set of pages on "Shots in the Dark", examining the evidence as to whether an officer committed suicide during the ship's last moments.

W.T. Stead Resource Site attackingthedevil.co.uk

This rather intriguing site is devoted to the life and works of English journalist and editor W.T. Stead, who died on the *Titanic*. It includes his two prescient articles, "How the Mail Steamer went down in Mid Atlantic" and "From the Old World to the New", as discussed on p.216.

Library of Congress Titanic Archives loc.gov/rr/program/bib/titanic/Titanic.html

Search the extraordinary archive of digitized newspapers and magazines held by the Library of Congress to find contemporary reports on every aspect of the tragedy, along with many contemporary photographs.

Jacques Futrelle futrelle.com

The "official" site of American author and *Titanic* victim Jacques Futrelle contains around fifty of his detective stories, many featuring his Sherlock Holmes-inspired sleuth Professor Van Dusen, a.k.a. "The Thinking Machine".

Thomas Whiteley tomwhiteley.info

A labour of love, put together by the descendants of *Titanic* steward Thomas Whiteley, a remarkable character who survived the sinking, appears to have picked up hush money from the White Star Line, and became a movie actor in both Hollywood and England.

Chapter 11
Remembering the *Titanic*

All the cities and ports of call associated with the *Titanic* and her brief career now commemorate the ill-fated liner with **museums** and other attractions. In addition, **memorials** to the victims of the disaster are scattered throughout the British Isles and North America, ranging from collective monuments in major cities to individual headstones in isolated cemeteries. Touring exhibitions of artefacts retrieved from the wreck itself also keep the memory of the *Titanic* alive.

Belfast

Proud citizens of **Belfast** have long insisted that while the story of the *Titanic* may be a global tragedy, it's also a local triumph. A large swathe of the

Titanic Belfast, on the site of the old Harland & Wolff shipyards where the Titanic *was launched.*

industrial core of the city where the great ship was built has been re-dubbed the **Titanic Quarter** (titanic-quarter.com).

This book went to press before its centrepiece, the futuristic jagged-aluminium **Titanic Belfast**, opened in April 2012 as part of the centenary commemorations. Its six storeys tell the entire *Titanic* saga from the very beginning, explaining how the ship came to be built, and why Belfast's Harland & Wolff shipyards were chosen as the construction site. All the displays are highly interactive, and never more so than in the so-called "dark ride", in which visitors voyage through a life-sized replica of the *Titanic* as she took shape. That's followed by the Launch section, in a gallery that overlooks the actual slipways used by both the *Titanic* and the *Olympic*.

Next the ship itself is celebrated in all her finery and opulence, before her maiden voyage heads to its terrible conclusion in a "dramatic sensory experience". There's also full coverage of the inquiries and the *Titanic's* afterlife in myth and media, while the **Ocean Exploration Centre** at the end, created in conjunction with Dr Robert Ballard (see p.167), holds extensive footage of the rediscovered wreck as well as a broader account of the science of oceanography. The topmost storeys of the building include a dining and function room equipped with a replica of the Grand Staircase, and the more exclusive "Astor Suite". For full details, including opening hours and prices, see titanicbelfast.com.

Several other *Titanic*-related attractions are located nearby; all were being revamped for the centenary as this book went to press, so it's impossible to give current access details. Highlights managed by the Titanic Quarter include the cavernous **drawing offices** where the blueprints of the *Titanic* and the *Olympic* were prepared, in the former Harland & Wolff headquarters building that also held the offices of Thomas Andrews and Lord Pirrie, and the **Thompson Graving Dock**, where the *Titanic* was fitted out after her launch. In addition, the *Nomadic* – the last White Star Line vessel still afloat, which served as a tender when the *Titanic* called at Cherbourg – is permanently moored at Hamilton Dock close to Titanic Belfast, and is undergoing renovation (nomadicbelfast.com). A memorial to the twenty-two "gallant Belfastmen" who perished in the sinking stands outside City Hall; the list of names is headed by Thomas Andrews. For a guided tour of Belfast's *Titanic* sites, contact **Titanic Tours** (02890/659971, titanictours-belfast.co.uk).

The **Ulster Folk & Transport Museum** (02890/428428, nmni.com), outside Holywood seven miles east of Belfast city centre, devotes an entire floor to a circular gallery called **TITANICa**, holding original artefacts, photos and displays. Outdoors, recreated streets allow visitors to explore the Belfast of 1912, complete with craft workshops, homes and shops.

Southampton

As the port from which the *Titanic* sailed on her maiden voyage, and the city hardest hit by the disaster, **Southampton** is filled with reminders of the ship. Sadly, the **dock** from which she sailed is not accessible to visitors, as it lies within the security-controlled port facility. It's no longer recognizable, in any case, forming part of an extensive but featureless paved quayside. The sheds that stood alongside the *Titanic*'s berth, number 43, were damaged by bombs during World War II, and replaced by the Ocean Terminal, which was in turned demolished in 1983.

Southampton marked the centenary of the disaster by replacing its long-standing Maritime Museum with the much larger **Sea City Museum** in the heart of town (seacity.co.uk). It had yet to open at the time of publication, but was expected to include the council's superb collection of *Titanic* artefacts and oral histories, which focuses especially on the ship's crew and their families.

The largest of Southampton's many **memorials** to the disaster, the **Engineer Officers' Memorial**, is in East Park, a short walk north of the museum. Topped by a bronze statue of Nike, the winged goddess of victory, it commemorates the 35 officers who remained at their posts as the ship

The Engineer Officers' Memorial in Southampton, which was restored in 2010.

OTHER *TITANIC* MEMORIALS

Colne, Lancashire, England. A monument to the memory of violinist Wallace Hartley, who led the musicians that played as the *Titanic* was sinking, is located in the cemetery where he was buried.

Godalming, Surrey, England. Wireless operator Jack Phillips, whose body was never recovered, is commemorated by an iceberg-shaped headstone in the town's Old Cemetery, and also by a large cloister and garden adjoining the Church of St Peter and St Paul.

Lichfield, Staffordshire, England. A statue of Captain Smith stands in Beacon Park. Sculpted by Lady Kathleen Scott, widow of "Scott of the Antarctic", it was unveiled by Smith's daughter Helen in July 1914, and bears the inscription "Be British".

New York City, USA. The marital devotion of Isidor and Ida Straus, who refused to be separated on the night of the sinking, is honoured by a memorial at Broadway and West 106th Street.

Washington DC, USA. Individual women donated no more than $1 each to build the city's Titanic Memorial, in honour of the men who sacrificed their lives to save women and children. Unveiled in Rock Creek Park in 1931, it was moved to a new site on P Street SW near Fort McNair in 1968.

went down. Other local monuments include the **Musicians' Memorial** across the road; the **Postal Workers' Memorial** in the Civic Centre; the **Crew Memorial** in Holy Rood Church on the High Street; and the **Gatti Memorial**, honouring Luigi Gatti and the ship's restaurant workers, in St Joseph's Church on Bugle Street.

The **Terminus Railway Station**, where the boat train arrived from London, is now a casino. Its platforms provided direct access to the **South Western Hotel**, across from the docks on Canute Road; guests on the night before the *Titanic*'s departure included J. Bruce Ismay and Thomas Andrews. Although the hotel has been converted into apartments, its lobby has been restored to its 1912 appearance. Also on Canute Road, a plaque marks the former offices of the **White Star Line**, where relatives of the crew and passengers waited for news. The **Grapes** pub, where some crew members famously lingered too long and missed the boat, still stands on nearby Oxford Street.

A map and brochure describing the **Titanic Trail** through the city is available from the local tourist board (visit-southampton.co.uk).

Cherbourg

The *Titanic* spent just over an hour and a half at anchor off the northern French port of **Cherbourg** on 10 April 1912. Although Cherbourg had been developed from an unpromising site into a major artificial harbour under Napoleon, such a large ship could not at the time enter the port itself, so passengers had to be ferried out to reach it on tenders. In the years that followed, the city became an important embarkation point for emigrants not merely from France but all Europe.

The former Transatlantic Terminal on the quayside – an Art Deco extravaganza unveiled in 1933 – is now the centrepiece of the **Cité de la Mer** (citedelamer.com), a museum that includes a decommissioned nuclear submarine. A new gallery for the centenary, "Emigration and Titanic", explores Cherbourg's heyday as a port of call for the great liners.

Cobh (Queenstown)

The pretty little southern Irish port that was known as **Queenstown** when the *Titanic* made her final stop here on 11 April 1912, changed its name to **Cobh** (pronounced "Cove") in 1922, after Ireland achieved independence. Set on the shoreline of a magnificent natural harbour, eight miles southeast of the city of **Cork**, it was the point of departure for more than 2.5 million emigrants to the United States in the century up to 1950. It was also a centre for shipbuilding and steel, although these days it's primarily a tourist destination. While it still welcomes cruise liners, Cork's principal ferry port is now Ringaskiddy, across the harbour.

As well as the history of Irish emigration, the waterfront **Cobh Heritage Centre** (cobhheritage.com) tells the story of the *Titanic*'s brief halt, and the 120 people who boarded her, of whom only 44 survived the voyage. It also covers the sinking of the *Lusitania*, which unfolded just thirty miles southwest, three years later. For a walking tour of Cobh, contact **Titanic Trail** (titanic.ie).

Halifax

The Canadian city of **Halifax**, in Nova Scotia, earned its place in the *Titanic* story because it was the closest port to the wreck site. It therefore served as the point of departure for the *Mackay-Bennett* and the two other ships that searched the bleak Atlantic for the bodies of the victims (see p.133). A total of 150 casualties of the disaster lie buried in three of the city's **cemeteries**; 44 of them have never been identified. Fairview Lawn

Cemetery holds 121, Mount Olivet Catholic Cemetery 19, and Baron de Hirsch Jewish Cemetery 10; a trust established by the long-defunct White Star Line still provides for their upkeep.

A sizeable section of the city's **Maritime Museum of the Atlantic** (museum.gov.ns.ca) is devoted to the *Titanic*. Prized exhibits include several chunks of woodwork from the *Titanic* that were picked up as souvenirs by the recovery crews. As well as an entire deck chair, they have an original piece of panelling from the entrance to the First Class Lounge, which served as the model for the (larger) segment seen in James Cameron's *Titanic*, on which Rose floats to safety.

Liverpool

Although the *Titanic* never actually visited **Liverpool**, the city nonetheless counted as being her **home port**. As the original base for the White Star Line, Liverpool had long been home to the Ismay family, and also to Captain Smith. White Star only started to operate their express services to the USA from Southampton in 1907, making the shift because Southampton had just developed large new port facilities, was much nearer to London, and also made it possible to pick up passengers from northern France as well. While Smith himself moved to Southampton, around a tenth of the *Titanic*'s crew came from Liverpool, including Chief Officer Wilde, fireman Fred Barrett, and Lookout Frederick Fleet.

The **Merseyside Maritime Museum**, on Liverpool's Albert Dock (liverpoolmuseums.org.uk/maritime), holds an extensive collection of *Titanic*-related artefacts, including a builder's model of the ship, a genuine

TITANIC MUSEUMS IN THE US

The United States holds three **museums** dedicated to the *Titanic*. The oldest, in **Indian Orchard**, Massachusetts (208 Main St; titanic1.org), is run by the Titanic Historical Society. Established in 1963, the Society opposes the salvage of artefacts from the wreck, so its collection centres on items donated by survivors or collected from other ships.

The museums in **Branson**, Missouri (3235 76 Country Blvd; titanicbranson. com), and **Pigeon Forge**, Tennessee (2134 Parkway; titanicpigeonforge.com), are housed in half-size *Titanic* replicas. Both also hold reconstructions of the Grand Staircase and sundry other features, as well as costumed guides, but neither has anything retrieved from the wreck itself.

first-class ticket and letters from survivors. Liverpool was also home to Captain Stanley Lord of the *Californian*, and the displays include sympathetic coverage of his long campaign to clear his name.

RMS Titanic, Inc.

The "salvor in possession" of the *Titanic* wreck site (see p.174) stages lavish *Titanic* exhibitions all over the world. These typically take over part of a big-city museum or gallery for six to nine months at a time. As well as artefacts recovered from the ocean depths, they feature reconstructions of various portions of the ship, and detailed displays on her passengers, crew, construction and fate.

Precise details vary from venue to venue. The one permanent location, incongruously located inside the pyramid-shaped Luxor hotel-casino in **Las Vegas**, incorporates the "Big Piece", a gigantic slab of the *Titanic*'s hull that was brought to the surface in 1998, as well as replicas of the Grand Staircase and part of the Promenade Deck. Exhibitions elsewhere include mock-ups of the bridge, cabins from different classes and even the iceberg itself.

The 22-ton "Big Piece", a segment of the C-deck hull, on display in Las Vegas.

While most of the actual artefacts on show tend to be essentially trivia, such as pots and pans, plates and tools, fragments and fittings or bus tickets and banknotes retrieved from abandoned suitcases, all have an undeniable emotional impact. Many items have been identified as belonging to specific passengers, and there are always one or two star attractions, such as Captain Smith's megaphone or the bell from the crow's nest.

A clever human touch is added by giving each visitor a "boarding pass" in the name of a particular passenger; you only find out at the end, from scanning the lists posted on the walls, whether your passenger survived. For details of current exhibitions, visit rmstitanic.net.

A *Titanic* glossary

The following glossary explains nautical and shipboard terms and phrases that figure throughout this book. As far as possible, definitions are given in terms of usage at the time of the *Titanic*'s maiden voyage.

abaft towards the stern.

aft in, near or towards the stern of the ship.

aft bridge structure that spanned the *Titanic*'s poop deck, close to the stern, and held a wheel and parallel controls for use in an emergency.

alleyway a corridor or passageway.

amidships in the middle of the ship, halfway between the bow and the stern.

bearing the compass direction from an observer to a specified object.

boatswain also known as the bosun, the boatswain is the petty officer on a ship in charge of the deck crew, as well as equipment such as cables, rigging and anchors.

bow the front, or forward end, of the ship.

bulkhead a vertical wall or partition within a ship. In the *Titanic*, these cut across the ship from side to side, but the term also applies to divisions that run fore and aft.

coaming a raised lip around a hatch or doorway, to stop flowing water.

commutator a small clock-like instrument that shows the extent to which a ship is listing.

crow's nest perch used by lookouts; on the *Titanic*, it was reached by climbing inside the hollow forward mast.

davit a crane-like device used (in pairs) for lowering or raising lifeboats; pronounced to sound like "David".

dead reckoning an estimate of a ship's position, produced by using her speed and course to extrapolate from a previous known position.

deck crew the eighty or so sailors who were responsible for actually moving the *Titanic* through the water.

displacement a ship's mass at a specific moment, most commonly when fully loaded.

engine crew the 320 men who worked below decks in the *Titanic*'s engine and boiler rooms.

expansion joint a sliding joint in the superstructure that allows the ship to flex under stress.

falls the ropes and mechanical apparatus used to lower a lifeboat.

fireman the primary role of the firemen aboard the *Titanic* was not to extinguish fires, but to keep the fires burning in the boilers.

fix an exact position for a ship, traditionally established by using the sun and stars.

forecastle a separate superstructure at the bow of a ship, traditionally used for crew accommodation, and topped by the forecastle deck.

gantry scaffolding used during a ship's construction, and extending over the top.

greaser a greaser's role on the *Titanic* was to keep moving machinery well greased.

guarantee group the nine-man group from shipbuilders Harland & Wolff, led by Thomas Andrews, that sailed on the *Titanic*'s maiden voyage.

gunwale the topmost edge of the side of a vessel.

hove to a ship that is "hove to" is stationary in the water, pointing into the wind, and using her engines to maintain that position.

keel the central spine of a ship, running fore to aft along the bottom of the hull.

knot a unit of speed, corresponding to one nautical mile per hour. A nautical mile, at 6080 feet, is longer than the 5280-feet geographical mile. Twenty knots equals just over 23 miles per hour.

log a device, trailed underwater, that measures a ship's speed and distance run.

log (book) the official written record of a ship and her voyages.

orlop deck the lowest deck of a ship that has at least four decks.

poop a separate superstructure at the stern of a ship, equivalent to the forecastle at the bow, and topped by the poop deck.

port the left side of a ship, when facing forward.

quartermaster a seaman whose main task is to steer the ship, following officers' orders. All seven of the *Titanic's* quartermasters survived the disaster.

slipway a ramp leading into the water, via which a ship is launched.

starboard the right side of a ship, when facing forward.

stern the rear, or aft end, of the ship.

stoker although Fred Barrett took pains at the UK inquiry to point out that a stoker and a fireman were not the same thing, the difference was of rank rather than role; both were responsible for feeding and maintaining the boiler-room fires.

superstructure the portion of a ship that rests above the main deck; on the *Titanic*, the superstructure consisted of B Deck, A Deck and the Boat Deck.

tender a vessel used to ferry cargo or passengers between the shore and a larger ship.

thwarts wooden crosspieces that serve as seats on a lifeboat.

tiller orders the system of orders in use on the *Titanic*, dating from the age of sail, under which an order such as "Hard a-starboard" referred to the movement of the tiller rather than the ship herself. For a full explanation, see p.185.

tramp a cargo ship that carries varying cargoes on varying routes.

trimmer the job of a trimmer aboard the *Titanic* was to keep the coal evenly distributed in the bunkers, in order to maintain the balance of the ship, and also to carry coal to the firemen.

victualling crew amounting to more than half the total crew of the *Titanic*, these five hundred men and women included stewards, cooks, barmen, bellboys and storekeepers.

weather deck a deck that's open to the elements.

well deck an open space on the main deck of a ship, lower than the forecastle and/or poop. The *Titanic* had two well decks, one forward and one aft.

Author's acknowledgements

Thanks above all to the international community of *Titanic* historians and enthusiasts who have spent a century researching the ship and her fate. I'd also like to thank my dear wife Sam Cook for her support, encouragement and invaluable input; Pam Cook for sparking my interest with her *Titanic* conference in Southampton back in 2000, and much exchange of ideas since; and the many other friends and family who have contributed valuable ideas and information, including Jim Cook, John Eglin, Robert Jones, Rob Humphreys, Kate Middleton and Julian Ward. At Rough Guides, thanks to Andrew Lockett; Joe Staines for his constructive editing and picture research; Richie Unterberger for his editorial input; Diana Jarvis for the cover; Tom Cabot for design work; Kate Berens for last-minute contributions; Ankur Guha for layout; and Katie Lloyd-Jones for the map and diagrams.

Picture credits

Front cover (top) Mary Evans Picture Library/Onslow Auctions Limited; front cover (bottom) © Ralph White/Corbis; inside front cover © Bettmann/Corbis; back cover; © Corbis; p.1 © Hulton-Deutsch Collection/Corbis; p.5 © Corbis; p.9 © Bettmann/Corbis; p.14 © The Mariners' Museum/Corbis; p.16 © Ralph White/Corbis; p.21 © Corbis; p.34 © Hulton-Deutsch Collection/Corbis; p.39 © Bettmann/Corbis; p.43 © Leonard de Selva/Corbis; p.45 © Bettmann/Corbis; p.52 © Ralph White/Corbis; p.57 © Bettmann/Corbis; p.61 © Bettmann/Corbis; p.62 Library of Congress; p.65 © Illustrated London News Ltd/Mary Evans; p.71 © Illustrated London News Ltd/Mary Evans; p.80 © Hulton-Deutsch Collection/Corbis; p.87 © Bettmann/Corbis; p.91 © Bettmann/Corbis; p.95 © Bettmann/Corbis; p.100 Getty Images; p.103 © Underwood & Underwood/Corbis; p.105 © Underwood & Underwood/Corbis; p.116 © Bettmann/Corbis; p.118 © Ralph White/Corbis; p.123 © Bettmann/Corbis; p.128 © Corbis; p.132 Library of Congress; p.140 © Bettmann/Corbis; p.144 © Hulton-Deutsch Collection/Corbis; p.147 © Bettmann/Corbis; p.150 Mary Evans Picture Library; p.160 Getty Images; p.169 © Ralph White/Corbis; p.170 © Ralph White/Corbis; p.177 © Illustrated London News Ltd/Mary Evans; p.181 © Underwood & Underwood/Corbis; p.186 © Ralph White/Corbis; p.193 © Lake County Museum/Corbis; p.196 Getty Images; p.202 © Bettmann/Corbis; p.208 Science Photo Library; p.214 © Corbis; p.219 © Bettmann/Corbis; p.227 © Bettmann/Corbis; p.227 Getty Images; p.229 The Moviestore Collection Ltd; p.232 © Ralph White/Corbis; p.239 Haynes Publishing; p.242 Little, Brown Book Group; p.246 © Donal McCann Photography; p.248 © Greg Ward; p.252 © Premier Exhibitions.

Index

Titles enclosed in quotation marks below are songs; titles in italics are books, films or plays.